Gifts *from* *the* Heart™

Edited by Laura Scott

HOUSE of
WHITE
BIRCHES
PUBLISHERS
SINCE 1947

Editor: Laura Scott
Editorial Assistant: Marla Freeman
Pattern Editor: Maggie Petsch Chasalow
Copy Editor: Cathy Reef

Photography: Nora Elsesser, Andree Petty, Teri Staub
Photography Assistants: Linda Quinlan, Jaclyn McCabe

Production Manager: Vicki Macy
Book Design/Production: Ronda Bollenbacher
Creative Coordinator: Shaun Venish
Traffic Coordinator: Sandra Beres
Production Assistants: Cheryl Lynch, Darren Powell, Miriam Zacharias

Publishers: Carl H. Muselman, Arthur K. Muselman
Chief Executive Officer: John Robinson
Marketing Director: Scott Moss
Editorial Director: Vivian Rothe
Production Director: Scott Smith

Printed in the United States of America
First Printing: 1997
Library of Congress Number: 97-71139
ISBN: 1-882138-25-2

Every effort has been made to ensure the accuracy and completeness of the instructions in this book. However, we cannot be responsible for human error or for the results when using materials other than those specified in the instructions, or for variations in individual work.

Cover project: Summer Breezes, page 48

~ *From the Heart* ~

There is a biblical proverb that reads, "It is more blessed to give than to receive." Did you know that crocheters around the world are one of the most generous groups of people?

The vast majority of hand-crocheted patterns are given as gifts. Gifts for holidays and birthdays, gifts for weddings and baby showers, and gifts for charity. These charitable gifts, given to groups such as Warm Up America, Caps for Kids and Habitat for Humanity, give warmth and comfort to thousands of needy people. It is no small wonder then that crocheters carry a certain amount of joy and pride, not only in their work, but in themselves, knowing that the fruit of their labor will be enjoyed by others. Crocheters are living proof that, indeed, giving is a blessed and happy event.

It is with this same kind of joy and pride that my staff, our many talented free-lance designers and I have brought together this collection of brand-new crochet patterns. Knowing that they will be enjoyed not only by you, our treasured crocheters, but also many others with whom you share your work, gives us tremendous satisfaction.

We hope your life is filled with many joyful gift-giving occasions, overflowing with love, family, friends and crochet.

Warmest regards,

Laura Scott

Editor,
Gifts From the Heart

~ Contents ~

Delicate Delights

Winter Warmers

The Christmas Home

Housewarming Gifts

Gifts for the Bride & Groom

Give the newlyweds a crocheted gift from your heart to warm up their first home.

Pretty yet practical items such as lacy hand towels, tissue toppers, quick-to-crochet rag baskets, handy table sets and other home accents will prove to be a gift used and appreciated again and again!

Pineapple Swirl

Timeless elegance is captured in this lovely Pineapple Swirl tablecloth. A dozen perfect pineapples circle the center floral motif while others add the finishing touch to the edging. This piece makes the perfect tablecloth for a round end table in either the living room or bedroom. Instructions begin on page 18.

Perfect Pastel Edgings

Intricate pastel edgings (right) tacked onto guest hand towels will make your visitors feel especially welcome and right at home. Instructions begin on page 22.

Lacy Tissue Box Cover

Small touches of crochet throughout your home will add a subtle beauty sure to be appreciated and admired. Stitch this sweet Lacy Tissue Box Cover (below) in colors to complement your bedroom or bath. Instructions begin on page 21.

Sweetheart Place Mat

Celebrate love with heart-shaped crocheted
gifts just right for bridal showers, weddings,
anniversaries and Valentine's Day! Rose-colored
hearts worked with cluster stitches stand out
beautifully against a pure white background on
this engaging Sweetheart Place Mat (above).
Instructions begin on pages 24.

Heart-Shaped Hot Pads

Protect your table with this pair of decorative
hot pads (right). Both sizes work up super-
quick with strips of colorful cotton fabric.
Instructions begin on page 24.

CROCHET PATTERNS

101052

House of White Birches — Publishers Since 1947

Angels of Blessing™

Designs by Jo Ann Maxwell

Charity

Hope

Faith

3 Delicate & Lacy Angels to Crochet

Angels of Blessing

Faith

Experience Level
Intermediate

Size
6½" tall x 5¾" wide at base

Materials
- South Maid crochet cotton size 10 (150 yds per ball): 1 ball cream
- Size 5 steel crochet hook
- Several cotton balls
- Funnel
- One & Only Creations curly doll hair
- 10½" length green metallic cording
- Small spray of ¾" iridescent blue silk flowers
- Small amount gold-glittered baby's breath
- 23 (¼"-diameter) emerald gem-stones
- Sugar and water
- Small paintbrush
- Plastic wrap
- Hot-glue gun

Gauge
Work evenly and consistently

Pattern Notes
Join rnds with a sl st unless otherwise stated.

To stiffen angel, bring 2 parts sugar and 1 part water to boil; stir to dissolve sugar. Let cool. Dip crocheted piece in solution; squeeze out excess. Use a small paintbrush to brush over sleeves. Do not saturate sleeves enough to wet cotton.

ANGELS OF BLESSING is published by House of White Birches, 306 East Parr Road, Berne, IN 46711. Printed in USA. Copyright 1996 House of White Birches. Editorial Director: Vivian Rothe; Editor: Laura Scott; Editorial Assistant: Marla Freeman; Production Manager: Vicki Macy; Production: Sandy Bauman; Cover Design: Shaun Venish; Product Marketing: Claudia Claussen.

RETAILERS: If you would like to carry this pattern book or any other House of White Birches publication, call The Needlecraft Shop at (903) 636-4011 to set up an account.

ADDITIONAL PUBLICATIONS: Write today for a complete listing of publications available from House of White Birches. Send to: Publications Listing, 306 East Parr Road, Berne, IN 46711

Every effort has been made to ensure that the instructions in this pattern book are complete and accurate. We cannot, however, take responsibility for human error, typographical mistakes or variations in individual work.

Pattern Stitches
Double treble (dtr): Yo 3 times, insert hook in st, yo, draw up a lp, [yo, draw through 2 lps on hook] 4 times.

Triple treble (trtr): Yo 4 times, insert hook in st, yo, draw up a lp, [yo, draw through 2 lps on hook] 5 times.

Dc picot: Dc in indicated st, ch 3, join in top of dc.

Love knot (Lk): Draw up ¼"-long lp on hook, yo, draw lp through, sc in back strand of long lp.

Head & Body
Rnd 1: Ch 4, join to form a ring, ch 3 (counts as first dc), 19 dc in ring, join in 3rd ch of beg ch-3. (20)

Rnds 2–6: Ch 2 (counts as first hdc), hdc in each dc around, join in 2nd ch of beg ch-2.

Rnd 7: Ch 1, sc in same sp, sk 1 st, [sc in next st, sk 1 st] rep around, join in beg sc. (10)

Rnd 8: Ch 5 (counts as first dc, ch 2), [dc, ch 2] in each st around, join in 3rd ch of beg ch-5.

Rnds 9 & 10: Sl st to next ch-2 sp, ch 5 (counts as first dc, ch 2), [dc, ch 2] in each sp around, join in 3rd ch of beg ch-5.

Rnd 11: Ch 3 (counts as first dc), dc in each st around, join in 3rd ch of beg ch-3. (30 dc)

Rnd 12: Ch 7 (counts as first dtr, ch 1), [dtr, ch 1] in each st around, join in 6th ch of beg ch-7.

Rnd 13: Ch 3 (counts as first dc), dc in same sp, [dc in next ch, dc picot in next dtr, dc in next ch, 2 dc in next dtr] rep around, join in 3rd ch of beg ch-3. (75 dc)

Rnd 14: Sl st to next dc, ch 1, sc in same sp, [ch 5, sk picot and 2 dc, sc in next dc] rep around, join in beg sc. (15 ch-5 lps)

Rnd 15: *Sc in first ch, [2 sc in next ch, sc in next ch] twice, sl st in sc, rep from * around, join in beg sp.

Rnd 16: Sl st to 4th sc of ch-5 lp, working in back lps only, ch 3 (counts as first dc), dc in same sp, [ch 1, Lk, 2 dc in 4th sc of next ch-5 lp] rep around, join in 3rd ch of beg ch-3.

Rnd 17: Ch 3 (counts as first dc), dc in next dc, [ch 5, dc in each of next 2 dc] rep around, join in 3rd ch of beg ch-3.

Rnd 18: Sl st in 2nd ch of next ch-5 lp, ch 8 (counts as first trtr, ch 1), trtr in next ch, ch 1, trtr in next ch, ch 2, [trtr, ch 1 in each of 2nd and 3rd chs, trtr in 4th ch, ch 2] rep around, join in 7th ch of beg ch-8. (45 trtr)

Rnd 19: Ch 3 (counts as first dc), [dc in next ch, dc picot in next st, dc in each of next 2 sts, ch 2, sc in ch-2 sp, ch 2, dc in next st] rep around, join in 3rd ch of beg ch-3.

Rnd 20: Ch 1, sc in same sp, [ch 5, sk picot and dc, sc in next dc, ch 3, sc in next dc] rep around, join in beg sc.

Rnd 21: Sl st to first ch of next ch-5 lp, ch 4 (counts as first hdc, ch 2), [hdc, ch 2] in each of next 3 chs, *hdc in next ch, sc in ch-3 sp, [hdc, ch 2] in each of next 4 chs of next lp, rep from * around, join in 2nd ch of beg ch-4, fasten off.

Wings
Row 1: Ch 4, join to form a ring, ch 3 (counts as first dc), 8 dc in ring, turn.

Row 2: Ch 9 (counts as first dtr, ch 3), *[dtr, ch 1] twice in next st, dtr in same sp, ch 3 *, rep from * to * twice, sk 1 st, rep from * to * 3 times, dtr in last dc, turn.

Row 3: Ch 3 (counts as first dc), dc in same sp, ch 1, Lk, *2 dc, ch 1, Lk in center ch of ch-3 sp, 2 dc, ch 1, Lk in center dtr *, rep from * to * once, 2 dc in center of ch-3 sp, ch 3, sc in center dtr, ch 3, sc in next ch-3 sp, ch 3, sc in center of next dtr, ch 3, rep from * to * twice, 2 dc in 2nd ch of ch-3 sp, ch 1, Lk, sk 1 ch, 2 dc in next ch, ch 1, turn.

Row 4: Sc in same sp, [ch 5, sk Lk, sc in next dc, ch 2, sc in next dc] 5 times, sk next ch-3 lp, [ch 3, sc in next ch-3 lp] twice, ch 3, sk next ch-3 lp, sc in next dc, ch 2, sc in next dc, [ch 5, sk Lk, sc in next dc, ch 2, sc in next dc] 4 times, ch 5, sc in dc at end, ch 1, turn.

Row 5: Sc in same sp, *[hdc, ch 2 in each of next 4 chs of ch-5 lp, hdc in next ch, sc in ch-2 sp] * 5 times, ch 3, sc in center lp, ch 3, sc in next ch-2 sp, rep from * to * 4 times, hdc, ch 2 in each of next 4 chs of ch-5 lp, hdc in next ch, sc in sc, fasten off.

Arms

[Ch 20, hdc in 5th ch from hook and in each rem ch across] twice, fasten off.

Stiffening

Apply fabric stiffener (see Pattern Notes).

Stuff head with cotton; cinch neck. Insert arms through body just below neck, curving toward front of body. Wrap cotton with plastic wrap; stuff in body. Shape angel over funnel; allow to dry.

Shape wings on plastic-covered flat surface; pin in place to dry.

Finishing

Glue wings to back of body, using photo as a guide.

Glue hair to head, following manufacturer's directions.

Cut 4½" length of cording; form in a circle around top of head. Secure with glue at back of head. Glue 1 silk flower and sprigs of baby's breath to hair, using photo as guide.

Glue rem cording around waist; secure with glue under wings. Arrange silk flowers down front of angel over ends of arms; glue in place with sprigs of baby's breath.

Glue emerald gemstones around edges of skirt and wings, using photo as guide. ❖

Hope

Experience Level

Intermediate

Size

12" tall x 6½" wide across wings

Materials

- South Maid crochet cotton size 10 (350 yds per ball): 1 ball cream
- Size 5 steel crochet hook
- 1½"-diameter plastic foam egg
- Small piece thin fabric
- Cereal bowl
- 9" x 3⅞" cone
- Drinking straw
- One & Only Creations mini curly hair
- 6½" length gold foil garland
- 15 (1¼") Darice mauve coil ribbon roses with leaves #7205-03
- 2 yds ¼"-wide mauve satin ribbon
- 3 (¾") plastic white bells with gold trim
- 24" gold metallic thread
- Polyester fiberfill
- White glue
- Gold glitter
- Sugar and water
- Small paintbrush
- Plastic wrap
- Hot-glue gun
- Pliers

Gauge

Work evenly and consistently

Pattern Notes

Join rnds with a sl st unless otherwise stated.

To stiffen angel, bring 2 parts sugar and 1 part water to boil; stir to dissolve sugar. Let cool. Dip crocheted piece in solution; squeeze out excess. Use a small paintbrush to brush over sleeves. Do not saturate sleeves enough to wet cotton.

Pattern Stitches

Love knot (Lk): Draw up ¼"-long lp on hook, yo, draw lp through, sc in back strand of long lp.

Double love knot (dlk): [Draw up ½"-long lp on hook, yo, draw lp through, sc in back strand of long lp] twice.

Head & Body

Rnd 1: Ch 6, join to form a ring, ch 3 (counts as first dc), 29 dc in ring, join in 3rd ch of beg ch-3. (30 dc)

Rnds 2–11: Ch 2 (counts as first hdc), hdc in each st around, join in 2nd ch of beg ch-2.

Slip in 1½" plastic foam ball after Rnd 11.

Rnd 12: Ch 1, sc in same sp, sk 1 st, [sc in next st, sk 1 st] rep around, join in beg sc. (15)

Rnd 13: Ch 3 (counts as first dc), dc in same sp, 2 dc in each rem st, join in 3rd ch of beg ch-3. (30)

Rnds 14–17: Ch 3 (counts as first dc), dc in each rem st around, join in 3rd ch of beg ch-3.

Rnd 18: Ch 4 (counts as first tr), tr in same sp, ch 3, [tr in each of next 2 sts, ch 3, 2 tr in next st, ch 3] rep around, join in 4th ch of beg ch-4. (20 2-tr groups and 20 ch-3 sps)

Rnd 19: Sl st to ch-3 sp, ch 3 (counts as first dc), *[dc, ch 2, dc] in same sp, dc in same sp working off 2 lps of dc only, yo, dc in next ch-3 sp, work off 2 lps, work off 3 lps (counts as 2 dc tog between shells), rep from * in each ch-3 sp around, [work off 2 lps from last dc, join in 3rd ch of beg ch-3, pull thread through all 3 lps] to join.

Rnd 20: Sl st to center of ch-2 sp, ch 4 (counts as first tr), tr in same sp, ch 3, [2 tr in next ch-2 sp, ch 3] rep around, join in 4th ch of beg ch-4.

Rnd 21: Rep Rnd 19.

Rnd 22: Rep Rnd 20.

Rnd 23: Sl st to ch-3 sp, ch 3, [dc, ch 2, 2 dc] in same ch-3 sp, shell of 2 dc, ch 2, 2 dc in each rem ch-3 sp around, join in 3rd ch of beg ch-3. (20 shells)

Rnd 24: Rep Rnd 20.

Rnd 25: Rep Rnd 23.

Rnd 26: Rep Rnd 20.

Rnd 27: Rep Rnd 23.

Rnd 28: Sl st to ch-2 sp of shell, ch 1, sc, ch 3, sl st in top of sc for picot in same sp, ch 5, sc, ch 3, sl st in top of sc for picot in each shell around, ending with ch 5, join in beg sc.

Rnd 29: Sl st to center of ch-5 sp, ch 1, sc in same sp, ch 1, [dlk, sc, ch 1] in each ch-5 sp around, join in beg sc.

Rnd 30: Ch 5, sc picot in center knot of dlk, [ch 7, sc picot in center knot of dlk] rep around, join in beg sc.

Rnd 31: Sl st to 2nd ch of next ch-7 lp, ch 5 (counts as first dc, ch 2), [dc, ch 2] in each of next 4 chs, *sl st in 3rd ch of next ch-7 lp, ch 3, sl st in same ch, sl st in next ch, ch 5, sl st in same sp, sl st in next ch, ch 3, sl st in same sp, ch 2, beg in 2nd ch of next ch-7 lp, [dc, ch 2] in each of 5 center chs, rep from * around, join in 3rd ch of beg ch-5, fasten off.

Wing Circle
Rnd 1: Ch 4, join to form a ring, ch 3 (counts as first dc), 19 dc in ring, join in 3rd ch of beg ch-3.

Rnd 2: Ch 5 (counts as first dc, ch 2), [dc, ch 2] in each st around, join in 3rd ch of beg ch-5.

Rnd 3: Ch 4 (counts as first tr), tr in same dc, [ch 3, 2 tr in next dc] rep around, join in 4th ch of beg ch-4.

Rnd 4: Sl st into ch-3 sp, ch 3, [dc, ch 2, 2 dc] in same ch-3 sp, shell of 2 dc, ch 2, 2 dc in each rem ch-3 sp, join in 3rd ch of beg ch-3.

Rnd 5: Sl st to ch-2 sp of shell, [sc picot, ch 5] in each shell around, join in beg sc.

Rnds 6–8: Rep Rnds 29–31 of Head & Body, fasten off.

Sleeves
Make 2
Rnd 1: Ch 4, join to form a ring, ch 3 (counts as first dc), dc in ring, [ch 3, 2 dc] 7 times, ch 3, join in 3rd ch of beg ch-3.

Rnd 2: Sl st to ch-3 sp, ch 4 (counts as first tr), tr in same sp, [ch 3, 2 tr in next ch-3 sp] rep around, join in 4th ch of beg ch-4.

Rnd 3: Sl st to ch-3 sp, ch 3 (counts as first dc), dc in same sp, [ch 1, 2 dc in next ch-3 sp] rep around, join in 3rd ch of beg ch-3.

Cover small amount of fiberfill with plastic wrap; slip into sleeve to shape.

Rnd 4: Sl st to ch-1 sp, sc in each ch-2 sp around, join in beg sc. (8 sc)

Rnd 5: Ch 3 (counts as first dc), dc in each sc around, join in 3rd ch of beg ch-3. (8 dc)

Rnds 6–10: Ch 3 (counts as first dc), dc in each st around, join in 3rd ch of beg ch-3, fasten off at end of Rnd 10.

Stiffening
Apply fabric stiffener (see Pattern Notes).

Cover small egg with thin fabric, then with plastic wrap. Insert into bodice wide end first.

Cut 1½" off of top of cone; press in sharp edges to round off. Place cone on bottom of bowl and cover cone and bowl with plastic wrap.

Shape angel skirt over cone and bowl; cinch neck and waist. Allow to dry completely.

Insert straws into sleeves; shape in desired position, using photo as a guide.

Shape wing circle on flat surface and separate love knots with a straight pin; allow to dry completely.

Finishing
Remove cinch thread from waist. Remove egg from bodice by grasping fabric with pliers and twisting and pulling out.

Using small paintbrush, brush white glue onto love knots on skirt and wing circle, sprinkling glitter as you go. Allow to dry.

Place 4½" length of ribbon around waist, overlapping ends in back and securing with glue.

Remove fiberfill and plastic wrap from sleeves with crochet hook. Using photo as a guide, hot-glue sleeves in place.

Glue hair in place following manufacturer's instructions.

Glue wing circle to back of angel so that center of circle is at lower back of head.

Thread 1 bell to center of gold metallic thread; knot loosely. Thread rem bells onto thread, knotting loosely at approximately 1½" intervals. Loop rem ends twice and glue into place at end of sleeve, using photo as a guide. Glue rem bells to skirt as shown.

Form bows from 2 (8"-long) pieces of ribbon; hot-glue 1 bow on each sleeve, using photo as guide. Hot-glue 1 ribbon rose over center of each bow.

Weave rem ribbon diagonally through base of skirt, skipping every other space as shown in photo; trim ends and secure with glue. Hot-glue ribbon roses in skipped spaces.

Hot-glue rem ribbon roses onto wings around head, as shown in photo. Form a circle from garland; hot-glue in place on head for halo. ❖

Charity

Experience Level
Intermediate

Size
14" tall x 7¼" wide across wings

Materials
- South Maid crochet cotton size 10 (350 yds per ball): 1 ball cream
- Size 5 steel crochet hook
- 1½"-diameter plastic foam ball
- 12" x 3⅞" plastic foam cone
- 2 chenille stems
- One & Only Creations curly doll hair
- 27" gold metallic cording
- 20" ¼"-wide lavender feather-edged ribbon
- 1½ yds ½"-wide lavender feather-edged ribbon
- 12 (1½") light orchid ribbon flowers with leaves
- Small amount gold-glittered baby's breath
- Sugar and water
- Small paintbrush
- Plastic wrap
- Hot-glue gun

Gauge
Work evenly and consistently

Pattern Notes
Join rnds with a sl st unless otherwise stated.

To stiffen angel, bring 2 parts sugar and 1 part water to boil; stir to dissolve. Let cool. Dip crocheted piece in solution; squeeze out excess. Use a small paintbrush to brush over sleeves. Do not saturate sleeves enough to wet cotton.

Head & Body
Rnd 1: Ch 6, join to form a ring, ch 3 (counts as first dc), 31 dc in ring, join in 3rd ch of beg ch-3. (32)

Rnds 2–10: Ch 2 (counts as first hdc), hdc in each st around, join in 2nd ch of beg ch-2.

Slip in plastic foam ball after Rnd 10.

Rnd 11: Ch 1, sc in same sp, sk 1 st, [sc in next st, sk 1 st] rep around, join in beg sc. (16)

Rnd 12: Ch 1, sc in same sp, ch 3, sc in each st around, join with [ch 1, hdc] in beg sc.

Rnds 13–16: [Sc, ch 3] in each sp around, join with [ch 1, hdc] in beg sc.

Rnds 17–21: [Sc, ch 4] in each sp around, join in beg sc, sl st to center of next ch-4 lp to beg next rnd.

Rnds 22–26: [Sc, ch 5] in each sp around, join in beg sc, sl st to center of next lp to beg next rnd.

Rnds 27–31: [Sc, ch 6] in each sp around, join in beg sc, sl st to center of next lp to beg next rnd.

Rnds 32–34: [Sc, ch 7] in each sp around, join in beg sc, sl st to center of next lp to beg next rnd in Rnds 32 and 33 only.

Rnd 35: Ch 1, sc in same sc as joining, ch 7, sk ch-7 sp, sc in each sc around, join in beg sc.

Rnd 36: Sl st to center of next lp, [sc, ch 7] in each lp around, join in beg sc.

Rnd 37: Rep Rnd 35.
Rnd 38: Rep Rnd 36.

Top ruffle

Rnd 39: Sl st to center of next ch-7 lp, ch 3 (counts as first dc), dc in same sp, [ch 16, sl st in 15th ch from hook, ch 2, 2 dc in 4th ch of next ch-7 lp] rep around, join in 3rd ch of beg ch-3.

Rnd 40: Sl st in next dc, *[hdc, ch 2] in each of next 13 chs of ch-16 lp, hdc in next ch, sl st in each of next 2 dc, rep from * around, join in sl-st sp, fasten off.

Middle ruffle

Rnd 41: Attach cotton from bottom in 4th ch of unworked ch-7 lp, 2 dc in 4th ch, [ch 14, sl st in 13th ch from hook, ch 2, 2 dc in 4th ch of next ch-7 lp] rep around, join in 3rd ch of beg ch-14.

Rnd 42: Sl st in next dc, *[hdc, ch 2] in each of next 11 chs of ch-14 lp, hdc in last ch, sl st in each of next 2 dc, rep from * around, join in sl-st sp, fasten off.

Bottom ruffle

Rnd 43: Attach cotton in 4th ch of ch-7 lp above middle ruffle, 2 dc in same sp, [ch 12, sl st in 11th ch from hook, ch 2, 2 dc in 4th ch of next ch-7 lp] rep around, join in 3rd ch of beg ch-12.

Rnd 44: Sl st to next dc, *[hdc, ch 2] in each of next 9 chs of lp, hdc in last ch, sl st in each of next 2 dc, rep from * around, join in beg sl-st sp, fasten off.

Wings

Row 1: Ch 5, join to form a ring, ch 3 (counts as first dc), 19 dc in ring, ch 6 (counts as first dc, ch 3 of following row), turn.

Row 2: Sc in next dc, [ch 3, sc in next dc] 7 times, ch 3, sk 2 sts, [sc, ch 3 in next st] 8 times, dc in last dc, ch 7 (counts as first dc, ch 4 of following row), turn.

Row 3: [Sc, ch 4 in next lp] 7 times, sc in next lp, [ch 1, sc, ch 1] in next lp, [sc, ch 4 in next lp] 8 times, dc in last dc, ch 7 (counts as first dc, ch 4 of following row), turn.

Row 4: [Sc, ch 4 in next lp] 7 times, sc in next lp, sk ch-1 sp, [ch 2, sc, ch 2] in center sc, sk ch-1 sp, [sc, ch 4 in next lp] 7 times, sc in next lp, [ch 4, dc] in last dc, ch 8 (counts as first dc, ch 5 of following row), turn.

Row 5: [Sc, ch 5 in next lp] 7 times, sc in next lp, ch 3, sk ch-2 sp, sc in next sc, ch 3, sk ch-2 sp, [sc, ch 5 in next lp] 7 times, sc in next lp, [ch 5, dc] in last dc, ch 9 (counts as first dc, ch 6 of following row), turn.

Row 6: [Sc, ch 6 in next lp] 7 times, sc in next lp, ch 4, sk ch-3 sp, sc in next sc, ch 4, sk ch-3 sp, [sc, ch 6 in next lp] 7 times, sc in next lp, [ch 6, dc] in last dc, ch 9 (counts as first dc, ch 6), turn.

Row 7: [Ch 1, sc, ch 3, sl st in top of sc for sc picot, ch 6 in next lp] 7 times, sc picot in next lp, ch 5, sk ch-4 sp, sc in next sc, ch 5, sk ch-4 sp, [sc picot, ch 6 in next lp] 7 times, sc picot in next lp, [ch 6, dc] in last dc, ch 3 (counts as first dc of following row), turn.

Row 8: Dc in same sp, [ch 13, sl st in 12th ch from hook, ch 2, dc in 3rd and 4th chs of next ch-6 lp] 8 times, ch 13, sl st in 12th ch from hook, [ch 2, sc] in next picot, *{ch 4, sc, ch 4} in ch-5 sp *, sc in next sc, rep from * to * once, sc in next picot, rep between {} 8 times, ch 13, sl st in 12th ch from hook, ch 2, 2 dc in last dc, ch 1, turn.

Row 9: Sl st in next dc, *[hdc, ch 2] in 10 chs of lp, hdc in next ch, sl st in each of next 2 dc *, rep from * to * 8 times, sl st in sc after 9th lp, [ch 3, sc] in next lp 4 times, ch 3, sl st in next sc, rep from * to * 9 times, fasten off.

Sleeves
Make 2

Rnd 1: Ch 8, join to form a ring, sc in each ch around, join in beg sc.

Rnds 2–5: [Sc, ch 3] in each st around, join with [ch 1, hdc] in beg sc.

Rnds 6–9: [Sc, ch 4] in each lp around, join in beg sc.

Rnds 10–13: Sl st to center of next lp, [sc, ch 5] in each lp around, join in beg sc.

Rnd 14: Sl st to center of next lp, ch 3 (counts as first dc), dc in same sp, [ch 13, sl st in 12th ch from hook, ch 2, 2 dc in center of next lp] rep around, join in 3rd ch of beg ch-3.

Rnd 15: Sl st to next dc, *[hdc, ch 2] in each of next 10 chs of next lp, hdc in last ch, sl st in each of next 2 dc, rep from * around, join in beg sl-st sp, fasten off.

Stiffening

Apply fabric stiffener (see Pattern Notes). Cinch neck; shape angel over cone.

Cover chenille wires with plastic wrap; insert into sleeves. Push ends of chenille wires into cone at angel's shoulders; shape sleeves.

Shape wings on plastic-covered flat surface; pin in place.

Allow pieces to dry completely.

Finishing

Cut 14" length of ½"-wide ribbon. Using photo as a guide, weave through first wing, across wing back and through 2nd wing; trim ends even with wing edges and glue in place.

Glue wings on angel back approximately 1" below neck.

Glue curly hair over angel's head according to manufacturer's directions. Cut 6" length of gold cording; shape in circle over hair. Join ends at back of head; secure in place with glue. Using photo as a guide, glue 1 ribbon flower and small sprigs of baby's breath over cording.

Cut 2 (6½") lengths of ½"-wide ribbon. Using photo as a guide, weave each piece through end of 1 sleeve just above ruffled edge. Trim ends and glue in place.

Cut rem ½"-wide ribbon into 2 equal lengths. Weave 1 piece through skirt just above top ruffle. Trim ends and glue in place. Rep for 2nd piece just above first.

Glue 8 ribbon flowers over ribbons evenly sp around skirt. Glue small sprig of baby's breath between each flower.

Make a bouquet from rem flowers and small amount of baby's breath; arrange in place through edge of 1 sleeve, using photo as guide. Secure with glue.

Glue ¼"-wide ribbon over ends of bouquet so that ends trail down front of angel. Knot each end of rem cording; glue in place over ends of bouquet in same manner as ribbon. ❖

STITCH GUIDE

Front Loop (a)
Back Loop (b)

Chain (ch)
Yo, draw lp through hook.

Slip Stitch Joining
Insert hook in beg ch, yo, draw lp through.

Front Post/Back Post Dc
Fpdc (a): Yo, insert hook from front to back and to front again around the vertical post (upright part) of next st, yo and draw yarn through, yo and complete dc.
Bpdc (b): Yo, reaching over top of piece and working on opposite side (right side) of work, insert hook from right to left around vertical post of next st, yo and draw yarn through, yo and complete dc.

Single Crochet (sc)
Insert hook in st (a), yo, draw lp through (b), yo, draw through both lps on hook (c).

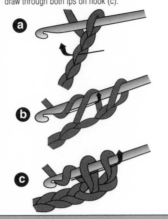

Half-Double Crochet (hdc)
Yo, insert hook in st (a), draw lp through (b), yo, draw through all 3 lps on hook (c).

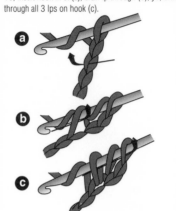

Double Crochet (dc)
Yo, insert hook in st (a), yo, draw through 1 lp (b), [yo, draw through 2 lps] twice (c, d).

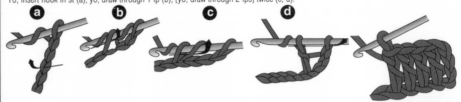

Treble Crochet (tr)
Yo hook twice, insert hook in st (a), yo, draw lp through (b), [yo, draw through 2 lps on hook] 3 times (c, d, e).

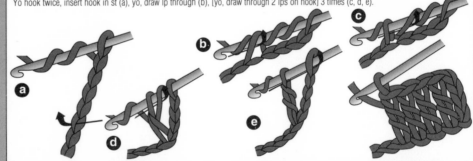

Stitch Abbreviations
The following stitch abbreviations are used throughout this book.

beg	begin(ning)
bl(s)	block(s)
bpdc	back post dc
ch(s)	chain(s)
cl(s)	cluster(s)
CC	contrasting color
dc	double crochet
dec	decrease
dtr	double treble crochet
fpdc	front post dc
hdc	half-double crochet
inc	increase
lp(s)	loop(s)
MC	main color
p	picot
rem	remain(ing)
rep	repeat
rnd(s)	round(s)
RS	right side facing you
sc	single crochet
sk	skip
sl st	slip stitch
sp(s)	space(s)
st(s)	stitch(es)
tog	together
tr	treble crochet
trtr	triple treble crochet
WS	wrong side facing you
yo	yarn over

Yarn Conversion

OUNCES TO GRAMS		GRAMS TO OUNCES	
1	28.4	25	⅞
2	56.7	40	1⅖
3	85.0	50	1¾
4	113.4	100	3½

DECREASING

Single Crochet Decrease
Dec 1 sc over next 2 sc as follows: Draw up a lp in each of next 2 sts, yo, draw through all 3 lps on hook.

Half-Double Crochet Decrease
Dec 1 hdc over next 2 hdc as follows: [Yo, insert hook in next st, yo, draw lp through] twice, yo, draw through all 5 lps on hook.

SPECIAL STITCHES

Chain Color Change (ch color change)
Yo with new color, draw through last lp on hook.

Double Crochet Color Change (dc color change)
Work dc until 2 lps rem, drop first color, yo with new color, draw through last 2 lps of st.

Reverse Single Crochet (reverse sc)
Working from left to right, insert hook in next st to the right (a), yo, draw through st, complete as for sc (b).

Charity

Hope

Faith

Lacy and delicate, each of these three exquisite angels will bring an aura of heavenly beauty into your home!

0 54525 30089 3

Quick Kitchen Helpers

Dress up your liquid dish detergent bottle with a cute apron! A matching dishcloth completes the set of Quick Kitchen Helpers (right). Both are made with 100 percent worsted weight cotton, so you can wash them again and again! Instructions begin on page 26.

Heart & Home Rug

Crocheted with a washable and durable polyester yarn, this charming Heart & Home Rug (below) adds a homey touch to the kitchen when placed by the sink. Instructions begin on page 27.

Napkin Rag & Apple Rag Baskets

Strips of cotton fabric work up quickly into these
handy baskets! Keep paper napkins tucked in our
Napkin Rag Basket and crisp apples in our Apple
Rag Basket. Both can be used for keeping a variety
of items close at hand. Instructions begin on page 28.

Satin Rag Basket

Strips of white satin give an elegant look to rag crochet. Our Satin Rag Basket (above) is just the right size for holding potpourri or after-dinner candies. Instructions begin on page 29.

Climbing Roses Place Mat

Anyone who likes roses will cherish a set of Climbing Roses Place Mats (right). Delicate flowers worked in filet make this piece heirloom quality. Instructions begin on page 28.

Blue Shell Tissue Topper

Our Blue Shell Tissue Topper (right) tastefully accents your bathroom while keeping spare bathroom tissue conveniently at hand. Instructions begin on page 31.

Pretty Bath Rug

Variegated yarn adds a lot of pleasing color without a lot of effort! Give your bathroom a fresh new look with this Pretty Bath Rug (below). Instructions begin on page 30.

Pineapple Swirl

EXPERIENCE LEVEL
Intermediate

SIZE
Approximately 46" in diameter

MATERIALS
- DMC® Cebelia® crochet cotton size 10 (50 grams per ball): 7 balls ecru naturel
- Size 7 steel crochet hook or size needed to obtain gauge

GAUGE
Rnds 1–6 = 4" in diameter
To save time, take time to check gauge.

PATTERN NOTE
Join rnds with a sl st unless otherwise stated.

PATTERN STITCHES

Beg cl: Ch 2, holding back on hook last lp of each st, work a total of 2 dc over indicated sts or in indicated st, yo, draw through all 3 lps on hook.

3-dc cl: Holding back on hook last lp of each st, work a total of 3 dc over indicated sts or in indicated st, yo, draw through all 4 lps on hook.

4-dc cl: Holding back on hook last lp of each st, work a total of 4 dc over indicated sts or in indicated st, yo, draw through all 5 lps on hook.

TABLECLOTH

Rnd 1: Ch 9, join to form a ring, ch 3 (counts as first dc throughout), 23 dc in ring, join in 3rd ch of beg ch-3. (24 dc)

Rnd 2: Ch 4 (counts as first dc, ch 1 throughout), [dc, ch 1] in each dc around, join in 3rd ch of beg ch-4.

Rnd 3: Ch 5 (counts as first dc, ch 2), [dc, ch 2] in each dc around, join in 3rd ch of beg ch-5.

Rnd 4: Sl st in next ch-2 sp, ch 3, 2 dc in same ch-2 sp, [ch 1, 3 dc in next ch-2 sp] rep around, ending with ch 1, join in 3rd ch of beg ch-3.

Rnd 5: Beg cl over next 2 dc, [ch 3, dc in next dc, 2 dc in next dc, dc in next dc, ch 3, 3-dc cl over next 3 dc] rep around, ending with ch 3, join in top of beg cl.

Rnd 6: Ch 1, sc in top of same beg cl, [ch 7, 4-dc cl over next 4 dc, ch 7, sc in top of next 3-dc cl] rep around, ending with ch 3, tr in beg sc to form last ch-7 sp.

Rnd 7: Ch 1, sc in sp just formed, [ch 7, sc in next ch-7 sp] rep around, ending with ch 3, tr in beg sc. (24 ch-7 sps)

Rnds 8–10: Rep Rnd 7.

Rnd 11: Ch 3, 3 dc in sp just formed, [dc in next sc, 7 dc in next ch-7 sp] rep around, ending with 3 dc in same sp as beg ch-3, join in 3rd ch of beg ch-3. (192 dc)

Rnd 12: Ch 3, dc in each of next 3 dc, *[dc, ch 2, dc] in next dc, dc in each of next 7 dc, ch 2, sk next dc **, dc in each of next 7 dc, rep from * around, ending last rep at **, dc in each of last 3 dc, join in 3rd ch of beg ch-3.

Rnd 13: Ch 3, dc in each of next 4 dc, *[dc, ch 2, dc] in next ch-2 sp, dc in each of next 6 dc, sk 2 dc, [dc, ch 3, dc] in next ch-2 sp, sk 2 dc **, dc in each of next 6 dc, rep from * around, ending last rep at **, dc in last dc, join in 3rd ch of beg ch-3.

Rnd 14: Sl st in next dc, ch 3, dc in each of next 4 dc, *[dc, ch 2, dc] in next ch-2 sp, dc in each of next 5 dc, ch 1, sk 3 dc, [dc, ch 3, dc] in next ch-3 sp, ch 1, sk 3 dc **, dc in each of next 5 dc, rep from * around, ending last rep at **, join in 3rd ch of beg ch-3.

Rnd 15: Sl st in next 2 dc, ch 3, dc in each of next 3 dc, *[dc, ch 3, dc] in next ch-2 sp, dc in each of next 4 dc, ch 2, [2 dc, ch 3, 2 dc] in next ch-3 sp, ch 2, sk ch-1 sp and next 2 dc **, dc in each of next 4 dc, rep from * around, ending last rep at **, join in 3rd ch of beg ch-3.

Rnd 16: Sl st in next 2 dc, ch 3, dc in each of next 2 dc, *ch 5, dc in each of next 3 dc, ch 3, sk 2 dc, dc in each of next 2 dc, 5 dc in next ch-3 sp, dc in each of next 2 dc, ch 3, sk 2 dc **, dc in each of next 3 dc, rep from * around, ending last rep at **, join in 3rd ch of beg ch-3.

Rnd 17: Ch 3, dc in each of next 2 dc, *ch 3, dc in 3rd ch of next ch-5 sp, ch 3, dc in each of next 3 dc, ch 1, [{dc, ch 1} in next dc] 9 times **, dc in each of next 3 dc, rep from * around, ending last rep at **, join in 3rd ch of beg ch-3.

Rnd 18: Ch 3, dc in each of next 2 dc, *ch 3, dc in next dc, ch 3, dc in each of next 3 dc, ch 3, sk next ch-1 sp, sc in next ch-1 sp, [ch 3, sc in next ch-1 sp] 7 times, ch 3, sk next ch-1 sp **, dc in each of next 3 dc, rep from * around, ending last rep at **, join in 3rd ch of beg ch-3.

Rnd 19: Ch 3, dc in each of next 2 dc, *ch 3, 2 dc in next dc, ch 3, dc in each of next 3 dc, ch 3, sk next ch-3 sp, sc in next ch-3 sp, [ch 3, sc in next ch-3 sp] 6 times, ch 3 **, dc in each of next 3 dc, rep from * around, ending last rep at **, join in 3rd ch of beg ch-3.

Rnd 20: Ch 3, dc in each of next 2 dc, *ch 3, 2 dc in each of next 2 dc, ch 3, dc in each of next 3 dc, ch 3, sk next ch-3 sp, sc in next ch-3 sp, [ch 3, sc in next ch-3 sp] 5 times, ch 3 **, dc in each of next 3 dc, rep from * around, ending last rep at **, join in 3rd ch of beg ch-3.

Rnd 21: Ch 3, dc in each of next 2 dc, *[ch 3, dc in each of next 2 dc] twice, ch 3, dc in each of next 3 dc, ch 3, sk next ch-3 sp, sc in next ch-3 sp, [ch 3, sc in next ch-3 sp] 4 times, ch 3 **, dc in each of next 3 dc, rep from * around, ending last rep at **, join in 3rd ch of beg ch-3.

Rnd 22: Ch 3, dc in each of next 2 dc, *ch 4, dc in next dc, 2 dc in next dc, ch 3, 2 dc in next dc, dc in next dc, ch 4, dc in each of next 3 dc, ch 3, sk next ch-3 sp, sc in next ch-3 sp, [ch 3, sc in next ch-3 sp] 3 times, ch 3 **, dc in each of next 3 dc, rep from * around, ending last rep at **, join in 3rd ch of beg ch-3.

Rnd 23: Ch 3, dc in each of next 2 dc, *ch 4, 2 dc in next dc, dc in each of next 2 dc, ch 3, dc in next ch-3 sp, ch 3, dc in each of next 2 dc, 2 dc in next dc, ch 4, dc in each of next 3 dc, ch 3, sk next ch-3 sp, sc in next ch-3 sp, [ch 3, sc in next ch-3 sp] twice, ch 3 **, dc in each of next 3 dc, rep from * around, ending last rep at **, join in 3rd ch of beg ch-3.

Rnd 24: Ch 3, dc in each of next 2 dc, *ch 4, dc in each of next 3 dc, 2 dc in next dc, ch 3, [dc, ch 3, dc] in next dc, ch 3, 2 dc in next dc, dc in each of next 3 dc, ch 4, dc in each of next 3 dc, ch 3, sk next ch-3 sp, sc in next ch-3 sp, ch 3, sc in next ch-3 sp, ch 3 **, dc in each of next 3 dc, rep from * around, ending last rep at **, join in 3rd ch of beg ch-3.

Rnd 25: Ch 3, dc in each of next 2 dc, *ch 4, dc in each of next 5 dc, [ch 3, 2 dc in next dc] twice, ch 3, dc in each of next 5 dc, ch 4, dc in each of next 3 dc, ch 3, sk next ch-3 sp, sc in next ch-3 sp, ch 3 **, dc in each of next 3 dc, rep from * around, ending last rep at **, join in 3rd ch of beg ch-3.

Rnd 26: Ch 3, dc in each of next 2 dc, *ch 3, sk 2 chs of next ch-4 sp, dc in each of next 2 chs, dc in each of next 3 dc, ch 4, sk 2 dc and next ch-3 sp, 2 dc in each of next 2 dc, ch 3, 2 dc in each of next 2 dc, ch 4, sk next ch-3 sp and 2 dc, dc in each of next 3 dc, dc in each of next 2 chs of ch-4 sp, ch 3, dc in each of next 3 dc, ch 1 **, dc in each of next 3 dc, rep from * around, ending last rep at **, join in 3rd ch of beg ch-3.

Rnd 27: Sl st in next 2 dc and first ch of ch-3 sp, ch 3, dc in each of next 2 chs, *dc in each of next 3 dc, ch 5, sk 2 dc, sk 2 chs of next ch-4 sp, dc in each of next 2 chs, dc in each of next 3 dc, ch 3, dc in next ch-3 sp, ch 3, sk next dc, dc in each of next 3 dc, dc in each of next 2 chs of ch-4 sp, ch 5, sk next 2 dc, dc in each of next 3 dc, dc in each of next 3 chs of ch-3 sp, ch 3, sk next [3 dc, ch-1 sp and 3 dc] **, dc in each of next 3 chs, rep from * around, ending last rep at **, join in 3rd ch of beg ch-3.

Rnd 28: Sl st in each of next 2 dc, ch 8 (counts as first dc, ch 5 throughout), *sk next 2 chs of ch-5 sp, dc in each of next 3 chs, dc in each of next 4 dc, ch 6, sk next ch-3 sp, sc in next dc, ch 6, sk first dc of next 5-dc group, dc in each of next 4 dc, dc in each of next 3 chs of ch-5 sp, ch 5, sk 3 dc, dc in next dc, ch 7, sk next [2 dc, ch-3 sp and 2 dc] **, dc in next dc, ch 5, rep from * around, ending last rep at **, join in 3rd ch of beg ch-8.

Rnd 29: Sl st in next 2 chs, ch 3, dc in each of next 3 chs, *dc in each of next 3 dc, ch 5, sk 3 dc, dc in next dc, [ch 5, dc in next ch-6 sp] twice, ch 5, dc in next dc, ch 5, sk 3 dc, dc in each of next 3 dc, dc in each of next 4 chs of ch-5 sp, ch 5, dc in next ch-7 sp, ch 5, sk first ch of next ch-5 sp **, dc in each of next 4 chs, rep from * around, ending last rep at **, join in 3rd ch of beg ch-3.

Rnd 30: Sl st in 3 dc, ch 8, dc in next ch-5 sp, [ch 5, dc in next ch-5 sp] 4 times, *ch 5, sk 3 dc, dc in next dc, [ch 5, dc in next ch-5 sp] twice **, ch 5, sk 3 dc, dc in next dc, [ch 5, dc in next ch-5 sp] 5 times, rep from * around, ending last rep at **, ch 2, dc in 3rd ch of beg ch-8 to form last ch-5 sp. (108 ch-5 sps)

Rnd 31: Ch 8, dc in next ch-5 sp, [ch 5, dc in next ch-5 sp] rep around, ending with ch 2, dc in 3rd ch of beg ch-8.

Rnd 32: Ch 8, dc in next ch-5 sp, [ch 5, dc in next ch-5 sp] twice, *ch 5, [dc, ch 5, dc] in next ch-5 sp **, [ch 5, dc in next ch-5 sp] 8 times, rep from * around, ending last rep at **, [ch 5, dc in next ch-5 sp] 4 times, ch 2, dc in 3rd ch of beg ch-8. (120 ch-5 sps)

Rnd 33: Rep Rnd 31. (120 ch-5 sps)

Rnd 34: Ch 3, dc over sp just made, *[ch 5, dc in next ch-5 sp] 5 times, ch 5 **, 2 dc in next ch-5 sp, rep from * around, ending last rep at **, join in 3rd ch of beg ch-3.

Rnd 35: Sl st in next dc, ch 3, dc in same dc, *ch 3, sc in next ch-5 sp, [ch 5, sc in next ch-5 sp] 5 times, ch 4, sk next dc **, 2 dc in next dc, rep from * around, ending last rep at **, join in 3rd ch of beg ch-3.

Rnd 36: Sl st in next dc, ch 3, dc in same dc, *ch 4, sk next sp, sc in next ch-5 sp, [ch 5, sc in next sp] 5 times, ch 4, sk dc **, 2 dc in next dc, rep from * around, ending last rep at **, join in 3rd ch of beg ch-3.

Rnd 37: Rep Rnd 36.

Rnd 38: Sl st in next dc, ch 3, dc in same dc, *ch 4, sk next ch-4 sp, sc in next ch-5 sp, [ch 6, sc in next ch-5 sp] twice, [2 dc, ch 2, 2 dc] in next sc, sc in next ch-5 sp, [ch 6, sc in next sp] twice, ch 4, sk dc **, 2 dc in next dc, rep from * around, ending last rep at **, join in 3rd ch of beg ch-3.

Rnd 39: Sl st in next dc, ch 3, dc in same dc, *ch 4, sk next ch-4 sp, [sc in next ch-6 sp, ch 6] twice, sc in next ch-2 sp, [ch 6, sc in next sp] 3 times, ch 4, sk dc **, 2 dc in next dc, rep from * around, ending last rep at **, join in 3rd ch of beg ch-3.

Rnd 40: Sl st in next dc, ch 3, dc in same dc, *ch 3, 4-dc cl in next sc, [ch 6, sc in next sp] 6 times, ch 4, sk dc **, 2 dc in next dc, rep from * around, ending last rep at **, join in 3rd ch of beg ch-3.

Rnd 41: Sl st in next dc, ch 3, dc in same dc, *ch 3, sc in next ch-6 sp, [ch 6, sc in next sp] 6 times, ch 4, sk dc **, 2 dc in next dc, rep from * around, ending last rep at **, join in 3rd ch of beg ch-3.

Rnd 42: Rep Rnd 41.

Rnd 43: Sl st in next dc, ch 3, dc in same dc, *ch 3, 4-dc cl in next sc, [ch 6, sc in next sp] 7 times, ch 4, sk dc **, 2 dc in next dc, rep from * around, ending last rep at **, join in 3rd ch of beg ch-3.

Rnd 44: Sl st in next dc, ch 3, dc in same dc, *ch 3, sc in next ch-6 sp, [ch 6, sc in next sp] 7 times, ch 4, sk dc **, 2 dc in next dc, rep from * around, ending last rep at **, join in 3rd ch of beg ch-3.

Rnd 45: Rep Rnd 44.

Rnd 46: Sl st in dc, ch 3, dc in same dc, *ch 2, 4-dc cl in next sc, [ch 6, sc in next sp] 8 times, ch 3, sk dc **, 2 dc in next dc, rep from * around, ending last rep at **, join in 3rd ch of beg ch-3.

Rnd 47: Sl st in next dc, ch 3, dc in same dc, *ch 2, sc in next ch-6 sp, [ch 6, sc in next ch sp] 7 times, ch 6, sk dc **, 2 dc in next dc, rep from * around, ending last rep at **, join in 3rd ch of beg ch-3.

Rnd 48: Rep Rnd 47.

Rnd 49: Sl st in next dc, ch 3, dc in same dc, *ch 1, 4-dc cl in next sc, [ch 6, sc in next ch sp] 8 times **, ch 6, sk dc, 2 dc in next dc, rep from * around, ending last rep at **, ch 3, dc in 3rd ch of beg ch-3.

Rnd 50: Ch 1, sc in sp just made, *ch 7, sc in next ch-6 sp **, [ch 6, sc in next ch sp] 8 times, rep from * around, ending last rep at **, [ch 6, sc in next sp] 7 times, ch 6, join in beg sc.

Rnd 51: Sl st in next ch-7 sp, ch 3, 8 dc in same sp, *ch 3, sc in next sp, [ch 6, sc in next sp] 7 times, ch 3 **, 9 dc in next ch-7 sp, rep from * around, ending last rep at **, join in 3rd ch of beg ch-3.

Rnd 52: Ch 3, dc in each of next 3 dc, *ch 3, sk next dc, dc in each of next 4 dc, ch 3, sc in next ch-6 sp, [ch 6, sc in next ch sp] 6 times, ch 3 **, dc in each of next 4 dc, rep from * around, ending last rep at **, join in 3rd ch of beg ch-3.

Rnd 53: Ch 3, dc in each of next 3 dc, *ch 5, sc in next ch sp, ch 5, dc in each of next 4 dc, ch 3, sc in next ch-6 sp, [ch 6, sc in next sp] 5 times, ch 3 **, dc in each of next 4 dc, rep from * around, ending last rep at **, join in 3rd ch of beg ch-3.

Rnd 54: Ch 3, dc in each of next 3 dc, *ch 5, dc in next sp, ch 1, dc in next sp, ch 5, dc in each of next 4 dc, ch 3, sc in next ch-6 sp, [ch 6, sc in next ch sp] 4 times, ch 3 **, dc in each of next 4 dc, rep from * around, ending last rep at **, join in 3rd ch of beg ch-3.

Rnd 55: Ch 3, dc in each of next 3 dc, *ch 4, sc in next sp, ch 4, sc in next ch-1 sp, ch 4, sc in next sp, ch 4, dc in each of next 4 dc, ch 4, sc in next ch-6 sp, [ch 6, sc in next sp] 3 times, ch 4 **, dc in each of next 4 dc, rep from * around, ending last rep at **, join in 3rd ch of beg ch-3.

Rnd 56: Ch 3, dc in each of next 3 dc, *[ch 4, dc in next sp] 4 times, ch 4, dc in each of next 4 dc, ch 5, sc in next ch-6 sp, ch 4, 5 sc in next sp, ch 4, sc in next sp, ch 5 **, dc in each of next 4 dc, rep from * around, ending last rep at **, join in 3rd ch of beg ch-3.

Rnd 57: Ch 3, dc in each of next 3 dc, *[ch 5, sc in next dc] 4 times, ch 5, dc in each of next 4 dc, ch 9, sk ch-5 sp and ch-4 sp, sc in each of next 5 sc, ch 9 **, dc in each of next 4 dc, rep from * around, ending last rep at **, join in 3rd ch of beg ch-3.

Rnd 58: Ch 3, dc in each of next 3 dc, *[ch 5, sc in next sp] 5 times, ch 5, dc in each of next 4 dc, ch 9, sk 1 sc, sc in each of next 3 sc, ch 9 **, dc in each of next 4 dc, rep from * around, ending last rep at **, join in 3rd ch of beg ch-3.

Rnd 59: Ch 3, dc in each of next 3 dc, *[ch 5, sc in next sp] 6 times, ch 5, dc in each of next 4 dc, dc in each of next 2 chs, ch 7, sc in each of next 3 sc, ch 7, sk 7 chs, dc in each of next 2 chs **, dc in each of next 4 dc, rep from * around, ending last rep at **, join in 3rd ch of beg ch-3.

Rnd 60: Ch 3, dc in next dc, *[ch 5, sc in next sp] 7 times, ch 5, sk 2 dc, dc in each of next 4 dc, dc in each of next 2 chs, ch 6, sk next sc, sc in next sc, ch 6, sk 5 chs, dc in each of next 2 chs **, dc in each of next 4 dc, rep from * around, ending last rep at **, dc in each of next 2 dc, join in 3rd ch of beg ch-3.

Rnd 61: Ch 8, sc in next sp, [ch 5, sc in next sp] 7 times, *ch 5, sk 1 dc, dc in each of next 5 dc, dc in each of next 2 chs, ch 2, sk 4 chs of next ch-6 sp, dc in each of next 2 chs **, dc in each of next 5 dc, [ch 5, sc in next sp] 8 times, rep from * around, ending last rep at **, dc in each of next 4 dc, join in 3rd ch of beg ch-8.

Rnd 62: Sl st in next 2 chs, ch 1, sc in same sp, [ch 6, sc in next sp] 8 times, *ch 6, sk 2 dc, dc in each of next 5 dc, 3 dc in next ch-2 sp, dc in each of next 5 dc **, [ch 6, sc in next sp] 9 times, rep from * around, ending last rep at **, ch 6, join in beg sc.

Rnd 63: Sl st in next 3 chs, ch 9 (counts as first tr, ch 5), tr in next sp, [ch 5, tr in next sp] 7 times, *ch 5, sk 3 dc, tr in next dc, ch 5, sk 5 dc, tr in next dc **, [ch 5, tr in next sp] 10 times, rep from * around, ending last rep at **, ch 5, tr in next sp, ch 5, join in 4th ch of beg ch-9.

Rnd 64: Sl st in next 3 chs, ch 1, sc in same sp, [ch 9, sk next sp, 5 dc in each of next 3 sps, ch 9, sk next sp, sc in next sp] rep around, join in beg sc. (15 dc in each dc group)

Rnd 65: Sl st in 9 chs, sl st in next 2 dc, ch 4, dc in next dc, [ch 1, dc in next dc] 11 times, *ch 7, dc near end of next sp, dc near beg of next sp, ch 7, sk dc **, dc in next dc, [ch 1, dc in next dc] 12 times, sk last dc, rep from * around, ending last rep at **, join in 3rd ch of beg ch-4. (13 dc in each dc group)

Rnd 66: Sl st in next ch-1 sp, ch 4, dc in next ch-1 sp, [ch 1, dc in next ch-1 sp] 10 times, *ch 5, dc in next dc, ch 3, dc in next dc, ch 5 **, dc in next ch-1 sp, [ch 1, dc in next ch-1 sp] 11 times, rep from * around, ending last rep at **, join in 3rd ch of beg ch-4. (12 dc in each dc group)

Rnd 67: Sl st in next ch-1 sp, ch 1, sc in same sp, *[ch 3, sc in next ch-1 sp] 10 times, ch 5, sk next ch-5 sp, dc in next dc, 4 dc in next sp, dc in next dc, ch 5 **, sc in next ch-1 sp, rep from * around, ending last rep at **, join in beg sc.

Rnd 68: Sl st in next sp, ch 1, sc in same ch-3 sp, *[ch 3, sc in next ch-3 sp] 9 times, ch 5, dc in each of next 3 dc, ch 2, dc in each of next 3 dc, ch 5 **, sc in next ch-3 sp, rep from * around, ending last rep at **, join in beg sc.

Rnd 69: Sl st in next sp, ch 1, sc in same ch-3 sp, *[ch 3, sc in next ch-3 sp] 8 times, ch 5, dc in each of next 3 dc, ch 3, dc in each of next 3 dc, ch 5 **, sc in next ch-3 sp, rep from * around, ending last rep at **, join in beg sc.

Rnd 70: Sl st in next sp, ch 1, sc in same ch-3 sp, *[ch 3, sc in next ch-3 sp] 7 times, ch 5, 2 dc in next dc, dc in each of next 2 dc, ch 4, dc in each of next 2 dc, 2 dc in next dc, ch 5 **, sc in next ch-3 sp, rep from * around, ending last rep at **, join in beg sc.

Rnd 71: Sl st in next sp, ch 1, sc in same ch-3 sp, *[ch 3, sc in next ch-3 sp] 6 times, [ch 5, dc in each of next 4 dc] twice, ch 5 **, sc in next ch-3 sp, rep from * around, ending last rep at **, join in beg sc.

Rnd 72: Sl st in next sp, ch 1, sc in same ch-3 sp, *[ch 3, sc in next ch-3 sp] 5 times, ch 5, dc in each of next 3 dc, 2 dc in next dc, ch 5, 2 dc in next dc, dc in each of next 3 dc, ch 5 **, sc in next ch-3 sp, rep from * around, ending last rep at **, join in beg sc.

Rnd 73: Sl st in next sp, ch 1, sc in same ch-3 sp, *[ch 3, sc in next ch-3 sp] 4 times, ch 5, dc in each of next 3 dc, ch 2, dc in each of next 2 dc, ch 2, sc in next ch-5 sp, ch 2, dc in each of next 2 dc, ch 2, dc in each of next 3 dc, ch 5 **, sc in next ch-3 sp, rep from * around, ending last rep at **, join in beg sc.

Rnd 74: Sl st in next sp, ch 1, sc in same ch-3 sp, *[ch 3, sc in next ch-3 sp] 3 times, ch 6, dc in each of 3 dc, ch 4, dc in each of next 2 dc, ch 5, dc in each of next 2 dc, ch 4, dc in each of next 3 dc, ch 6 **, sc in next ch-3 sp, rep from * around, ending last rep at **, join in beg sc.

Rnd 75: Sl st in next sp, ch 1, sc in same ch-3 sp, *[ch 3, sc in next ch-3 sp] twice, ch 6, sk 5 chs, dc in next ch, dc in each of next 3 dc, ch 5, dc in each of next 2 dc, ch 2, sc in next sp, ch 2, dc in each of next 2 dc, ch 5, dc in each of next 3 dc, dc in first ch of next sp, ch 6 **, sc in next ch-3 sp, rep from * around, ending last rep at **, join in beg sc.

Rnd 76: Sl st in next sp, ch 1, sc in same ch-3 sp, *ch 3, sc in next ch-3 sp, ch 6, sk 4 chs, dc in each of next 2 chs, dc in each of next 4 dc, ch 3, sc in next sp, ch 3, dc in each of next 2 dc, ch 3, dc in each of next 2 dc, ch 3, sc in next ch sp, ch 3, dc in each of next 4 dc, dc in each of next 2 chs, ch 6 **, sc in next ch-3 sp, rep from * around, ending last rep at **, join in beg sc.

Rnd 77: Sl st in next sp, ch 1, sc in same ch-3 sp, *ch 6, sk 4 chs, dc in each of next 2 chs, dc in each of next 4 dc, ch 5, dc in next sc, ch 5, dc in each of next 2 dc, ch 1, dc in each of next 2 dc, ch 5, dc in next sc, ch 5, sk 2 dc, dc in each of next 4 dc, dc in each of next 2 chs, ch 6 **, sc in next ch-3 sp, rep from * around, ending last rep at **, join in beg sc.

Rnd 78: Sl st in first 4 chs, ch 3, dc in each of next 2 chs, *dc in each of next 4 dc, [ch 5, dc in next sp] twice, ch 5, sk dc, dc in next dc, dc in next ch-1 sp, dc in next dc, [ch 5, dc in next sp] twice, ch 5, sk 2 dc, dc in each of next 4 dc, dc in each of next 3 chs, ch 2, sk 3 chs of next ch-6 sp **, dc in each of next 3 chs, rep from * around, join in 3rd ch of beg ch-3.

Rnd 79: Sl st in first 2 dc, ch 1, *sc in next dc, ch 5, dc in next sp, ch 5, sl st in dc just made (picot), [ch 5, {dc, picot} in next sp] twice, ch 3, [3-dc cl, picot] over next 3 dc, ch 3, [{dc, picot} in next sp, ch 5] 3 times, sk 3 dc, sc in next dc, ch 1, [dc, picot, ch 1] 5 times in next ch-2 sp, sk 3 dc, rep from * around, join in beg sc, fasten off.

—*Designed by Lucille LaFlamme*

Lacy Tissue Box Cover

EXPERIENCE LEVEL
Beginner

SIZE
Fits boutique-style tissue box

MATERIALS
- Crochet cotton size 10: 200 yds white (MC) and 25 yds mauve (CC)
- Size 0 steel crochet hook or size needed to obtain gauge

GAUGE
Rows 1–6 = 1"
To save time, take time to check gauge.

SIDE
Make 4

Row 1 (WS): Beg at bottom with MC, ch 27, sc in 2nd ch from hook and in each ch across, turn. (26 sc)

Row 2: Ch 3, sk first sc, *[sc, ch 4, sc] in next sc, sk 1 sc, rep from * across to last 2 sts, sk next st, sc in last st, turn. (12 ch-4 sps)

Rows 3–23: Ch 3, [sc, ch 4, sc] in each ch-4 sp across, sc in 3rd ch of turning ch-3, turn.

Row 24: Ch 3, 2 sc in each ch-4 sp across, dc in 3rd ch of turning ch-3, fasten off.

TOP
Make 2

Rows 1–9: Rep Rows 1–9 of side, at end of Row 9, fasten off, turn.

Row 10 (RS): Attach CC with a sl st in first sc, ch 3, [sc, ch 4, sc] in each ch-4 sp across, sc in 3rd ch of turning ch-3, fasten off.

JOINING SIDES
Holding 2 sides with WS tog, matching Rows 1–24, beg at bottom edge with CC, working through both thicknesses, [sc, ch 3, sc] in first st, *[sc, ch 3, sc] over end st of next row, sk next row, rep from * across, fasten off. (13 ch-3 sps)

Rep 3 times to join rem sides.

JOINING TOP & SIDES
With RS up, place foundation-ch edge of either top piece across last row of any side piece. Beg over end st at right edge of last row of top piece and working through both top and side pieces at the same time, attach CC with a sl st, work joining border around 3 edges as for sides, working [sc, ch 3, sc] in every other st across foundation-ch edge, place 2nd top piece on opposite side and continue joining around rem 3 sides of 2nd top piece, join in beg sc, fasten off.

—*Designed by Debbi Everett*

Perfect Pastel Edgings

E X P E R I E N C E   L E V E L
Advanced beginner

S I Z E
Fit 16"-wide hand towel

M A T E R I A L S
- DMC® Cebelia® crochet cotton size 10 (50 grams per ball): 90 yds medium pink #818, 88 yds pale delft #800, 73 yds pale yellow #745, 48 yds blue #799, 40 yds light melon #3326 and 33 yds light orange #743
- Size 7 steel crochet hook or size needed to obtain gauge
- Sewing needle and matching thread
- 3 (16"-wide) white hand towels

G A U G E
Yellow Diamonds Edging: Motif = 2¼" square
Pink Floral Edging: Motif = 4" in diameter
Blue Pineapple Edging: 7 rows of band = 2"
To save time, take time to check gauge.

P A T T E R N   N O T E
Join rnds with a sl st unless otherwise stated.

P A T T E R N   S T I T C H E S
3-dc cl: [Yo, draw up a lp in indicated sp, yo and draw through 2 lps] 3 times, yo and draw through all 4 rem lps.
Beg shell: [Ch 3, dc, ch 2, 2 dc] in same sp.
Shell: [2 dc, ch 2, 2 dc] in same sp.

·

Yellow Diamonds Edging

F I R S T   M O T I F
Rnd 1: With light orange, ch 7, join to form a ring, ch 1, 16 sc in ring, join in beg sc.

Rnd 2: Ch 1, sc in same st as joining, [ch 5, sk 3 sc, sc in next sc] 3 times, ch 5, join in beg sc.

Rnd 3: Ch 1, sc in same st as joining, [ch 3, {3-dc cl, ch 2, dc, ch 2, 3-dc cl} in next ch-5 sp, ch 3, sc in next sc] rep around, join in beg sc, fasten off.

Rnd 4: Attach pale yellow with a sl st in any dc, ch 1, sc in same st, [sc in next ch-2 sp, ch 9, sk 2 ch-3 sps, sc in next ch-2 sp, sc in next dc] rep around, join in beg sc.

Rnd 5: Ch 1, sc in same sc as joining, [15 dc in next ch-9 sp, sk next sc, sc in next sc] rep around, join in beg sc.

Rnd 6: Ch 1, [sc, ch 3, sc] in same sc as joining, [sc in each of next 7 dc, {sc, ch 3, sc} in next dc, sc in each of next 7 dc, {sc, ch 3, sc} in next sc], rep around, join in beg sc, fasten off.

S U B S E Q U E N T   M O T I F S
Make 8
Rnds 1–5: Rep Rnds 1–5 of first motif.

Joining
Note: Join motifs as shown in Fig. 1.

FIG. 1
Attaching Motifs to Towel

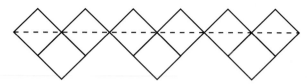

Dotted line indicates lower edge of towel

Rnd 6: Ch 1, [sc, ch 3, sc] in same sc as joining, *sc in each of next 8 dc, ch 1, sl st in corner ch-3 sp of previous motif, ch 1, sc in same dc of working motif *, sc in each of next 7 dc, sc in next sc, ch 1, sl st in corresponding ch-3 sp of previous motif, ch 1, sc in same sc of working motif, rep from * to * once, complete rem of rnd as for first motif.

F I N I S H I N G
With sewing needle and matching thread, center motifs over towel edge as in Fig. 1; stitch in place.

Tassels (make 3)
Cut 10 (8") strands of pale yellow. Holding all strands tog, fold in half, insert crochet hook from WS to RS through ch-3 sp at lower corner of motif, pull folded ends through, remove hook, pull free ends through lp and tighten. Trim ends evenly.

Pink Floral Edging

F I R S T   M O T I F
Rnd 1: With light melon, ch 7, join to form a ring, ch 1, 16 sc in ring, join in beg sc.

Rnd 2: Ch 1, sc in same sc as joining, [ch 3, sk 1 sc, sc in next sc] rep around, join in beg sc. (8 ch-3 sps)

Rnd 3: [Sc, ch 1, 2 dc, ch 1, sc] (1 petal made) in each ch-3 sp around, ending with sl st in same sc as joining st of Rnd 2.

Rnd 4: Ch 8 (counts as first dc, ch 5), holding petals forward, dc behind petals in next sk sc of Rnd 2 between petals, [ch 5, dc in next sk sc] rep around, ending with ch 5, join in 3rd ch of beg ch-8.

Rnd 5: Ch 1, sc in same ch as joining, [ch 1, 5 dc in next ch-5 sp, ch 1, sc in next dc] rep around, ending with ch 1, join in beg sc, fasten off.

Rnd 6: Attach medium pink with a sl st in any sc, ch 11 (counts as first dc, ch 8), dc in next sc, [ch 8, dc in next sc] rep around, join in 3rd ch of beg ch-11. (8 ch-8 sps)

Rnd 7: Ch 3 (counts as first dc), [9 dc in next ch-8 sp, dc in next dc] rep around, join in 3rd ch of beg ch-3. (80 dc)

Rnd 8: Ch 1, sc in same st as joining, [ch 5, sk 4 dc, sc in next dc] rep around, join in beg sc. (16 ch-5 sps)

Rnd 9: Ch 1, sc in same sc as joining, [7 dc in next ch-5 sp, sc in next sc] rep around, join in beg sc, fasten off.

Make 3

Rnds 1–8: Rep Rnds 1–8 of first motif.

Joining

Rnd 9: Ch 1, sc in same sc as joining, 7 dc in next ch-5 sp, sc in next sc, 4 dc in next ch-5 sp, sl st in 4th dc of any petal on previous motif that immediately precedes a Rnd 6 dc, 3 dc in same ch-5 sp on working motif, sc in next sc, 4 dc in next ch-5 sp, sl st in 4th dc of next corresponding petal on previous motif, 3 dc in same ch-5 sp on working motif, sc in next sc, [7 dc in next ch-5 sp, sc in next sc] rep around, join in beg sc, fasten off.

Join rem 2 motifs to previous motif so that 6 petals rem unworked on each side between each joining.

FILL-IN MOTIF

With RS facing, attach medium pink with a sl st in 4th dc of first petal to the right above joining, ch 7, sl st in 4th dc on first free petal above joining of next motif to the left, sl st in next 8 sts of same motif, turn, ch 7, sc in ch-7 sp, ch 7, sl st in 4th dc of next free petal of first motif, ch 1, turn, sc in each of next 4 chs, [ch 2, dc] 3 times in sc in first ch-7 sp, ch 2, sk 3 chs, sc in each of next 4 chs, turn, ch 5, sk first dc, shell in next dc, ch 5, sk 3 sc, join in next sc, fasten off.

Rep between rem motifs.

FINISHING

Tassels (make 3)

Cut 10 (8") strands of medium pink; complete same as for tassel in Yellow Diamonds Edging, attaching in each shell ch-2 sp in center of fill-in motif.

Attach to towel in same manner as for Yellow Diamonds Edging.

Blue Pineapple Edging

BAND

Row 1: With blue, ch 17, dc in 6th ch from hook and in each of next 2 chs, sk 2 chs, 5 dc in next ch, ch 1, sk 3 chs, dc in each of last 3 chs, turn.

Row 2: Ch 5, dc in each of first 3 dc, 5 dc in first dc of next 5-dc group, ch 1, sk 4 dc, dc in each of next 3 dc, turn.

Rows 3–56: Rep Row 2, fasten off at end of Row 56.

UPPER EDGING

Row 1: Attach pale delft with a sl st in first ch-5 sp on right end of band, ch 1, sc in same sp, working across longer edge, [ch 7, sc in next ch-5 sp, ch 5, sc in next ch-5 sp] rep across, ending with ch 7, sc in last ch-5 sp, turn. (14 ch-7 sps; 13 ch-5 sps)

Row 2 (RS): Sl st in ch-7 sp, ch 3 (counts as first dc), [4 dc, ch 4, sl st in last dc made (picot), 5 dc] in same sp, sc in next ch-5 sp, *[5 dc, picot, 5 dc] in next ch-7 sp **, sc in next ch-5 sp, rep from * across, ending last rep at **, fasten off.

PINEAPPLE MOTIFS

Base

Row 1: With RS facing and upper edging facing down, attach pale delft with a sl st in first free ch-5 sp on opposite side of band, beg shell in same ch-5 sp, *ch 7, sk next ch-5 sp, sc in next ch-5 sp, [ch 5, sc in next ch-5 sp] twice, ch 7, sk next ch-5 sp, [shell in next ch-5 sp] twice, rep from * across, ending with shell in last ch-5 sp, turn.

First pineapple motif

Row 2: Ch 4, shell in first shell sp, ch 5, dc in next sc, [[ch 1, dc] 3 times in next ch-5 sp, ch 1, dc in next sc] twice, ch 5, shell in next shell sp, tr in end dc of same shell, turn.

Row 3: Ch 4, shell in shell sp, ch 5, sc in next ch-1 sp, [ch 3, sc in next ch-1 sp] 7 times, ch 5, shell in next shell sp, tr in end dc of same shell, turn.

Row 4: Ch 4, shell in shell sp, ch 4, sc in next ch-3 sp, [ch 3, sc in next ch-3 sp] 6 times, ch 4, shell in next shell sp, tr in end dc of same shell, turn.

Row 5: Ch 4, shell in shell sp, ch 4, sc in next ch-3 sp, [ch 3, sc in next ch-3 sp] 5 times, ch 4, shell in next shell sp, tr in end dc of same shell, turn.

Row 6: Ch 4, shell in shell sp, ch 4, sc in next ch-3 sp, [ch 3, sc in next ch-3 sp] 4 times, ch 4, shell in next shell sp, tr in end dc of same shell, turn.

Row 7: Ch 4, shell in shell sp, ch 4, sc in next ch-3 sp, [ch 3, sc in next ch-3 sp] 3 times, ch 4, shell in next shell sp, tr in end dc of same shell, turn.

Row 8: Ch 4, shell in shell sp, ch 4, sc in next ch-3 sp, [ch 3, sc in next ch-3 sp] twice, ch 4, shell in next shell sp, tr in end dc of same shell, turn.

Row 9: Ch 4, shell in shell sp, ch 4, sc in next ch-3 sp, ch 3, sc in next ch-3 sp, ch 4, shell in next shell sp, tr in end dc of same shell, turn.

Row 10: Ch 4, shell in shell sp, shell in next shell sp, tr in end dc of same shell, turn.

Row 11: Ch 4, 2 dc in shell sp, 2 dc in next shell sp, tr in end dc of same shell, turn.

Row 12: Ch 4, sk 4 dc, sl st in 4th ch of turning ch-4, fasten off.

Subsequent pineapple motifs (make 3)

Rows 2–12: Attach pale delft with a sl st in first dc of next shell of Row 1 of base, rep Rows 2–12 of first motif.

PINEAPPLE EDGING

With RS facing, attach blue with a sl st in first blue ch-5 sp with pineapple shell, ch 1, sc in same sp, sc in each of next 3 chs of pineapple beg ch-3, [4 sc over each tr or in each ch-4 sp] 24 times around edges of same pineapple and next pineapple, ending over end st of Row 4 of next pineapple, *ch 6, turn, sl st in corresponding sc on previous pineapple, ch 1, turn, 7 sc in ch-6 sp just made, 4 sc in each of next 2 sps, ch 7, turn, sc in 4th sc of 7-sc group, ch 7, sl st in corresponding sc on previous pineapple, ch 1, turn, 7 sc in ch-7 sp just made, [sc, ch 4, sc] in next sc, 7 sc in next ch-7 sp, [4

sc over each tr and in each ch-4 sp] 19 times, rep from *
across, ending with 3 sc in last dc of last pineapple, sl st in
blue ch-5 sp, fasten off.

FINISHING

Tassels (make 3)

Cut 10 (8") strands of pale delft; complete in same manner
as for tassels for Yellow Diamond Edging, attaching in ch-4
sps between pineapple motifs.

Attach to towel in same manner as for Yellow Diamond
Edging.

—Designed by Lucille LaFlamme

Sweetheart Place Mat

EXPERIENCE LEVEL
Advanced

SIZE
Approximately 12" x 16"

MATERIALS
- DMC® Cebelia® crochet cotton size 10 (50 grams per
  ball): 1 ball each white (MC) and medium shell pink
  #223 (CC)
- Size 7 steel crochet hook or size needed to obtain gauge
- 6 bobbins

GAUGE
4 sps and 4 rows = 1"
To save time, take time to check gauge.

PATTERN NOTES
Join rnds with a sl st unless otherwise stated.

Wind 6 bobbins of medium shell pink before beg.

To change color in dc, work dc with first color until 2 lps
rem on hook, drop first color to WS of work, yo with next
color and complete dc.

To carry color not in use across sp to its next working area
after completing a CC popcorn, wrap color not in use
around working color while working ch sts of sp.

Do not carry CC across more than 1 sp; attach new bobbin.

MC may be carried at WS of work, working over it with CC
when 2–3 successive CC popcorn blocks are worked.

PATTERN STITCHES
Block (bl): Dc in each of next 3 sts.

Beg bl: Ch 3 (counts as first dc), dc in each of next 3 sts.

Sp: Ch 2, sk next 2 dc or next ch-2 sp, dc in next st.

Popcorn (pc): 5 dc in indicated st or sp, remove hook
from lp, insert hook from RS to WS in top of first dc, pull lp
through dc to form pc, ch 1 to close.

Pc bl: Pc in indicated st or sp, dc in next indicated st.

Bl over a bl: Dc in each of next 3 dc.

Bl over a sp: 2 dc in indicated ch-2 sp, dc in next dc.

Sp over a bl: Ch 2, sk 2 dc, dc in next dc.

Sp over a sp: Ch 2, dc in next dc.

Sp over a pc bl: Ch 2, sk pc, dc in next dc.

Pc bl over a sp: Pc in indicated ch-2 sp, dc in next dc.

Pc bl over a pc bl: Pc in top of indicated pc, dc in next dc.

3-tr cl: Holding back on hook last lp of each st, work 3 tr in
same sp, yo, draw through all 4 lps on hook.

Beg 3-tr cl: Ch 3, holding back on hook last lp of each st,
work 2 tr in same sp, yo, draw through all 3 lps on hook.

Picot: Ch 3, sl st in 3rd ch from hook.

———————————•———————————

PLACE MAT
Row 1 (RS): With white, ch 132, dc in 4th ch from hook
and in each ch across, turn. (130 dc, counting last 3 chs of
foundation ch as first dc; 43 bls)

Row 2: Ch 3 (counts as first dc throughout), dc in each of
next 3 dc, [ch 2, sk 2 dc, dc in next dc] rep across, working
dc in each of last 4 dc, turn.

Row 3: Beg bl over a bl, 41 sps over 41 sps, bl over a bl, turn.

Rows 4–65: Follow graph, at end of Row 65, do not fasten off, do not turn.

EDGING
Rnd 1 (RS): Ch 1, [sc, ch 5, sc] in last dc worked, *[ch 5, sk
1 row, sc over end st of next row] rep across side to next
corner, ending with ch 5, [sc, ch 5, sc] in top of corner st,
[ch 5, sk 2 dc, sc in next dc, [ch 5, sk 3 dc, sc in next dc] rep
across to next corner, ending with ch 5, sk 1 dc *, [sc, ch 5,
sc] in end dc, rep from * to *, join in beg sc, do not turn.
(136 ch-5 sps)

Rnd 2: [Sl st, beg 3-tr cl] in corner ch-5 sp, [ch 1, picot, ch 1,
3-tr cl] 3 times in same sp, *sc in next ch-5 sp, [3-tr cl, ch 1,
picot, ch 1] twice in next ch-5 sp, 3-tr cl in same sp, rep
from * around, working [[3-tr cl, ch 1, picot, ch 1] 3 times, 3-
tr cl] in each corner sp, join in top of beg 3-tr cl, fasten off.
Block to size.

—Designed by Nancy Hearne

Heart-Shaped Hot Pads

EXPERIENCE LEVEL
Beginner

SIZE
Small Heart: Approximately 7" x 6"
Large Heart: Approximately 12" x 10"

MATERIALS
- 3 yds pink fabric cut into 1" strips (MC)
- ¼ yd white fabric cut into 1" strips (CC)

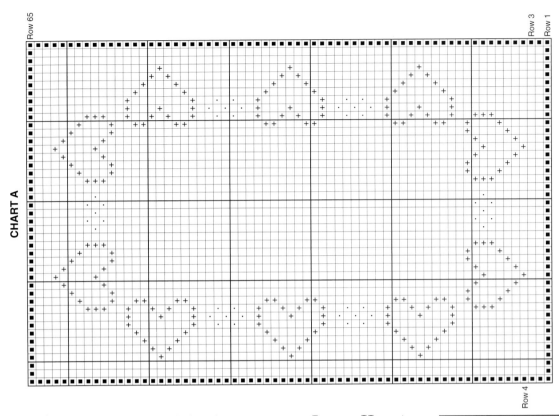

CHART A

Row 65 ... Row 3 ... Row 1 ... Row 4

- Size K/10½ crochet hook or size needed to obtain gauge

GAUGE

First 2 rnds of small heart = 6¼" wide x 4¾" tall

To save time, take time to check gauge.

PATTERN NOTES

Read General Instructions for Crocheting With Fabric Strips (page 26) before beginning.

Join rnds with a sl st unless otherwise stated.

Small Heart

Rnd 1: With MC, ch 12, 5 dc in 4th ch from hook, hdc in next ch, sc in next ch, sk 3 chs, sc in next ch, hdc in next ch, 6 dc in next ch, working on opposite side of foundation ch, dc in each of next 3 chs, 3 dc in next ch (bottom tip), dc in each of next 3 chs, join in last ch of beg ch-12. (25 sts, counting last 3 chs of beg ch-12 as first dc)

Rnd 2: Ch 3 (counts as first dc), dc in same ch as joining, 2 dc in each of next 4 sts, hdc in next st, sc in next st, sk 2 sts, sc in next st, hdc in next st, 2 dc in each of next 6 sts, dc in each of next 3 sts, 5 dc in next st, dc in each of next 3 sts, 2 dc in next st, join in 3rd ch of beg ch-3, fasten off. (39 sts)

EDGING

With RS facing, attach CC between 2 sc at center top between curves, ch 1, sc in same sp, ch 3, sk next st, [sc in next st, ch 3, sk next st] rep around, join in beg sc, fasten off. (20 ch-3 sps)

Weave in loose ends.

Large Heart

Rnd 1: With MC, ch 14, 5 dc in 4th ch from hook, dc in next ch, hdc in next ch, sc in next ch, sk 3 chs, sc in next ch, hdc in next ch, dc in next ch, 6 dc in next ch, working on opposite side of foundation ch, dc in each of next 4 chs, 3 dc in next ch (bottom tip), dc in each of next 4 chs, join in last ch of beg ch-14. (29 sts, counting last 3 chs of beg ch-14 as first dc)

Rnd 2: Ch 3 (counts as first dc throughout), dc in same ch as joining, 2 dc in each of next 5 sts, hdc in next st, sc in next st, sk 2 sts, sc in next st, hdc in next st, 2 dc in each of next 6 sts, dc in each of next 5 sts, 5 dc in next st, dc in each of next 5 sts, join in 3rd ch of beg ch-3. (43 sts)

Rnd 3: Ch 3, [2 dc in next st, dc in next st] 4 times, dc in each of next 2 sts, hdc in next st, sc in next st, sk 2 sts, sc in next st, hdc in next st, dc in each of next 3 sts, [2 dc in next st, dc in next st] 6 times, dc in each of next 3 sts, 3 dc in next dc, dc in each of next 3 sts, [2 dc in next st, dc in next st] twice, join in 3rd ch of beg ch-3. (55 sts)

Rnd 4: Ch 3, dc in next st, 2 dc in next st, [dc in each of next 2 sts, 2 dc in next st] 3 times, dc in each of next 2 sts, hdc in next st, sc in next st, sk 2 sts, sc in next st, hdc in next st, dc in each of next 2 sts, [2 dc in next st, dc in each of next 2 sts] 6 times, dc in each of next 4 sts, 5 dc in next dc, dc in each of next 6 sts, 2 dc in next st, dc in each of next 2 sts, 2 dc in last st, join in 3rd ch of beg ch-3, fasten off. (69 sts)

STITCH AND COLOR KEY
- ⊞ CC popcorn bl
- ■ MC block
- · MC popcorn bl
- ☐ MC sp

General Instructions for Crocheting With Fabric Strips

Fabric amounts given are based on 54" fabric width. If using 45" fabric width, add 1 yard; if using 60" fabric width, delete 1 yard.

Fold fabric in half lengthwise several times, making sure you can still cut through all thicknesses. Beg at folded edge and cutting toward selvage edge, cut 3"-wide strips unless otherwise stated in pattern. *Note: Lighter weight fabric may be cut into 3½"–4" strips.*

Hand- or machine-stitch short ends of strips tog with RS tog, using a ½" seam allowance.

Leaving long ends at beg and end, crochet with strips in same manner as with yarn or thread.

Weave ends in using a large blunt needle or smaller crochet hook.

Work projects with raw edges showing for a more ragged look, or fold edges under as follows for a more finished look: Fold outer edges of strip into center; fold in half again. Holding edges tog in this manner, make a beg sl knot; continue to fold edges as work progresses. *Note: If you prefer, you may iron edges of strips before you beg crocheting.*

When crocheting baskets, do not join rnds unless otherwise stated; mark last st of each rnd with a safety pin or other marker.

EDGING
With RS facing, attach CC between 2 sc at center top between curves, ch 1, sc in same sp, ch 3, sk next st, [sc in next st, ch 3, sk next st] rep around, join in beg sc, fasten off. (35 ch-3 sps)

Weave in loose ends.

—Designed by Maggie Weldon

Quick Kitchen Helpers

EXPERIENCE LEVEL
Beginner

SIZE
Dishcloth: Approximately 6¾" wide x 7" long

Apron: Fits 22-oz bottle

MATERIALS
- Worsted weight 100 percent cotton yarn: 1 oz pink and small amount variegated
- Size I/9 crochet hook or size needed to obtain gauge

GAUGE
17 dc = 5"

To save time, take time to check gauge

PATTERN NOTE
Join rnds with a sl st unless otherwise stated.

PATTERN STITCH
Dc dec: Holding back on hook last lp of each st, dc in each of next 2 sts, yo, draw through all 3 lps on hook.

Dishcloth

Row 1: With pink, ch 24, sc in 2nd ch from hook and in each rem ch across, fasten off, turn. (23 sc)

Row 2: Attach variegated with a sl st in first sc, ch 3 (counts as first dc throughout), dc in each of next 2 sc, [ch 1, sk next sc, dc in each of next 3 sc] rep across, fasten off, turn.

Row 3: Attach pink with a sl st in first dc, ch 1, sc in each dc and ch-1 sp across, turn. (23 sc)

Rows 4–12: Ch 3, dc in each rem st across, turn, at end of Row 12, ch 1, turn. (23 dc)

Row 13: Sc in each dc across, fasten off, turn.

Row 14: Rep Row 2.

Row 15: Attach pink with a sl st in first dc, ch 1, sc in each dc and ch-1 sp across, fasten off.

Apron

Rnd 1: With pink, ch 18, join to form a ring, ch 1, sc in each ch around, join in beg sc. (18 sc)

Row 2: Ch 3, dc in same st, [dc in each of next 2 sc, 2 dc in next sc] twice, turn. (10 dc)

Rows 3 & 4: Ch 3, dc in each rem dc across, turn.

Row 5: Ch 3, dc in each of next 3 dc, dc dec, dc in each of next 4 dc, turn. (9 sts)

Row 6: Ch 4 (counts as first dc, ch 1), sk next dc, dc in next dc, [ch 1, sk next dc, dc in next dc] rep across, turn. (4 ch-1 sps)

Row 7: Ch 3, dc in same st, [dc in next ch-1 sp, 2 dc in next dc] rep across, turn. (14 dc)

Row 8: Ch 3, dc in each rem dc across, turn. (14 dc)

Row 9: Rep Row 8, ch 1, turn.

Row 10: Sc in each dc across, fasten off, turn.

Row 11: Attach variegated with a sl st in first sc, ch 3, dc in next sc, [ch 1, sk next sc, dc in each of next 2 sc] rep across, fasten off, turn.

Row 12: Attach pink with a sl st in first dc, ch 1, sc in each dc and ch-1 sp across, fasten off.

TIE
With variegated, ch 67, fasten off. Weave through Row 6 of apron.

—Designed by Debi Yorston

Heart & Home Rug

EXPERIENCE LEVEL
Beginner

SIZE
Approximately 16" x 30" excluding fringe

MATERIALS
- Ruby Mills® 100 percent Ecospun® polyester yarn (1 lb per cone): 1 cone light pink
- Size G/6 crochet hook or size needed to obtain gauge
- 4½" piece of cardboard

GAUGE
24 sc = 5" with 3 strands held tog

To save time, take time to check gauge.

PATTERN NOTES
Wind yarn into 3 separate balls. Rug is worked holding 3 strands tog throughout.

Only RS rows are shown on chart; chart is read from right to left.

All WS rows are worked in sc.

Beg all RS rows with ch 2 for first hdc.

PATTERN STITCH
Popcorn (pc): 5 hdc in indicated sc, remove hook from lp, insert from RS to WS in top of first hdc of 5-hdc group, draw lp through, ch 1 to secure.

RUG
Row 1 (WS): Ch 145, sc in 2nd ch from hook and in each rem ch across, turn. (144 sc)

Row 2: Ch 2 (counts as first hdc), hdc in each rem sc across, turn. (144 sts)

Row 3 and all WS rows: Ch 1, sc in each st across, turn. (144 sc)

Rows 4–75: Follow Chart A for RS rows, working each open square as 1 hdc and each dotted square as 1 pc, ending with a WS row. Fasten off at end of Row 75.

Weave in all loose ends.

FRINGE
Wind yarn around cardboard 6 times; cut 1 end. Insert hook in first row end on short edge of rug; draw lp end of fringe through, pull cut ends through lp, tighten.

Rep in each row end along both short edges of rug.

Wet rug; pin to size to block. Let dry thoroughly.

–Designed by Maureen Egan Emlet

STITCH KEY
☐ 1 hdc
● 1 popcorn (pc)
Note: *Only RS rows are shown on graph. All WS rows are worked in sc.*

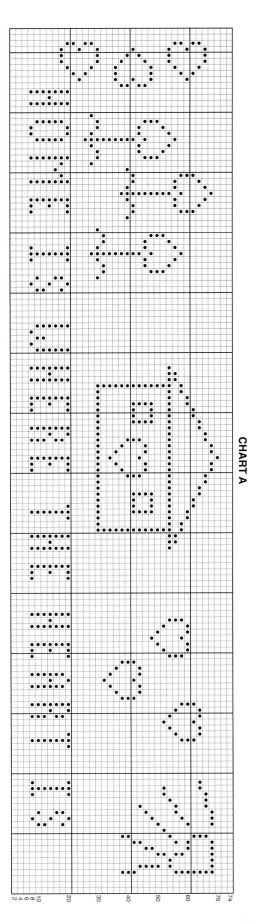

CHART A

Napkin Rag Basket

EXPERIENCE LEVEL
Beginner

SIZE
Approximately 8" in diameter at base x 4" deep

MATERIALS
- 3 yds fabric cut in 3" strips
- Size Q crochet hook
- Pinking shears
- Medium-size safety pin

GAUGE
First 4 rnds = 8" square
To save time, take time to check gauge.

PATTERN NOTES
Read General Instructions for Crocheting With Fabric Strips (page 26) before beginning.

Join rnds with a sl st.

BASKET
Rnd 1: Ch 1 (center ch), ch 1 more, [sc in center ch, ch 2] 4 times, join in beg sc. (4 sc)

Rnd 2: Ch 1, sc in same st as joining, [sc, ch 2, sc] in next ch-2 sp (corner), *sc in next sc, [sc, ch 2, sc] in next ch-2 sp, rep from * around, join in beg sc. (12 sc)

Rnd 3: Ch 1, sc in same st as joining, *sc in each st to corner, [sc, ch 2, sc] in corner ch-2 sp, rep from * around, ending with sc in last st, join in beg sc. (20 sc)

Rnd 4: Ch 1, sc in same st as joining, *sc in each st to corner, [sc, ch 2, sc] in corner ch-2 sp, rep from * around, ending with sc in each of last 2 sts, join in back lp of beg sc. (28 sc)

Rnd 5: Ch 1, working in back lps only this rnd, sc in same st as joining, sc in each st around, sk ch-2 sps, join in both lps of beg sc. (28 sc)

Rnds 6–8: Ch 1, sc in same st as joining, sc in each st around, join in beg sc. (28 sc)

Rnd 9: Sl st in each st around, sl st in beg sl st, fasten off.
Weave in loose ends.

BOW
Cut 3"-wide fabric strip 24" long with pinking shears. Tie in a bow; pin to center front of basket with safety pin, as shown in photo. Trim ends diagonally.

—Designed by Maggie Weldon

Apple Rag Basket

EXPERIENCE LEVEL
Beginner

SIZE
Approximately 10" in diameter x 5" deep

MATERIALS
- 4 yds heavyweight cotton fabric cut into 3"-wide strips
- Size Q crochet hook

GAUGE
First 2 rnds = approximately 5¼" in diamter
To save time, take time to check gauge.

PATTERN NOTE
Read General Instructions for Crocheting With Fabric Strips (page 32) before beginning.

BASKET
Rnd 1: Ch 2, 6 sc in 2nd ch from hook. (6 sc)

Rnd 2: Working in back lps only this rnd and throughout, 2 sc in each st around. (12 sc)

Rnd 3: [Sc in next st, 2 sc in next st] rep around. (18 sc)

Rnd 4: [Sc in each of next 2 sts, 2 sc in next st] rep around. (24 sc)

Rnd 5: Sc in each st around, inc 8 sts evenly sp. (32 sc)

Rnds 6–8: Sc in each st around. (32 sc)

Rnd 9: Sc in next st, ch 6, sk 3 sts, sc in each of next 13 sts, ch 6, sk 3 sts, sc in each of next 12 sts, join with a sl st in beg sc, fasten off.
Weave in loose ends.

—Designed by Maggie Weldon

Climbing Roses Place Mat

EXPERIENCE LEVEL
Advanced

SIZE
Approximately 16" x 12½"

MATERIALS
- DMC® Cebelia® crochet cotton size 10 (50 grams per ball): 2 balls ecru #712 (MC), 1 ball each medium shell pink #223 (A), shell pink #224 (B), very light fern green #524 (C) and light antique blue #932 (D)
- Size 7 steel crochet hook or size needed to obtain gauge
- 15 bobbins

GAUGE
19 sps = 5"; 9 rows = 2"
To save time, take time to check gauge.

PATTERN NOTES
Join rnds with a sl st unless otherwise stated.

Wind 6 bobbins of C, 4 bobbins of D, 3 bobbins of B and 2 bobbins of MC.

To change color in dc, work dc with first color until 2 lps rem on hook, drop first color to WS of work, yo with next color and complete dc.

To carry color not in use across sp to its next working area, wrap color not in use around working color while working ch sts of sp.

Do not carry CCs across more than 1 sp; attach new bobbin.

With the exception of bl and sp sections worked with A at the center of the mat, MC may be carried on WS of work when not in use, working over it with color in use.

PATTERN STITCHES

Block (bl): Dc in each of next 3 sts.

Sp: Ch 2, sk next 2 dc or next ch-2 sp, dc in next st.

Popcorn (pc): 5 dc in indicated st or sp, remove hook from lp, insert hook from RS to WS in top of first dc, pull lp through dc to form pc, ch 1 to close.

Beg pc bl: Ch 3 (counts as first dc), pc in next indicated st or pc, dc in next dc.

Pc bl: Pc in indicated st or sp, dc in next indicated st.

Bl over a bl: Dc in each of next 3 dc.

Bl over a sp: 2 dc in indicated ch-2 sp, dc in next dc.

Sp over a bl: Ch 2, sk 2 dc, dc in next dc.

Sp over a sp: Ch 2, dc in next dc.

Sp over a pc bl: Ch 2, sk pc, dc in next dc.

Pc bl over a sp: Pc in indicated ch-2 sp, dc in next dc.

Pc bl over a pc bl: Pc in top of indicated pc, dc in next dc.

Pc bl over a bl: Sk 1 dc, pc in next dc, dc in next dc.

———————•———————

PLACE MAT

Row 1 (RS): With MC, ch 147, pc in 5th ch from hook, dc in next ch, [sk 1 ch, pc in next ch, dc in next ch] rep across, turn. (48 pc bls)

STITCH AND COLOR KEY
⊡ MC pc
■ A bl
⊠ B bl
▲ C bl
⊞ D bl
☐ MC sp*
*In bl and sp section worked with A at center of mat, sp is worked with A.

Row 2: Ch 3, pc in top of pc, dc in next dc, [ch 2, sk pc, dc in next dc] 46 times, pc in top of last pc, dc in next ch of foundation ch, turn.

Row 3: Beg pc bl over a pc bl, sp over a sp, 44 pc bls over 44 sps, sp over a sp, pc bl over a pc bl, turn.

Rows 4–72: Follow graph, fasten off at end of Row 72. Block place mat to size.

—Designed by Nancy Hearne

Satin Rag Basket
———————•———————

EXPERIENCE LEVEL
Beginner

SIZE
Approximately 5½" in diameter x 4" deep

MATERIALS
• 3 yds white satinlike fabric cut into 4" strips

CHART A

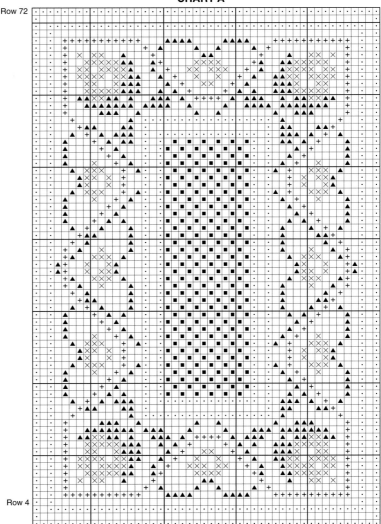

Row 72

Row 4

Row 3

Row 1

- Size P/16 crochet hook or size needed to obtain gauge
- Sewing needle and white thread

GAUGE
Rnds 1–3 = 5" in diameter
To save time, take time to check gauge.

PATTERN NOTE
Read General Instructions for Crocheting With Fabric Strips (page 32) before beginning.

BASKET
Rnd 1: Ch 2, 6 sc in 2nd ch from hook.(6 sc)

Rnd 2: 2 sc in each st around. (12 sc)

Rnd 3: [Sc in next st, 2 sc in next st] rep around. (18 sc)

Rnd 4: Working in back lps only this rnd, sc in each st around. (18 sc)

Rnds 5–7: Sc in each st around, at end of Rnd 7, join with a sl st in beg sc, do not fasten off.

HANDLE
Ch 16, remove hook, insert hook from RS in top lps of corresponding sc on opposite side of basket, draw last ch of beg ch-16 through lps, ch 1, working on opposite side of foundation ch, sl st in each ch across, fasten off.

Weave ends into basket.

BOW
Cut 24" length from fabric strip; fold in half lengthwise with RS tog, forming strip 24" x 2". Sew long edge, using ¼" seam allowance; turn RS out. Press flat, turning raw edges at ends under ½". Tie in a bow; sew to basket with sewing needle and thread, as shown in photo.

—Designed by Maggie Weldon

Pretty Bath Rug

EXPERIENCE LEVEL
Beginner

SIZE
Approximately 48" x 25"

MATERIALS
- Bernat® Berella® "4" worsted weight yarn (3½ oz per skein): 6 skeins seashore #8972 and 1 skein pale antique rose #8814
- Size H/8 crochet hook or size needed to obtain gauge
- Size Q crochet hook or size needed to obtain gauge
- Sewing needle and thread

GAUGE
4 dc = 1" with size H hook with 3 strands held tog
7 dc = 5" with size Q hook with 3 strands held tog
To save time, take time to check gauge.

PATTERN NOTES
Work rug holding 3 strands of yarn tog.

Join rnds with a sl st unless otherwise stated.

RUG
Rnd 1: With seashore and larger hook, ch 33, dc in 4th ch from hook, dc in each of next 28 chs, 3 dc in last ch, working on opposite side of foundation ch, dc in each of next 29 chs, join in last ch of foundation ch. (62 dc, counting last 3 chs of foundation ch as first dc)

Rnd 2: Ch 3 (counts as first dc throughout), 2 dc in same st, 2 dc in next dc, dc in each of next 28 dc, 2 dc in next dc, 3 dc in next dc, 2 dc in next dc, dc in each of next 28 dc, 2 dc in last dc, join in 3rd ch of beg ch-3. (70 dc)

Rnd 3: Ch 3, dc in same st, *3 dc in next dc, 2 dc in each of next 3 dc, dc in each of next 28 dc *, 2 dc in each of next 3 dc, rep from * to * once, 2 dc in each of next 2 dc, join in 3rd ch of beg ch-3. (86 dc)

Rnd 4: Ch 3, dc in same st, [2 dc in next dc] twice, *3 dc in next dc, 2 dc in each of next 7 dc, dc in each of next 28 dc *, 2 dc in each of next 7 dc, rep from * to * once, 2 dc in each of next 4 dc, join in 3rd ch of beg ch-3. (118 dc)

Rnd 5: Ch 3, dc in each of next 4 dc, 2 dc in each of next 5 dc, dc in each of next 54 dc, 2 dc in each of next 5 dc, dc in each of next 49 dc, join in 3rd ch of beg ch-3. (128 dc)

Rnd 6: Ch 3, dc in each dc around, join in 3rd ch of beg ch-3. (128 dc)

Rnd 7: Ch 3, dc in each of next 8 dc, 2 dc in next dc, dc in each of next 63 dc, 2 dc in next dc, dc in each of next 54 dc, join in 3rd ch of beg ch-3. (130 dc)

Rnd 8: Ch 3, dc in same st, *[dc in each of next 9 dc, 2 dc in next dc] twice, dc in each of next 44 dc *, 2 dc in next dc, rep from * to * once, join in 3rd ch of beg ch-3. (136 dc)

Rnd 9: Ch 3, dc in same st, *dc in each of next 5 dc, 2 dc in next dc, dc in each of next 10 dc, 2 dc in next dc, dc in each of next 5 dc, 2 dc in next dc, dc in each of next 44 dc *, 2 dc in next dc, rep from * to * once, join in 3rd ch of beg ch-3. (144 dc)

Rnd 10: Ch 3, dc in same st, *dc in each of next 6 dc, 2 dc in next dc, dc in each of next 5 dc, 2 dc in each of next 2 dc, dc in each of next 5 dc, 2 dc in next dc, dc in each of next 6 dc, 2 dc in next dc, dc in each of next 44 dc *, 2 dc in next dc, rep from * to * once, join in 3rd ch of beg ch-3. (156 dc)

Rnd 11: Ch 1, rev sc in each dc around, join in beg rev sc, fasten off.

ROSE
Make 6

Rnd 1: With pale antique rose and smaller hook, ch 8, join to form a ring, ch 1, 16 sc in ring, join in beg sc.

Rnd 2: [Ch 3, sk 1 sc, sl st in next sc] rep around, join in beg sc. (8 ch-3 sps)

Rnd 3: Ch 1, *[sc, hdc, 3 dc, hdc, sc] in next ch-3 sp, rep from * around, join in beg sc. (8 petals)

Rnd 4: Working in back of Rnd 3 in unworked sc of Rnd 1, sl st in first unworked sc, [ch 5, sl st in next unworked sc] rep around, join in beg sl st. (8 ch-5 sps)

Rnd 5: Ch 1, *[sc, hdc, 5 dc, hdc, sc] in next ch-5 sp, rep from * around, join in beg sc, fasten off.

FINISHING

With sewing needle and thread, sew roses on rug, using photo as a guide.

—Designed by Nazanin S. Fard

Blue Shell Tissue Topper

EXPERIENCE LEVEL
Advanced beginner

SIZE
4½" x 5" in diameter

MATERIALS
- Red Heart® Classic™ worsted weight yarn: 3 oz true blue #822 (MC) and small amount white #1 (CC)
- Size I/9 crochet hook or size needed to obtain gauge
- 8" ⅜"-wide white satin ribbon
- Hot-glue gun

GAUGE
First 2 rnds = 2½" in diameter

To save time, take time to check gauge.

PATTERN NOTE
Join rnds with a sl st unless otherwise stated.

Do not turn rnds unless otherwise stated.

PATTERN STITCH
Shell: [{Dc, ch 1} 4 times, dc] in indicated sp.

TOP
Rnd 1: With MC, ch 1 (center ch), ch 3 (counts as first dc throughout), 11 dc in center ch, join in top of beg ch-3. (12 dc)

Rnd 2: Ch 3, dc in same st as joining, 2 dc in each rem st around, join in 3rd ch of beg ch-3. (24 dc)

Rnd 3: Ch 3, 2 dc in next st, [dc in next st, 2 dc in next st] rep around, join in 3rd ch of beg ch-3. (36 dc)

Rnd 4: Ch 3, dc in next st, 2 dc in next st, [dc in each of next 2 sts, 2 dc in next st] rep around, join in 3rd ch of beg ch-3. (48 dc)

Rnd 5: Working in back lps only this rnd, ch 1, sc in same st as joining and in each rem st around, join in back lp only of beg sc. (48 sc)

SIDE
Rnd 1: Working in back lps only this rnd, ch 3, dc in each rem st around, join in 3rd ch of beg ch-3. (48 dc)

Rnds 2–7: Ch 3, dc in each rem st around, join in 3rd ch of beg ch-3, at the end of Rnd 7, fasten off. (48 dc)

Rnd 8: Attach CC with sl st in any st of Rnd 7, ch 1, rev sc in same st and in each rem st around, join in beg rev sc, fasten off.

SHELL BORDER
Rnd 1: With top facing you, attach MC in rem lp of any sc on Rnd 5, ch 1, sc in same lp, sk 2 lps, shell in next lp, sk 2 lps, *sc in next lp, sk 2 lps, shell in next lp, sk 2 lps, rep from * around, join in beg sc, fasten off. (8 shells)

Rnd 2: With top of cover facing you, attach CC with a sl st between any sc and first dc to its right, ch 1, sc in same sp, ch 3, sc between same sc and next dc to its left, *[ch 3, sc in next ch-1 sp] 4 times, ch 3 **, sc between next dc and sc, ch 3, sc between same sc and next dc, rep from * around, ending last rep at **, join in beg sc, fasten off.

With top facing you, attach CC with a sl st in any rem lp of Rnd 4, ch 1, beg in same st, rev sc around, join in beg rev sc, fasten off.

Weave in loose ends.

FINISHING
Tie ribbon into 3" bow; glue to center top of cover, as shown in photo.

—Designed by Maggie Weldon

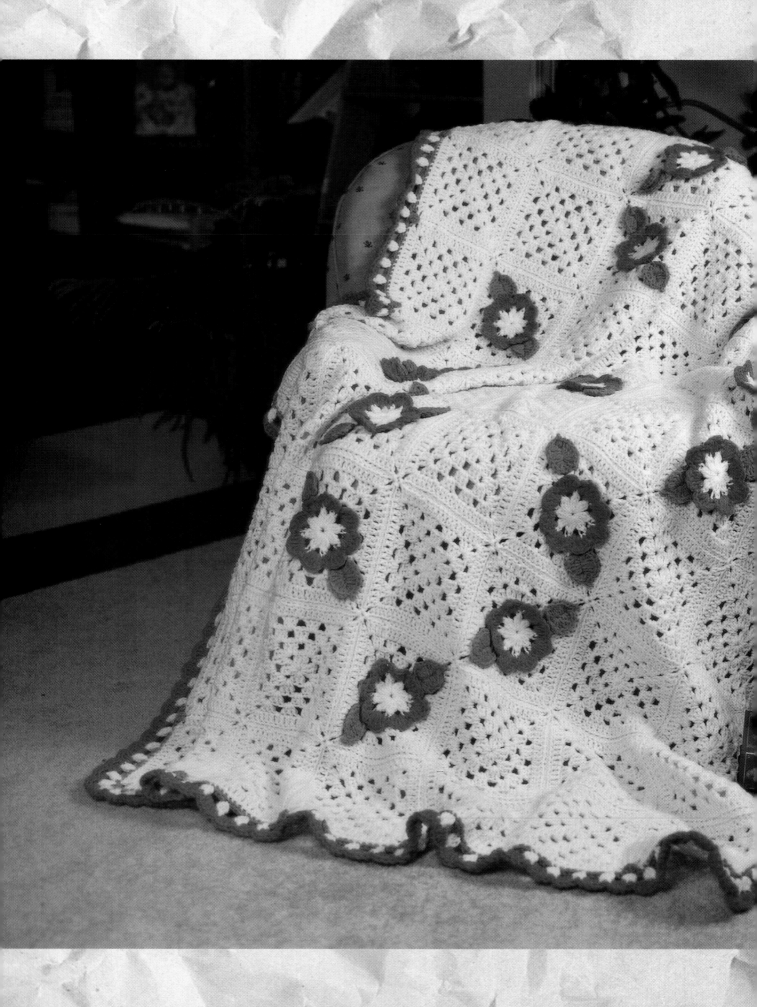

Cozy Afghans

Gifts to Keep You & Yours Warm & Cozy

The perfect gift for someone who has

everything, an afghan is always

appreciated! Crochet this warm gift in

colors to match the recipient's bedroom

or living room for an extra-special

touch. Everyone from college students

to nursing home residents will love

snuggling up in this thoughtful gift

from your heart.

Raspberry Cream Floral

Vibrant raspberry-colored flowers arranged on a pretty cream background make this charming granny square afghan a delight to crochet and display. Instructions begin on page 42.

Reversible Rickrack

Let your daughter or granddaughter pick her
favorite colors for this enchanting reversible afghan!
Reversible Rickrack (above) looks just as lovely
from either side. Worked in a brushed, mohair-look
acrylic yarn, this afghan has a soft look and oh-so-
cozy feel! Instructions begin on page 43.

White-on-White

The bride-to-be will surely add this pretty
White-on-White afghan (right) to her collection
of treasured keepsakes tucked away in her hope
chest. A floral pattern worked in pure white will
be a lasting reminder of her day as a beautiful
bride. Instructions begin on page 43.

Ripple Rhapsody

Ripple Rhapsody (right) features cascades of beautiful colors worked in a ravishing ripple pattern. It makes a lovely addition to a sunroom or bedroom. Instructions begin on page 45.

Easy Clusters Pillow

Pillows can add the perfect, finishing touch to a comfortable living room decor. This eye-catching accent pillow, Easy Clusters (below) will complement your sofa or an over-stuffed chair. Instructions begin on page 44.

Starburst Ripple Pillow

Crochet one Starburst Ripple Pillow (above) as a sofa or chair accent, or three or four to dress up a bed, in colors to match your upholstery or bedspread. Instructions begin on page 46.

Double Border Granny

Soft hues of pink and green blend perfectly together against a background of classic cream in this delightful Double Border Granny afghan (left). Crocheters of all ages will love this variation on an all-time favorite afghan style, the granny square. Instructions begin on page 45.

Summer Breezes

Summer Breezes (above) with its lacy, openwork pattern, is the perfect throw for enjoying those cool summer evenings on the veranda. Instructions begin on page 48.

Winter Pineapple

Celebrate the onset of cooler weather with this luscious afghan. Winter Pineapple (left) is a super-warm afghan crocheted with richly colored chenille yarn. Instructions begin on page 47.

Raspberry Cream Floral

EXPERIENCE LEVEL
Beginner

SIZE
Approximately 52" x 79" including border

MATERIALS

- Coats & Clark Red Heart® Classic™ worsted weight yarn (3½ oz per skein): 9 skeins eggshell #111 and 2 skeins each cherry pink #746 and light seafoam #683
- Size J/10 crochet hook or size needed to obtain gauge
- Tapestry needle

GAUGE
Plain granny square = 6¾" square
To save time, take time to check gauge.

PATTERN NOTE
Join rnds with a sl st unless otherwise stated.

PATTERN STITCHES
Beg shell: Ch 3, [2 dc, ch 2, 3 dc] in indicated sp.

Shell: [3 dc, ch 2, 3 dc] in indicated sp.

Beg 3-dc cl: Ch 2, holding back on hook last lp of each st, 2 dc in indicated sp, yo, draw through all 3 lps on hook.

3-dc cl: Holding back on hook last lp of each st, 3 dc in indicated sp, yo, draw through all 4 lps on hook.

———————•———————

PLAIN GRANNY SQUARE
Make 60
Rnd 1: With eggshell, ch 4, join to form a ring, ch 3 (counts as first dc throughout), 2 dc in ring, [ch 2, 3 dc in ring] 3 times, ch 2, join in 3rd ch of beg ch-3.

Rnd 2: Sl st in next 2 dc and in next ch-2 sp, beg shell in same ch-2 sp, [ch 1, shell in next ch-2 sp] rep around, ending with ch 1, join in 3rd ch of beg ch-3.

Rnd 3: Sl st in next 2 dc and in next shell sp, beg shell in same sp, [ch 1, 3 dc, ch 1] in next ch-1 sp, *shell in next shell sp, [ch 1, 3 dc, ch 1] in next ch-1 sp, rep from * around, join in 3rd ch of beg ch-3.

Rnd 4: Sl st in next 2 dc and in shell sp, beg shell in same sp, *ch 1, [3 dc in next ch-1 sp, ch 1] twice **, shell in next shell sp, rep from * around, ending last rep at **, join in 3rd ch of beg ch-3.

Rnd 5: Ch 3, dc in each of next 2 dc, *[2 dc, ch 2, 2 dc] in next ch-2 sp, dc in each dc and ch-1 sp across to next corner ch-2 sp, rep from * around, ending with dc in last ch-1 sp, join in 3rd ch of beg ch-3, fasten off. (76 dc)

FLOWER GRANNY SQUARE
Make 17
Rnd 1: With eggshell, ch 4, join to form a ring, beg 3-dc cl in ring, [ch 2, 3-dc cl in ring] 7 times, ch 2, join in top of beg 3-dc cl.

Rnd 2: Ch 1, sc in same st, ch 4, *[sc, ch 2] in next 3-dc cl, [sc, ch 4] in next 3-dc cl, rep from * around, ending with [sc, ch 2] in last 3-dc cl, join in beg sc.

Rnd 3: Sl st in ch-4 sp, beg shell in same sp, *ch 1, [3 dc, ch 1] in next ch-2 sp **, shell in next ch-4 sp, rep from * around, ending last rep at **, join in 3rd ch of beg ch-3.

Rnds 4 & 5: Rep Rnds 4 and 5 of plain granny square.

FLOWER
Attach cherry pink with a sl st in top of any 3-dc cl, ch 1, sc in same sp, *5 dc in next ch-2 sp, sc in top of next 3-dc cl, rep from * around, join in beg sc, fasten off.

LEAVES
Make 34
With light seafoam, ch 6, sl st in 2nd ch from hook, sc in next ch, hdc in next ch, 2 dc in next ch, 9 dc in next ch, working on opposite side of foundation ch, 2 dc in next ch, hdc in next ch, sc in next ch, sl st in last ch, fasten off, leaving end for sewing.

JOINING
With RS tog, working through both thicknesses in outer lps only of each square, sc squares tog with eggshell as shown in Fig. 1.

FIG. 1
Joining Diagram

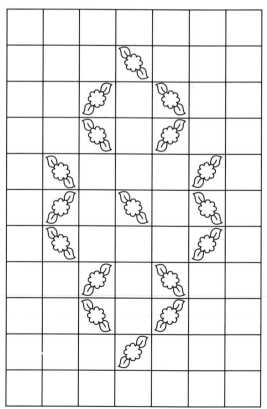

EDGING

Rnd 1: With RS facing, attach light seafoam with a sl st in any corner shell sp, ch 1, 5 sc in same sp, working in back lps only this rnd, *sc in each of next 19 dc, [ch 1, 3-dc cl, ch 1] in joining seam between squares, rep from * around, working 5 sc in each corner shell sp of afghan, join in beg sc, fasten off light seafoam, attach eggshell in same st as joining, do not turn.

Rnd 2: Beg 3-dc cl in joining st, [ch 3, sk next sc, 3-dc cl in next sc] 3 times, *[ch 3, sk next 3 sc, 3-dc cl in next sc] 4 times **, ch 3, 3-dc cl in next 3-dc cl, ch 3, sk next sc, 3-dc cl in next sc, rep from * across to corner 5-sc group, ending last rep at **, [ch 3, sk 1 sc, 3-dc cl in next sc] 4 times, rep from * around, ending with ch 3, join in top of beg 3-dc cl, fasten off.

Rnd 3: Attach cherry pink in joining st, ch 1, sc in same st, [4 dc in next ch-3 sp, sc in top of next 3-dc cl] rep around, join in beg sc, fasten off.

FINISHING

With tapestry needle, sew 1 leaf on each side of each flower, using photo as a guide.

Place damp cloth over flowers and steam lightly 5–6 seconds.

—Designed by Jo Ann Maxwell

Reversible Rickrack

EXPERIENCE LEVEL
Intermediate

SIZE
43" x 54"

MATERIALS
- Caron® Simply Soft® 4-ply yarn (3 oz per skein): 10 skeins dark sage #2612 (MC) and 3 skeins white #2601 (CC)
- Size G/6 crochet hook or size needed to obtain gauge

GAUGE
5 sc = 1"; 14 rows = 5" in patt st
To save time, take time to check gauge.

PATTERN NOTES
To change colors in sc, work last sc until 2 lps rem on hook, fasten off current color, yo with next color and draw through 2 lps on hook.

AFGHAN

Row 1: With CC, ch 218, working in center strand of each ch on WS of ch, sc in 2nd ch from hook, sk 1 ch, sc in next ch, 3 sc in next ch, sc in next ch, *sk 2 chs, sc in next ch, 3 sc in next ch, sc in next ch, rep from * to last 2 chs, sk 1 ch, sc in last ch, ch 1, turn. (217 sc)

Row 2: Working in both lps of first and last sc of row and in back lps only of rem sc, sc in first sc, sk next sc, sc in next sc, 3 sc in next sc, sc in next sc, *sk 2 sc, sc in next sc, 3 sc in next sc, sc in next sc, rep from * across to last 2 sc, sk 1 sc, sc in last sc, changing to MC, ch 1, turn. (217 sc)

Rows 3–46: Rep Row 2, alternating 2 rows CC and 2 rows MC, ending with CC, at end of Row 46, change to MC.

Continue in patt with MC only until piece meas 38" from beg, changing to CC at end of last row, ch 1, turn.

[Rep Row 2] 46 times for top border, alternating 2 rows CC and 2 rows MC, fasten off at end of last row.

Weave in loose ends.

—Designed by Loa Ann Thaxton

White-on-White

EXPERIENCE LEVEL
Intermediate

SIZE
Approximately 46" x 58"

MATERIALS
- Caron® Dawn® Sayelle worsted weight yarn (3½ oz per skein): 14 skeins white #301
- Size I/9 crochet hook or size needed to obtain gauge
- Tapestry needle

GAUGE
Motif = 9" wide x 9½" long
To save time, take time to check gauge.

PATTERN NOTE
Join rnds with a sl st unless otherwise stated.

PATTERN STITCH
Picot: Ch 3, sl st in 3rd ch from hook.

MOTIF
Make 30

Row 1 (RS): Ch 34, dc in 6th ch from hook, [ch 1, sk next ch, dc in next ch] rep across, turn. (15 ch-1 sps, counting last 4 chs of foundation ch as first dc, ch 1)

Row 2: Ch 4 (counts as first dc, ch 1 throughout), [dc in next dc, ch 1] rep across, ending with sk next ch of turning ch, dc in next ch, turn. (15 ch-1 sps)

Rows 3–15: Rep Row 2, do not turn at end of Row 15.

Border

Rnd 16: Ch 3 (counts as first dc throughout), working over ends of rows, dc over last dc made, *2 dc over end of each of next 13 rows, [2 dc, ch 3, 2 dc] in corner sp, 2 dc in each of next 13 sps across to corner *, [2 dc, ch 3, 2 dc] in corner sp, rep from * to * once, [2 dc, ch 3] in next sp, join in 3rd ch of beg ch-3. (120 dc)

Rnd 17: Ch 3, dc in each dc around, working [2 dc, ch 3, 2 dc] in each corner ch-3 sp, join in 3rd ch of beg ch-3, fasten off. (136 dc)

FLOWER

Make 20

Rnd 1: Leaving a 6" length for sewing, ch 4, join to form a ring, ch 1, 10 sc in ring, join in beg sc.

Rnd 2: [Ch 4, sk 1 sc, sl st in next sc] rep around, ending with ch 4, join at base of beg ch-4. (5 ch-4 sps)

Rnd 3: Ch 1, [sc, hdc, 3 dc, hdc, sc] in each ch-4 sp around, join in back of Rnd 2 joining st. (5 petals)

Rnd 4: [Ch 4, working behind Rnd 3 petals, sl st in next sl st of Rnd 2] rep around, ending with ch 4, join in Rnd 3 joining st.

Rnd 5: Ch 1, [sc, hdc, 5 dc, hdc, sc] in each ch-4 sp around, join in back of Rnd 4 joining st.

Rnd 6: [Ch 6, working behind Rnd 5 petals, sl st in next sl st of Rnd 4] rep around, ending with ch 6, join in Rnd 5 joining st.

Rnd 7: Ch 1, [sc, hdc, ch 1, {dc, ch 1} 5 times, hdc, sc] in each ch-6 sp around, join in back of Rnd 6 joining st, fasten off.

JOINING

With RS facing, whipstitch motifs tog through back lps of Rnd 17, joining 5 rows of 6 motifs each.

EDGING

Rnd 1: With RS facing, attach yarn with a sl st in any corner sp, ch 3, 2 dc in same sp, dc in each dc around, working 2 dc in each of 2 sps at seams and [3 dc, ch 1, 3 dc] in each corner sp, ending with [3 dc, ch 1] in same sp as beg ch-3, join in 3rd ch of beg ch-3, do not turn.

Rnd 2: Ch 1, sc in same st as joining and in each of next 2 dc, *[picot, sk next st, sc in each of next 3 dc] rep across to next corner, [sc, picot, sc] in corner sp, sc in each of next 3 dc, rep from * around, join in beg sc, fasten off.

FINISHING

Using tapestry needle and 6" length, sew flowers on afghan over points where 4 motifs meet.

–Designed by Melissa Leapman
for Monsanto's Designs for America Program

Easy Clusters Pillow

EXPERIENCE LEVEL
Beginner

SIZE
20" square

MATERIALS
- Bernat® Berella "4"® worsted weight yarn (3½ oz/240 yds per skein): 5 skeins medium colonial blue #8861

(MC) and 3 skeins winter white #8941 (CC)
- Size Q crochet hook or size needed to obtain gauge
- 20" square pillow form
- 3" x 5" piece cardboard

GAUGE
First 2 rnds = 7½" square

To save time, take time to check gauge.

PATTERN NOTES
Pillow is worked using 3 strands of yarn held tog throughout.

Join rnds with a sl st unless otherwise stated.

PATTERN STITCHES
Beg 3-dc cl: Ch 2, holding back on hook last lp of each st, 2 dc in indicated sp, yo and draw through all 3 lps on hook.

3-dc cl: Holding back on hook last lp of each st, 3 dc in indicated sp, yo and draw through all 4 lps on hook.

———•———

SIDE

Make 2

Rnd 1 (RS): With MC, ch 3, join to form a ring, ch 3 (counts as first dc throughout), 2 dc in ring, ch 2, [3 dc in ring, ch 2] 3 times, join in 3rd ch of beg ch-3, fasten off. (12 dc)

Rnd 2: With RS facing, attach CC in any ch-2 sp, [beg 3-dc cl, ch 2, 3-dc cl] in same sp, ch 1, sk next dc, 3-dc cl in next dc, ch 1, *[3-dc cl, ch 2, 3-dc cl] in next ch-2 sp (for corner), ch 1, sk next dc, 3-dc cl in next dc, ch 1, sk next dc, rep from * around, join in top of beg 3-dc cl, fasten off. (12 3-dc cls)

Rnd 3: With RS facing, attach MC in any corner ch-2 sp, ch 3, [2 dc, ch 1, 3 dc] in same sp, *2 dc in next ch-1 sp, dc in next 3-dc cl, 2 dc in next ch-1 sp **, [3 dc, ch 1, 3 dc] in next corner ch-2 sp, rep from * around, ending last rep at **, join in 3rd ch of beg ch-3. (44 dc)

Rnd 4: Ch 3, dc in each st to corner, *[2 dc, ch 2, 2 dc] in corner ch-1 sp, dc in each st to next corner, rep from * around, join in 3rd ch of beg ch-3, fasten off. (60 dc)

Rnd 5: With RS facing, attach CC in any corner sp, [beg 3-dc cl, ch 2, 3-dc cl] in same sp, *ch 1, sk next dc, [3-dc cl in next dc, ch 1, sk next dc] rep across to next corner, [3-dc cl, ch 2, 3-dc cl] in next corner sp, rep from * around, join in top of beg 3-dc cl, fasten off. (36 3-dc cls)

Rnd 6: With RS facing, attach MC in any corner ch-2 sp, ch 3, [2 dc, ch 1, 3 dc] in same sp, *2 dc in each of next 4 ch-1 sps, dc in next 3-dc cl, 2 dc in each of next 4 ch-1 sps **, [3 dc, ch 1, 3 dc] in next corner ch-2 sp, rep from * around, ending last rep at **, join in 3rd ch of beg ch-3. (92 dc)

Rnd 7: Rep Rnd 4, fasten off. (108 dc)

Weave in loose ends.

JOINING

With WS tog, working through both thicknesses, attach MC in any corner sp, ch 1, 3 sc in same sp, sc in each st around, working 3 sc in each corner, inserting pillow form before closing, join in beg sc, fasten off.

TASSELS

Make 4

Wind triple strand of CC around cardboard 20 times. Cut 18" piece of CC; insert 1 end under all strands at top of cardboard. Pull up tightly; tie securely.

Slip yarn off cardboard. Sew tassel at tied end to corner of pillow. Wrap strand of CC around tassel 1" from top; tie securely.

Cut lps at bottom of tassel; trim evenly.

—Designed by Maggie Weldon

Ripple Rhapsody

EXPERIENCE LEVEL

Intermediate

SIZE

55" x 72"

MATERIALS

- Bernat® Berella "4"® worsted weight yarn: 33½ oz meadow variegated #8967 (MC) and 16½ oz pale lagoon #8819 (CC)
- Size J/10 crochet hook or size needed to obtain gauge

GAUGE

3 dc = 1"

To save time, take time to check gauge.

PATTERN STITCHES

Beg 3-tr cl: Ch 3, holding back on hook last lp of each st, tr in each of next 2 sts, yo, draw through all 3 lps on hook.

3-tr cl: Holding back on hook last lp of each st, tr in each of next 3 indicated sts, yo, draw through all 4 lps on hook.

7-tr cl: Holding back on hook last lp of each st, tr in each of next 7 sts, yo, draw through all 8 lps on hook.

AFGHAN

Row 1: With MC, ch 193, holding back on hook last lp of each st, tr in 4th ch from hook and in next ch, yo, draw through all 3 lps on hook, *[ch 1, tr in next ch] 4 times, ch 1, 3 tr in next ch, [ch 1, tr in next ch] 4 times, ch 1 **, 7-tr cl over next 7 chs, rep from * across, ending last rep at **, 3-tr cl over last 3 chs, turn.

Row 2: Ch 3 (counts as first dc throughout), dc in each of next 5 tr, *3 dc in next tr, dc in each of next 4 tr **, dc in next ch-1 sp, dc in next tr, sk 7-tr cl, dc in next ch-1 sp, dc in next tr, dc in next ch-1 sp, dc in each of next 4 tr, rep from * across, ending last rep at **, dc in next tr, dc in top of beg 3-tr cl, turn.

Row 3: Beg 3-tr cl, *[ch 1, tr in next dc] 4 times, ch 1, 3 tr in

next dc, [ch 1, tr in next dc] 4 times, ch 1 **, 7-tr cl over next 7 dc, rep from * across, ending last rep at **, 3-tr cl over last 3 sts, turn.

Rep Rows 2 and 3, working 4 rows of MC and 2 rows of CC, ending when piece meas approximately 72" or desired length after 4th row of MC stripe, fasten off at end of last row.

Weave in loose ends.

—Designed by Darla J. Fanton

Double Border Granny

EXPERIENCE LEVEL

Intermediate

SIZE

45" x 63" excluding fringe

MATERIALS

- Brunswick® Windrush® 100 percent acrylic worsted weight yarn (3½ oz/100 grams per skein): 10 skeins Aran #90400 and 5 skeins each light wicker green #90461 and faded rose #9006
- Size H/8 crochet hook or size needed to obtain gauge
- Tapestry needle

GAUGE

Motif = 9" square

To save time, take time to check gauge.

PATTERN NOTE

Join rnds with a sl st unless otherwise stated.

MOTIF

Make 35

Rnd 1: With Aran, ch 4, join to form a ring, ch 6 (counts as first dc, ch 3 throughout), [3 dc in ring, ch 3] 3 times, 2 dc in ring, join in 3rd ch of beg ch-6.

Rnd 2: Sl st in ch-3 sp, ch 3 (counts as first dc throughout), [2 dc, ch 3, 3 dc] in same sp, [ch 1, {3 dc, ch 3, 3 dc} in next ch-3 sp] 3 times, ch 1, join in 3rd ch of beg ch-3, fasten off.

Rnd 3: Attach light wicker green with a sl st in any ch-3 sp, ch 3, [dc, ch 1, tr, ch 1, 2 dc] in same sp, *sc in each of next 2 dc, ch 3, sk next [dc, ch-1 sp, dc], sc in each of next 2 dc **, [2 dc, ch 1, tr, ch 1, 2 dc] in next ch-3 sp, rep from * around, ending last rep at **, join in 3rd ch of beg ch-3, fasten off.

Rnd 4: Attach Aran with a sl st in any ch-3 sp, ch 4 (counts as first tr), [tr, ch 3, 2 tr] in same sp, *ch 2, sk next [2 sc, dc], working from behind, sc over post of next dc, ch 2, sk next [ch-1 sp, tr, ch-1 sp], working from behind, sc over post of next dc, ch 2 **, [2 tr, ch 3, 2 tr] in next ch-3 sp, rep from * around, ending last rep at **, join in 4th ch of beg ch-4.

Rnd 5: Sl st in next tr and in corner ch-3 sp, ch 3, [2 dc, ch 1, 3 dc] in same sp, *dc in each of next 2 tr, [2 dc in next ch-

2 sp] 3 times, dc in each of next 2 tr **, [3 dc, ch 1, 3 dc] in next corner ch-3 sp, rep from * around, ending last rep at **, join in 3rd ch of beg ch-3, fasten off. (64 dc)

Rnd 6: Attach faded rose with a sl st in any corner ch-1 sp, ch 1, [sc, ch 1, sc] in same sp, *sc in each rem st across to next corner **, [sc, ch 1, sc] in corner sp, rep from * around, ending last rep at **, join in beg sc, fasten off. (72 sc)

Rnd 7: Attach Aran with a sl st in any corner ch-1 sp, ch 6, dc in same sp, *sk 1 sc, 3 dc in next sc, [sk 2 sc, 3 dc in next sc] 5 times, sk 1 sc **, [dc, ch 3, dc] in corner sp, rep from * around, ending last rep at **, join in 3rd ch of beg ch-6, fasten off. (80 dc)

Rnd 8: Attach faded rose with a sl st in any corner ch-3 sp, ch 1, [sc, ch 3, sc] in same sp, *sc in each rem st across to next corner **, [sc, ch 3, sc] in corner sp, rep from * around, ending last rep at **, join in beg sc, fasten off. (88 sc)

Rnd 9: Attach Aran with a sl st in first sc to right of any ch-3 corner sp, ch 3, 2 dc in same st, *ch 3, sk corner sp, 3 dc in next sc **, [sk 2 sc, 3 dc in next sc] 7 times, rep from * around, ending last rep at **, [sk 2 sc, 3 dc in next sc] 6 times, join in 3rd ch of beg ch-3, fasten off. (96 dc)

Rnd 10: Attach light wicker green with a sl st in any corner ch-3 sp, ch 1, [sc, ch 3, sc] in same sp, *sc in each rem st across to next corner **, [sc, ch 3, sc] in corner sp, rep from * around, ending last rep at **, join in beg sc, fasten off. (104 sc)

JOINING

Arrange motifs in 7 rows of 5 motifs each.

With tapestry needle and light wicker green, working from RS, overcast motifs tog in back lps.

FRINGE

Cut 4 (18") lengths of Aran; fold in half. Pull lp end through end st on short edge of afghan; draw loose ends through lp. Pull to tighten.

Rep in every other st across both short edges of afghan.

–Designed by Mary Lamb Becker
for Monsanto's Designs for America Program

Starburst Ripple Pillow

EXPERIENCE LEVEL
Beginner

SIZE
16" in diameter

MATERIALS
- Bernat® Berella "4"® worsted weight yarn (3½ oz/240 yds per ball): 1 ball each white #8942 (MC) and dark oxford hunter #8893 (CC)
- Size H/8 crochet hook or size needed to obtain gauge
- 16" round pillow form
- Yarn needle

GAUGE
7 sc = 2"

To save time, take time to check gauge.

PATTERN NOTES
If round 16" pillow form is not available you may purchase a square 16" pillow form and round corners on a sewing machine.

Pillow is worked flat from center to outside edge to opposite center. One seam joins piece to form cylinder.

Work all sts through back lps only.

———————•———————

PILLOW

Row 1 (RS): With MC, ch 132, 2 sc in 2nd ch from hook, *sc in each of next 4 chs, sk 1 ch, sc in each of next 4 chs **, [sc, ch 1, sc] in next ch, rep from * across, ending last rep at **, 2 sc in last ch, ch 1, turn. (132 sc; 12 ch-1 sps)

Row 2: 2 sc in first sc, *sc in each of next 4 sc, sk 2 sc, sc in each of next 4 sc **, [sc, ch 1, sc] in next ch, rep from * across, ending last rep at **, 2 sc in last sc, fasten off MC, attach CC in front lp only of last st, ch 1, turn. (132 sc; 12 ch-1 sps)

Row 3: 2 sc in first sc, *sc in each of next 10 sc **, [sc, ch 1, sc] in next ch, rep from * across, ending last rep at **, 2 sc in last sc, ch 1, turn. (158 sc; 12 ch-1 sps)

Rows 4–8: 2 sc in first sc, *sc in each of next 5 sc, sk 2 sc, sc in each of next 5 sc **, [sc, ch 1, sc] in next ch, rep from * across, ending last rep at **, 2 sc in last sc, ch 1, turn, do not ch 1 at end of Row 8, fasten off CC, attach MC in front lp only of last st, ch 1, turn. (158 sc; 12 ch-1 sps)

Row 9: 2 sc in first sc, *sc in each of next 12 sc **, [sc, ch 1, sc] in next ch, rep from * across, ending last rep at **, 2 sc in last sc, ch 1, turn. (184 sc; 12 ch-1 sps)

Rows 10–16: 2 sc in first sc, *sc in each of next 6 sc, sk 2 sc, sc in each of next 6 sc **, [sc, ch 1, sc] in next ch, rep from * across, ending last rep at **, 2 sc in last sc, ch 1, turn, do not ch 1 at end of Row 16, fasten off MC, attach CC in front lp only of last st, ch 1, turn. (184 sc; 12 ch-1 sps)

Row 17: 2 sc in first sc, *sc in each of next 14 sc **, [sc, ch 1, sc] in next ch, rep from * across, ending last rep at **, 2 sc in last sc, ch 1, turn. (210 sc; 12 ch-1 sps)

Rows 18–31: 2 sc in first sc, *sc in each of next 7 sc, sk 2 sc, sc in each of next 7 sc **, [sc, ch 1, sc] in next ch, rep from * across, ending last rep at **, 2 sc in last sc, ch 1, turn, do not ch 1 at end of Row 31, fasten off CC, attach MC in front lp only of last st, ch 1, turn. (210 sc; 12 ch-1 sps)

Begin decreases

Row 32: 2 sc in first sc, *sc in each of next 5 sc, sc dec, sk next 2 sc, sc dec, sc in each of next 5 sc **, [sc, ch 1, sc] in next ch, rep from * across, ending last rep at **, 2 sc in last sc, ch 1, turn. (184 sts; 12 ch-1 sps)

Rows 33–39: 2 sc in first sc, *sc in each of next 6 sts, sk 2 sts, sc in each of next 6 sts **, [sc, ch 1, sc] in next ch, rep from * across, ending last rep at **, 2 sc in last st, ch 1, turn, do not ch 1 at end of Row 39, fasten off MC, attach CC in front lp only of last st, ch 1, turn. (184 sc; 12 ch-1 sps)

Row 40: 2 sc in first sc, *sc in each of next 4 sc, sc dec, sk next 2 sc, sc dec, sc in each of next 4 sc **, [sc, ch 1, sc] in next ch, rep from * across, ending last rep at **, 2 sc in last sc, ch 1, turn. (158 sts; 12 ch-1 sps)

Rows 41–45: 2 sc in first sc, *sc in each of next 5 sts, sk 2 sts, sc in each of next 5 sts **, [sc, ch 1, sc] in next ch, rep from * across, ending last rep at **, 2 sc in last st, ch 1, turn, do not ch 1 at end of Row 45, fasten off CC, attach MC in front lp only of last st, ch 1, turn. (158 sc; 12 ch-1 sps)

Row 46: 2 sc in first sc, *sc in each of next 3 sc, sc dec, sk next 2 sc, sc dec, sc in each of next 3 sc **, [sc, ch 1, sc] in next ch, rep from * across, ending last rep at **, 2 sc in last sc, ch 1, turn. (132 sts; 12 ch-1 sps)

Row 47: 2 sc in first sc, *sc in each of next 4 sts, sk 2 sts, sc in each of next 4 sts **, [sc, ch 1, sc] in next ch, rep from * across, ending last rep at **, 2 sc in last st, ch 1, turn. (132 sc; 12 ch-1 sps)

Row 48: Insert hook into center ch of first point, draw up a lp, [insert hook into center ch of next point, draw up a lp] rep across, ending with draw up a lp in last sc of row, yo, draw through all 14 lps on hook, ch 1 tightly to secure, fasten off, leaving length for sewing side seam.

BOBBLES

Make 2

With CC, ch 4, leaving 6" length, 7 dc in 4th ch from hook, drop lp from hook, insert in top of first dc of 7-dc group, pick up dropped lp, draw through, ch 1 to secure, fasten off, leaving 6" tail.

FINISHING

Sew side seam; insert pillow form.

Attach MC at base of end sc of Row 1, rep Row 48.

Center starbursts over pillow form. With yarn needle, pull 1 (6") length of bobble through center of pillow through all thicknesses; remove needle. Pull 2nd 6" length through in same manner ⅛" from first. Pull snugly, but not too tight; tie in knot. Hide ends inside cover.

Rep for 2nd bobble on opposite side of pillow.

–Designed by Maureen Egan Emlet

Winter Pineapple

EXPERIENCE LEVEL
Intermediate

SIZE
Approximately 54" x 64" excluding fringe

MATERIALS
- Lion Brand® Chenille Sensations® 100% Monsanto Acrylic Fiber yarn (1¼ oz/87 yds per skein): 27 skeins forest green #131
- Size H/8 crochet hook or size needed to obtain gauge

GAUGE
7 dc = 2"

PATTERN STITCHES
2-dc cl: Holding back on hook last lp of each st, work 2 dc in indicated st, yo, draw through all 3 lps on hook.

V-st: [Dc, ch 2, dc] in indicated st.

———————•———————

AFGHAN

Row 1: Ch 198 (foundation ch), ch 5 (counts as first dc, ch 2), dc in 8th ch from hook, [ch 2, sk 2 chs, dc in next ch] rep across, turn. (66 ch-2 sps)

Row 2: Ch 3 (counts as first dc throughout), *[2 dc in next sp, dc in next dc] 3 times, ch 2, dc in next dc, ch 1, V-st in next dc, ch 1, dc in next dc, ch 2, dc in next dc **, rep from * across, ending last rep at **, [2 dc in next sp, dc in next dc] twice, 2 dc in last sp, dc in 3rd ch of beg ch-5, turn.

Row 3: Ch 3, dc in each of next 9 dc, *ch 3, sk [ch-2 sp, dc, ch-1 sp], 5 dc in next V-st sp, ch 3, sk [ch-1 sp, dc, ch-2 sp], dc in each of next 10 dc, rep from * across, turn.

Row 4: Ch 3, dc in each of next 9 dc, *ch 1, [2-dc cl, ch 1] in each of next 5 dc, dc in each of next 10 dc, rep from * across, turn.

Row 5: Ch 3, dc in each of next 9 dc, *ch 3, sk next ch-1 sp, sc in next ch-1 sp, [ch 5, sc in next ch-1 sp] 3 times, ch 3, dc in each of next 10 dc, rep from * across, turn.

Row 6: Ch 3, dc in each of next 9 dc, *ch 3, sc in next ch-5 sp, [ch 5, sc in next ch-5 sp] twice, ch 3, dc in each of next 10 dc, rep from * across, turn.

Row 7: Ch 3, dc in each of next 9 dc, *ch 3, sc in next ch-5 sp, ch 5, sc in next ch-5 sp, ch 3, dc in each of next 10 dc, rep from * across, turn.

Row 8: Ch 3, dc in each of next 9 dc, *ch 5, sc in next ch-5 sp, ch 5, dc in each of next 10 dc, rep from * across, turn.

Row 9: Ch 3, dc in each of next 9 dc, *ch 2, dc in next ch-5 sp, ch 1, V-st in next sc, ch 1, dc in next ch-5 sp, ch 2, dc in each of next 10 dc, rep from * across, turn.

Rep Rows 3–9 until afghan meas approximately 64", ending with Row 8.

Last Row: Ch 5 (counts as first dc, ch-2), *[sk next 2 dc, dc in next dc, ch 2] 3 times, dc in next ch-5 sp, ch 2, dc in next sc, ch 2, dc in next ch-5 sp, ch 2, dc in next dc, ch 2, rep from * across, ending with dc in next dc, [ch 2, sk 2 dc, dc in next dc] 3 times, fasten off. (66 ch-2 sps)

FINISHING

Cut 11 (6") lengths of yarn. Holding all strands tog, fold in half; insert hook from WS to RS in first ch-2 sp at either shorter edge of afghan. Pull folded end of strands through to form lp; bring free ends of strands through lp and pull to tighten. Rep for each ch-2 sp across both shorter edges of afghan. Trim fringe evenly.

—*Designed by Melissa Leapman*
for Monsanto's Designs for America Program

Summer Breezes

EXPERIENCE LEVEL
Intermediate

SIZE
Approximately 48" x 54" including border

MATERIALS
- Coats & Clark Red Heart® Super Sport® Art. E.327 sport weight yarn (5 oz/140 grams per skein): 5 skeins off-white #4 (MC)
- Coats & Clark Red Heart® Sport yarn Art. E.289 (2.5 oz/70 grams per skein): 1 skein each cherry red #912 and hunter green #689
- Size H/8 crochet hook or size needed to obtain gauge

GAUGE
5 V-sts and 7 rows = 4" in body patt
To save time, take time to check gauge.

PATTERN NOTES
To change color in V-st, [dc, ch 1] in indicated sp, dc in same sp until 2 lps rem on hook, fasten off working color, complete dc with next color.

To change color in pc st, work 4 dc, work 5th dc until 2 lps rem on hook, fasten off working color, complete dc and pc with new color.

PATTERN STITCHES
V-st: [Dc, ch 1, dc] in indicated st.

V-st in V-st: V-st in ch-1 sp of indicated V-st.

Popcorn (pc): Work 5 dc in indicated sp, remove hook, insert from front to back into first dc of 5-dc group, pick up dropped lp, draw through.

Dtr: Yo hook 3 times, insert hook in indicated st, yo, draw up a lp, [yo, draw through 2 lps on hook] 4 times.

3-dtr cl: Holding back on hook last lp of each st, work 3 dtr, yo and draw through all 4 lps on hook.

AFGHAN
Row 1 (RS): Beg at lower edge with MC, ch 209, dc in 4th ch from hook, [sk 2 chs, V-st in next ch] rep across to last 4 chs, sk 2 chs, dc in each of last 2 chs, turn. (67 V-sts; 2 dc at each edge, counting last 3 chs of foundation ch as first dc)

Row 2: Ch 3 (counts as first dc throughout), dc in next dc,

[V-st in next V-st] rep across, ending with dc in each of 2 edge dc, turn.

Rows 3–6: Rep Row 2.

Row 7: Ch 3, dc in next dc, *[V-st in V-st] 11 times **, changing to hunter green in last dc, ch 5, sk 1 V-st, sc in ch-1 sp of next V-st, ch 5, fasten off hunter green, leaving 6" tail, attach MC in last ch, sk 1 V-st, rep from * across, ending last rep at **, dc in each of 2 edge dc, turn.

Row 8: Ch 3, dc in next dc, *[V-st in next V-st] 11 times **, [ch 3, sc in next ch-5 sp] twice, ch 3, rep from * across, ending last rep at **, dc in each of 2 edge dc, turn.

Row 9: Ch 3, dc in next dc, *[V-st in next V-st] 11 times **, changing to cherry red in last dc, sk first ch-3 sp, [pc, ch 2] twice in next ch-3 sp, pc in same sp, changing to MC, fasten off cherry red, leaving 6" tail, sk next ch-3 sp, rep from * across, ending last rep at **, dc in each of 2 edge dc, turn.

Row 10: Ch 3, dc in next dc, *[V-st in next V-st] 11 times **, [ch 3, sc in next ch-2 sp] twice, ch 3, rep from * across, ending last rep at **, dc in each of 2 edge dc, turn.

Row 11: Ch 3, dc in next dc, *[V-st in next V-st] 11 times **, [V-st in next ch-3 sp] 3 times, rep from * across, ending last rep at **, dc in each of 2 edge dc, turn.

Rows 12–15: Rep Row 2.

Rows 16–72: Rep Rows 2–15 alternately, ending with Row 2, fasten off.

TOP BORDER
Row 1: With WS facing, attach MC with a sl st in first dc at end of Row 72, ch 1, sc in same dc and in next dc, *ch 15, sk next 3 V-sts **, sc in ch-1 sp of next V-st, rep from * across, ending last rep at **, sc in each of last 2 dc, turn.

Row 2: Ch 5 (counts as first dtr), *[[3-dtr cl, ch 6] twice] in 8th ch of next ch-15 sp, 3-dtr cl in same ch **, dtr in next sc, rep from * across, ending last rep at **, sk 1 sc, dtr in last sc, fasten off.

BOTTOM BORDER
Row 1: With RS facing, attach MC with a sl st in first ch of foundation ch, ch 3, dc in next ch, [V-st in same ch as V-st of Row 1] rep across, ending with dc in each of last 2 chs, turn. (67 V-sts; 2 dc at each edge, counting beg ch-3 as first dc)

Rows 2–3: Rep Rows 1 and 2 of top border.

Weave in loose ends.

—*Designed by Ann E. Smith*

~ *Crochet Notes* ~

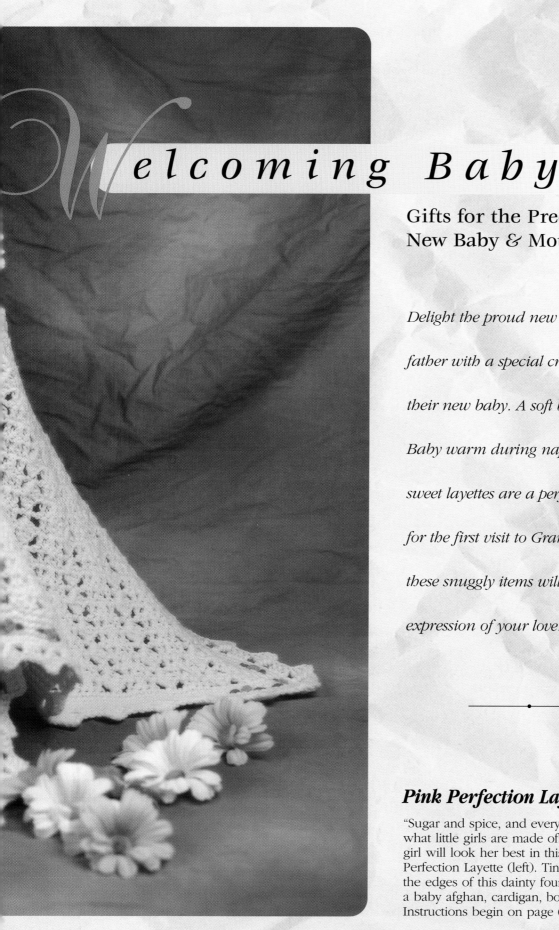

Welcoming Baby

Gifts for the Precious New Baby & Mother

Delight the proud new mother and father with a special crocheted gift for their new baby. A soft blanket will keep Baby warm during naptime, while sweet layettes are a perfect gift to wear for the first visit to Grandma's. Each of these snuggly items will be a tender expression of your love.

———•———

Pink Perfection Layette

"Sugar and spice, and everything nice—that's what little girls are made of!" Your sweet little girl will look her best in this adorable Pink Perfection Layette (left). Tiny rosebuds adorn the edges of this dainty four-piece set including a baby afghan, cardigan, bonnet and booties. Instructions begin on page 62.

Mother & Child Set

Delight the new mother by giving a coordinating sweater and bunting set to her and her newborn baby. A delicate lace collar is repeated on both patterns, giving this set a soft, feminine look that she'll feel beautiful wearing. Instructions begin on page 65.

White Lace

White Lace Blanket (above) has a pure white stitch pattern accented with satin ribbon, tulle and roses around the edges to make an exquisite keepsake afghan. Instructions begin on page 64.

Rainbow of Hearts

Row upon row of pink, yellow, blue and green textured hearts decorate this lovely Rainbow of Hearts crib coverlet (above), perfect for either a baby boy or baby girl. Instructions begin on page 67.

Precious Pink Roses

Precious Pink Roses (right) combines granny squares accented with a soft pink rose with an abundant, slightly ruffled edging. Instructions begin on page 69.

Little Boy Blue Layette

Baby will love playing with the soft pom-pons on this snuggly Little Boy Blue afghan (left). An open cardigan, warm winter hat and booties complete this attractive set. A simple stitch pattern is easy to remember and will work up quickly. Work it in blue as pictured for a little boy, or pink for that sweet little girl! Instructions begin on page 69.

Cream Lattice

Cream Lattice (left) combines several different techniques and styles to create a delicate, airy effect. This pretty blanket is just right for covering your napping baby in slightly warmer temperatures. Instructions begin on page 72.

Sherbet Stripes

Sherbet Stripes (above) is quick and fun to crochet. Delight the mother-to-be by crocheting it in colors to match the nursery. Instructions begin on page 74.

Lilac Lace

Pretty shells offset between a chain-latticed pattern make this clever Lilac Lace afghan (above) reversible. The closed pattern worked with super-soft yarn will keep Baby extra warm! Instructions begin on page 74.

Striped Ripple Set

Perfect for playtime, this colorful jumper and cardigan set is crocheted in a delightful ripple pattern. Work it in a variety of pastels as shown, a solid color, or perhaps in alternating solid and white cotton. Instructions begin on page 75.

Pink Perfection Layette

EXPERIENCE LEVEL
Intermediate

SIZE
Afghan: Approximately 40" x 38"
Sweater, Bonnet & Booties: 3–6 months

FINISHED MEASUREMENTS
Chest: 22½"
Length: 11"

MATERIALS
- Sport weight yarn: 24 oz pink
- Baby yarn: ½ oz each bright pink and green for embroidery
- Size F/5 crochet hook
- Size G/6 crochet hook or size needed to obtain gauge
- Size H/8 crochet hook or size needed to obtain gauge
- Yarn needle
- 2⅔ yds ⅜"-wide pink satin ribbon

GAUGE
[Dc, X-st, dc] = 1⅛"; 8 rows = 5" over patt with size H hook
7 sts and 8 rows = 2" in sc with size G hook
To save time, take time to check gauge.

PATTERN NOTE
Join rnds with a sl st unless otherwise stated.

PATTERN STITCH
X-st: Sk next st, dc in next st, dc in sk st.

Afghan

Row 1 (RS): With pink sport weight yarn and largest hook, ch 139, dc in 4th ch from hook and in next ch, *sk next 2 chs, dc in next ch, ch 3, 3 dc across bar of dc just made, sk 2 chs, dc in next ch **, X-st, dc in next ch, rep from * across, ending last rep at **, dc in each of last 2 chs, turn.

Row 2: Ch 3 (counts as first dc throughout), dc in each of next 2 dc, *ch 2, sc in next ch-3 sp, ch 2, dc in next dc **, X-st over next X-st, dc in next dc, rep from * across, ending last rep at **, dc in each of last 2 sts, turn.

Row 3: Ch 3, dc in each of next 2 dc, *dc in next sc, ch 3, 3 dc across bar of dc just made, dc in next dc **, X-st over next X-st, dc in next dc, rep from * across, ending last rep at **, dc in each of last 2 sts, turn.

Rows 4–58: Rep Rows 2 and 3 alternately, ending with Row 2, ch 1, turn at end of last row.

BORDER

Rnd 1: With RS facing, 3 sc in first st, sc in each dc, ch st and sc across to last st, 3 sc in last st, *working over row ends, 3 sc over end st of each row to corner **, 3 sc in first rem lp of foundation ch, sc in each rem lp of foundation ch across to last st, 3 sc in last st, rep from * to **, join in beg sc, ch 1, do not turn. (630 sc)

Rnds 2–5: Beg in same st as joining, sc in each sc around, working 3 sc in 2nd sc of each 3-sc group at corners, join in beg sc, ch 1, do not turn, fasten off at end of Rnd 5. (662 sc at end of Rnd 5)

Rnd 6: With RS facing and largest hook, attach sport weight pink with a sl st in 2nd sc of 3-sc group at any corner, ch 3, 2 dc in same st, *sk 2 sts, dc in next st, ch 3, 3 dc across bar of dc just made, sk 2 sts **, dc in each of next 3 sts, rep from * across to corner, sk 1 st instead of 2 sts 4 times evenly sp across, ending last rep at **, join in 3rd ch of beg ch-3, fasten off.

ROSEBUDS
Using photo as a guide, embroider 3 rosebuds with leaves in each corner and in center of each side as follows: With yarn needle and bright pink baby yarn, work 2 long French knots side by side, secure with knot. With yarn needle and green baby yarn, work 1 lazy-daisy st on each side of French-knot rosebuds.

Sweater

YOKE BACK & FRONTS
Row 1 (WS): With sport weight pink yarn and middle size hook, ch 34, sc in 2nd ch from hook and in each rem ch across, ch 1, turn. (33 sc)

Rows 2–16: Sc in each sc across, ch 1, turn.

Left shoulder
Row 17: Sc in each of first 10 sc, ch 1, turn.

Row 18: Sc in each sc across, ch 1, turn.

Left front
Rows 19 & 20: Rep Row 18.

Row 21: Sc in each sc across to last 2 sc, 2 sc in next sc, sc in last sc, ch 1, turn. (11 sc)

Row 22: Rep Row 18.

Rows 23–34: Rep Rows 21 and 22 alternately, fasten off at end of Row 34. (17 sc on Rows 33 and 34)

Right shoulder & right front
Row 17: With WS facing, sk next 13 unworked sts of Row 16, attach sport weight pink with a sl st in next st, sc in same st and in each rem st across, ch 1, turn. (10 sc)

Rows 18–34: Rep Rows 18–34 for left shoulder and front, reversing shaping at neckline, at end of Row 34, do not fasten off, ch 1, turn.

BODY
Row 1: Sc in each sc across right front yoke, ch 6, sc in each sc across yoke back, ch 6, sc in each sc across left front, turn. (79 sts)

Row 2: Ch 3, dc in each of next 2 sts, *sk 1 st, dc in next st,

ch 3, 3 dc across bar of dc just made, sk 1 st, dc in next st
**, X-st, dc in next st, rep from * across, ending last rep at **,
dc in each of last 2 sts, turn.

Row 3: Ch 3, dc in each of next 2 dc, *ch 2, sc in next ch-3 sp,
ch 2, dc in next dc **, X-st over next X-st, dc in next dc, rep
from * across, ending last rep at **, dc in each of last 2 sts, turn.

Row 4: Ch 3, dc in each of next 2 dc, *dc in next sc, ch 3, 3
dc across bar of dc just made, dc in next dc **, X-st over
next X-st, dc in next dc, rep from * across, ending last rep at
**, dc in each of last 2 sts, turn.

Rows 5–11: Rep Rows 3 and 4 alternately, ending with
Row 3, fasten off at end of Row 11.

Sleeve

Make 2

Rnd 1: With sport weight pink and middle size hook, ch
45, join to form a ring, ch 1, sc in each ch around, join in
beg sc, do not turn. (45 sc)

Rnd 2: Ch 3, *X-st, dc in next st, sk next 2 sts, dc in next sc,
ch 3, 3 dc across bar of dc just made, sk 2 sts **, dc in next
st, rep from * around, ending last rep at **, join in 3rd ch of
beg ch-3, turn.

Rnd 3: Ch 5 (counts as first dc, ch 2), *sc in next ch-3 sp,
ch 2, dc in next dc, X-st over next X-st **, dc in next dc, ch
2, rep from * around, ending last rep **, join in 3rd ch of
beg ch-5, turn.

Rnds 4–9: Rep Rnds 2 and 3 alternately, do not fasten off
at end of Rnd 9, ch 1, turn.

Cuff

Rnd 1: Sc in same st as joining and in each sc and dc
around, sk all ch-2 sps, join in beg sc, ch 1, turn. (25 sc)

Rnd 2: Sk first sc, sc in each rem sc around, join in beg sc,
ch 1, turn. (24 sc)

Rnds 3 & 4: Sc in each sc around, join in beg sc, ch 1, turn.
(24 sc)

Rnd 5: Ch 2, 2 sc in 2nd ch from hook, [sk next sc, sc in next
sc, ch 1, 2 sc over vertical bar of last sc made] rep around,
ending with sk last sc, join in same st as beg ch-2, fasten off.
Sew sleeve into armhole.

Edging

Rnd 1: With RS facing, using middle size hook, attach sport
weight pink with a sl st at center back neckline, ch 1, beg
in same st and working in sts and row ends, sc evenly
around sweater, working 3 sc at each front bottom corner,
join in beg sc, ch 1, do not turn.

Rnd 2: Rep Rnd 5 of cuff.

Finishing

Using photo as a guide, embroider rosebuds with leaves on
yoke and sleeve cuffs in same manner as for afghan.

Cut 2 (12") lengths of ⅜"-wide pink satin ribbon. Make a lp
at end of each piece; tack lp end of each piece to each
yoke front.

Bonnet

Row 1: With middle size hook and sport weight pink, beg
at center back, ch 15, sc in 2nd ch from hook and in each
of next 10 chs, 2 sc in each of next 3 chs, working on
opposite side of foundation ch, 2 sc in each of next 2 chs,
sc in each of next 11 chs, ch 1, turn. (32 sc)

Row 2: Sc in each sc across, ch 1, turn.

Row 3: Sc in each of first 13 sc, 2 sc in each of next 6 sc, sc
in each rem sc across, ch 1, turn. (38 sc)

Row 4: Sc in each of first 14 sc, 2 sc in each of next 10 sc,
sc in each rem sc across, ch 1, turn. (48 sc)

Row 5: Rep Row 2.

Row 6: Sc in each of first 20 sc, 2 sc in each of next 8 sc, sc
in each rem sc across, turn. (56 sc)

Row 7: Ch 3, dc in each of next 2 sts, *sk 2 sts, dc in next
sc, ch 3, 3 dc across bar of dc just made, sk 2 sts, dc in next
st **, X-st, dc in next st, rep from * across, ending last rep at
**, dc in each of last 2 sts, turn.

Row 8: Ch 3, dc in each of next 2 sts, *ch 2, sc in next ch-3 sp,
ch 2, dc in next dc **, X-st over next X-st, dc in next dc, rep
from * across, ending last rep at **, dc in each of last 2 sts, turn.

Rows 9–12: Rep Rows 7 and 8 alternately, at end of Row
12 ch 1, turn.

Rows 13–16: Sc in each st across, ch 1, turn. (56 sc)

Rnd 17: Sc in first sc, [sk 2 sts, sc in next sc, ch 1, 2 sc over
vertical bar of sc just made] rep across, ending with sk 2 sts,
sc in each of last 2 sts, working across neckline, 32 sc evenly sp over row ends, join in beg sc, fasten off.

Finishing

Using photo as a guide, embroider rosebuds with leaves
across front of bonnet in same manner as for afghan.

Cut 2 (18") lengths of ⅜"-wide satin ribbon. Make a lp at 1
end of each ribbon; sew lp ends at front corners for ties.

Booties

Instep

Row 1: With sport weight pink and smallest hook, ch 8, sc
in 2nd ch from hook and in each ch across, ch 1, turn. (7 sc)

Rows 2–8: Sc in each sc across, ch 1, turn, do not fasten off
at end of last row.

Sides

Rnd 1: Ch 19, being careful not to twist ch, sl st at opposite
end of last row, ch 1, turn, sc in each of next 19 chs, work
1 sc over end of each of next 8 rows of instep, working on
opposite side of foundation ch, sc in each of next 7 sts
across, work 1 sc over end of each of next 8 rows of instep,
join in beg sc, ch 1, do not turn. (42 sc)

Rnds 2–4: Sc in each st around, join in beg sc, ch 1, do not
turn. (42 sc)

Rnd 5: Sc in each of first 6 sc, sc dec, sc in each of next 3
sc, sc dec, sc in each of next 14 sc, sc dec, sc in each of

next 3 sc, sc dec, sc in each of last 8 sc, join in beg sc, ch 1, do not turn. (38 sts)

Rnd 6: Sc in each of first 6 sts, sc dec, sc in next st, sc dec, sc in each of next 14 sts, sc dec, sc in next st, sc dec, sc in each of next 8 sts, join in beg sc, ch 1, do not turn. (34 sc)

Rnd 7: Sc in each of first 5 sts, [sc dec] twice, sc in each of next 13 sts, [sc dec] twice, sc in each of next 8 sts, join in beg sc, fasten off. (30 sts)

Sew sole seams.

CUFF

Rnd 1: With smallest hook and RS facing, attach sport weight pink with a sl st at center back of bootie, ch 2, 25 hdc evenly sp around top edge, join in 2nd ch of beg ch-2, ch 1, do not turn. (26 hdc, counting beg ch-2 as first hdc)

Rnd 2: Sc in each hdc around, join in beg sc, do not turn.

Rnd 3: Rep Rnd 5 of sleeve cuff.

FINISHING

Using photo as a guide, embroider rosebuds with leaves on insteps of booties.

Cut 2 (14") lengths of ⅜"-wide pink satin ribbon; weave 1 piece through Rnd 1 of cuff of each bootie, beg and ending at center front; tie ends in a bow.

—Designed by Ruth Shepherd

White Lace

EXPERIENCE LEVEL
Intermediate

SIZE
Approximately 36" square including border

MATERIALS
- Coats & Clark Red Heart® Classic™ worsted weight yarn (3½ oz per skein): 4 skeins white #1
- Size J/10 crochet hook or size needed to obtain gauge
- 6 yds ⅜"-wide pale peach feather-edged satin ribbon
- 4 (18" x 4") pieces white tulle
- 4 (1¼") rose satin ribbon roses
- Sewing needle and white thread
- Fabric glue

GAUGE
[Hdc, Lk, hdc] = 1¼" in patt st

To save time, take time to check gauge.

PATTERN NOTE
Join rnds with a sl st unless otherwise stated.

PATTERN STITCHES
Love knot (Lk): Ch 1, draw up 1¼" lp, yo, draw through lp, insert hook between lp and long single strand and work sc.

Dc dec: Holding back on hook last lp of each st, work dc in each of next 2 indicated sts or 2 dc in next indicated sp, yo and draw through all 3 lps on hook.

———•———

AFGHAN

Row 1: Ch 108, hdc in 3rd ch from hook, [Lk, sk 3 chs, hdc in next ch] rep across, ending with hdc in each of last 2 chs, turn. (26 Lks; 29 hdc, counting last 2 chs of foundation ch as first hdc)

Row 2: Ch 2 (counts as first hdc throughout), [hdc in next hdc, ch 3] rep across, ending with hdc in each of last 2 hdc, turn.

Row 3: Ch 2, hdc in next hdc, [Lk, hdc in next hdc] rep across, ending with hdc in each of last 2 hdc, turn.

Rows 4–52: Rep Rows 2 and 3, ending with Row 2, do not turn at end of Row 52.

EDGING

Rnd 1: Ch 3 (counts as first dc throughout), 4 dc in same hdc, working down side of afghan, *2 dc over post of same hdc, [dc dec over post of next hdc, 2 dc over post of next hdc] rep across to next corner, ending with 2 dc over posts of each of last 2 hdc, 5 dc in top of last hdc, dc in next hdc, [dc in each of next 2 chs, dc dec over next ch and hdc] rep across to next corner, 5 dc in last hdc, rep from * around, join in 3rd ch of beg ch-3.

Rnd 2: Ch 5 (counts as first dc, ch 2), [dc, ch 2] in each of next 3 dc, *dc in next dc, ch 1, [sk 1 st, dc in next st, ch 1] rep across to next corner, [dc, ch 2] in each of first 4 dc of corner 5-dc, rep from * around, join in 3rd ch of beg ch-5.

Rnd 3: Ch 3, dc in each dc and in each ch around, working 3 dc in center dc of each corner 5-dc group, join in 3rd ch of beg ch-3.

Rnd 4: Ch 3, Lk, working in back lps only this rnd, [dc, Lk] in each dc around, join in 3rd ch of beg ch-3.

Rnd 5: Ch 3, Lk, [dc, Lk] in each rem dc around, join in 3rd ch of beg ch-3.

Rnd 6: Ch 1, beg in same st as joining, [sc, ch 5] in each dc around, join in beg sc, fasten off.

FINISHING
Beg and ending at 1 corner, weave ribbon through Rnd 2 of edging; cut off excess and set aside. Glue or sew ends tog.

Cut rem ribbon into 4 equal lengths; tie into bows. Set aside.

Fold tulle piece in half, forming 18" x 2" strip. Sewing raw edges tog, make gathering st by machine or hand along 18" edge; pull tight to gather, overlapping ends to form a circle. Tack ends tog. Rep for rem 3 tulle pieces.

Place ribbon bow in center of tulle circle; with sewing needle and thread, sewing through all thicknesses, stitch to corner of afghan, securing ribbon to dc post of Rnd 2 at same time. Rep for rem corners.

Glue ribbon rose over center of each corner bow.

—Designed by Jo Ann Maxwell

Mother & Child Set

EXPERIENCE LEVEL

Intermediate

SIZE

Sweater: Ladies small/34–36(medium/38–40)(large/42–44)

Bunting: 0–3(3–6) months

Instructions are given for smallest size, with larger sizes in parentheses. When only 1 number is given, it applies to all sizes.

FINISHED MEASUREMENTS

Sweater

Chest: 40⅝(45¼)(51½)"

Length: 19¼(20¾)(22¼)"

Bunting

Chest: 26½(28½)"

Length: 27(28¼)"

MATERIALS

- Coats & Clark Red Heart® baby fingering yarn, Art. E.254 (1¾ oz/50 grams per skein): 5(6)(7) skeins baby blue #802 (for sweater) and 3(4) skeins baby blue #802 (for bunting)
- Size E/4 crochet hook or size needed to obtain gauge
- Tapestry needle
- 3(3)(3½) yds ¼"-wide white satin ribbon (for sweater)
- 2 yds ¼"-wide ecru satin ribbon (for bunting)
- 6 (½"-diameter) white satin buttons (for sweater)
- 3 (½"-diameter) white buttons (for bunting)

GAUGE

3 shells = 5"; 5 rows = 2" in Body Patt

Gauge swatch (4" wide x 2" tall)

Row 1: Ch 21, sc in 2nd ch from hook and in each ch across, ch 1, turn. (20 sc)

Rows 2–12: Sc in each sc across, ch 1, turn.

To save time, take time to check gauge.

PATTERN NOTES

Join rnds with a sl st unless otherwise stated.

Bunting is made in 1 piece to the underarm.

PATTERN STITCHES

Shell: 5 dc in indicated st or sp.

Body Pattern (multiple of 12 sts + 1 st + 3 base chs)

Foundation Row (RS): 2 dc in 4th ch from hook, *sk 2 chs, sc in next ch, ch 5, sk 5 chs, sc in next ch, sk 2 chs **, shell in next ch, rep from * across, ending last rep at **, 3 dc in last ch, ch 1, turn.

Row 1: Sc in first dc, *ch 5, sc in next ch-5 sp, ch 5 **, sc in

3rd dc of next shell, rep from * across, ending last rep at **, sc in 3rd ch of turning ch-3, turn.

Row 2: Ch 5 (counts as first dc, ch 2, *sc in next ch-5 sp, shell in next sc, sc in next ch-5 sp **, ch 5, rep from * across, ending last rep at **, ch 2, dc in last sc, ch 1, turn.

Row 3: Sc in first dc, *ch 5, sc in 3rd dc of next shell, ch 5, sc in next ch-5 sp, rep from * across, ending with sc in 3rd ch of turning ch-5, turn.

Row 4: Ch 3 (counts as first dc), 2 dc in first sc, *sc in next ch-5 sp, ch 5, sc in next ch-5 sp **, shell in next sc, rep from * across, ending last rep at **, 3 dc in last sc, ch 1, turn.

Rep Rows 1–4 for patt.

Sweater

BACK

Row 1: Beg at lower edge, ch 136(148)(160), work Foundation Row of Body Patt. (10, 11, 12 shells + a partial shell at each edge)

Rows 2–46(50)(54): Rep Rows 1–4 of Body Patt, ending with Row 1, fasten off. *Note: Piece should meas 20⅝(22)-(24¼)" wide x 18½(20)(21½)" long.*

RIGHT FRONT

Row 1: Beg at lower edge, ch 64(76)(88), work Foundation Row of Body Patt. (4, 5, 6 shells + a partial shell at each edge)

Rows 2–38(42)(46): Rep Rows 1–4 of Body Patt, ending with Row 1, fasten off at end of last row.

Neck shaping

Row 39(43)(47): With RS facing, sk first 2 ch-5 sps, attach yarn with a sl st in sc before next ch-5 sp, work Row 2 of Body Patt as est.

Rows 40(44)(48)–46(50)(54): Beg with Row 3, continue in Body Patt on rem sts, ending with Row 1, fasten off. *Note: Front should meas 9⅝(11¼)(13¼)" wide.*

LEFT FRONT

Rows 1–38(42)(46): Work as for right front to neck shaping, do not fasten off after last rep of Row 1 of Body Patt, turn.

Neck shaping

Row 39(43)(47): Work Row 2 of Body Patt across, leaving last 2 ch-5 sps unworked, ending with ch 2, dc in next sc, ch 1, turn.

Rows 40(44)(48)–46(50)(54): Work as for right front.

SLEEVE

Make 2

Row 1: Beg at lower edge above cuff, ch 124(136)(148), work Foundation Row of Body Patt. (9, 10, 11 shells + a partial shell at each edge)

Rep Rows 1–4 of Body Patt until piece meas 17" long, ending with Row 1 or Row 3, fasten off.

Join shoulder seams. Place markers at each side edge in

7th(6th)(5th) partial shell from lower edge. Set in sleeves between markers. Join underarm and side seams.

COLLAR

Rnd 1: Ch 86, sl st in 11th ch from hook, [ch 5, sk 4 chs, sl st in next ch] rep across, ch 4 (counts as first tr), [4 tr, dc] in same sp, working in opposite side of foundation ch, [{sc, dc, 5 tr, dc} in next sp] 14 times, [sc, dc, 10 tr, dc] in next sp, do not turn.

Row 2: Ch 1, [{sc, dc, 5 tr, dc} in next sp] 14 times, [sc, dc, 5 tr] in next sp, join in 4th ch of beg ch-4, do not turn.

Row 3: Ch 4 (counts as first dc, ch 1), [dc, ch 1] in same st, [{dc, ch 1} twice] in each of next 4 tr, *sk [dc, sc, dc], [{dc, ch 1} twice] in each of next 5 tr, rep from * 13 times, sk [dc, sc, dc], [{dc, ch 1} twice] in each of next 4 tr, [dc, ch 1, dc] in last tr, ch 1, turn. (9 ch-1 sps for each pineapple)

Row 4: *Sc in first ch-1 sp of pineapple, [ch 3, sc in next sp] 8 times **, sk next sp, rep from * across, ending last rep at **, ch 1, turn.

Row 5: *Sc in first ch-3 sp of pineapple, [ch 3, sc in next ch-3 sp] 7 times, rep from * across, ch 1, turn.

Row 6: *Sc in first ch-3 sp of pineapple, [ch 3, sc in next ch-3 sp] 6 times, rep from * across, ch 1, turn.

Row 7: *Sc in first ch-3 sp of pineapple, [ch 3, sc in next ch-3 sp] 5 times, rep from * across, ch 1, turn.

Row 8: *Sc in first ch-3 sp of pineapple, [ch 3, sc in next ch-3 sp] 4 times **, ch 3, sk 2 sc, rep from * across ending last rep at **, ch 1, turn.

Row 9: *Sc in first ch-3 sp of pineapple, [ch 3, sc in next ch-3 sp] 3 times **, ch 5, sk next ch-3 sp, rep from * across, ending last rep at **, ch 1, turn.

Row 10: *Sc in first ch-3 sp of pineapple, [ch 3, sc in next ch-3 sp] twice **, ch 7, sk next ch-5 sp, rep from * across, ending last rep at **, ch 1, turn.

Row 11: *Sc in first ch-3 sp of pineapple, ch 5, sc in next ch-3 sp **, ch 5, sc in 4th ch of ch-7, ch 5, rep from * across, ending last rep at **, ch 1, turn.

Row 12: *[Sc, hdc, 3 dc, hdc, sc] in next ch-5 sp **, [ch 3, sc in 3rd ch of next ch-5 sp] twice, ch 3, rep from * across, ending last rep at **, fasten off.

Leaving Rnd 1 free, sew collar to neck edge with tapestry needle and yarn.

EDGINGS

Sleeve edging

Rnd 1: With RS facing, attach yarn with a sl st in ch-5 sp of foundation ch near seam, ch 3 (counts as first dc), 4 dc in same sp, shell in each ch-5 sp around, join in 3rd ch of beg ch-3, ch 1, turn.

Rnd 2: Sk first dc, *sc in next dc, [sc, ch 3, sc] in next dc, sc in next dc, sk next 2 dc, rep from * around, join in beg sc, fasten off.

Bottom edging

Row 1: With RS facing, attach yarn with a sl st in first ch-5 sp of foundation ch at lower edge of sweater, ch 3 (counts as first dc), 4 dc in same sp, shell in each ch-5 sp across, fasten off.

Outer edging

Row 1: With RS facing, attach yarn with a sl st at left front neck edge, ch 1, 59(63)(67) sc evenly sp across left front edge to corner, [sc, hdc] in corner, sc in each dc across bottom edge to next corner, [hdc, sc] in corner, 59(63)(67) sc evenly sp across right front edge, ch 1, turn.

Row 2: Sc in first sc, [ch 1, sk 1 sc, sc in each of next 10 sc] 5 times (buttonholes), ch 1, sk 1 sc, sc in each rem sc around, working 3 sc in each corner hdc, ch 1, turn.

Row 3: Sc in each sc around, working 3 sc in center sc of each corner and 1 sc in each ch-1 sp, ch 1, do not turn.

Row 4: Rev sc in each sc around, fasten off.

FINISHING

Cut 2 pieces of ribbon each meas ½(½)(¾) yard. Thread both pieces through ch-5 sps of Row 4 of sleeve so that ends are on side opposite seam. Tie in square knot and bow to fit wrist. Rep for 2nd sleeve.

Weave rem ribbon through ch-5 sps of Rnd 1 of collar; tie in bow at front.

Sew buttons on left front edge to correspond with buttonholes.

Bunting

Row 1: Beg at center back of lower edge, ch 172(184), work Foundation Row of Body Patt. (13, 14 shells + a partial shell at each edge)

Rows 2–54(58): Work Rows 1–4 of Body Patt, ending with Row 1.

LEFT BACK

Row 55(59): [Ch 5, sc in next ch-5 sp, shell in next sc, sc in next ch-5 sp] 4 times, ch 2, dc in next sc, ch 1, turn.

Rows 56(60)–68(72): Beg with Row 3, continue in Body Patt on rem sts, ending with Row 3, fasten off.

FRONT

Row 55(59): With RS facing, attach yarn with a sl st in same sc as last dc of Row 55(59) of left back, [ch 5, sc in next ch-5 sp, shell in next sc, sc in next ch-5 sp] 6(7) times, ch 2, dc in next sc, ch 1, turn.

Rows 56(60)–66(70): Beg with Row 3, continue in Body Patt on rem sts, ending with Row 1.

LEFT SHOULDER

Size 0–3 months only

Row 67: [Ch 5, sc in next ch-5 sp, shell in next sc, sc in next ch-5 sp] twice, ch 5, sc in next ch-5 sp, 3 dc in next sc, turn.

Row 68: Ch 3, sc in first ch-5 sp, ch 5, sc in 3rd dc of next shell, ch 5, sc in next ch-5 sp, ch 5, sc in 3rd dc of next shell, ch 5, sc in 3rd ch of turning ch-5, fasten off.

Size 3–6 months only

Row 71: [Ch 5, sc in next ch-5 sp, shell in next sc, sc in next ch-5 sp] 3 times, ch 2, dc in next sc, ch 2, turn.

Row 72: *Sc in 3rd dc of next shell, ch 5, sc in next ch-5 sp **, ch 5, rep from * across, ending last rep at **, fasten off.

RIGHT SHOULDER

Size 0–3 months only

Row 67: With RS facing, sk next 2 ch-5 sps at center front on Row 66, attach yarn with a sl st in next sc, ch 3, 2 dc in same sp, sc in next ch-5 sp, [ch 5, sc in next ch-5 sp, shell in next sc, sc in next ch-5 sp] twice, ch 2, dc in next sc, ch 1, turn.

Row 68: Sc in first dc, [ch 5, sc in 3rd dc of next shell, ch 5, sc in next ch-5 sp] twice, ch 3, sc in 3rd ch of turning ch-3, fasten off.

Size 3–6 months only

Row 71: With RS facing, sk next 2 ch-5 sps at center front on Row 70, attach yarn with a sl st in next sc, rep Row 71 of left shoulder, ch 1, turn.

Row 72: Rep Row 3 of Body Patt, ending with a sc in 3rd dc of last shell, ch 2, sc in 3rd ch of next ch-5 sp, fasten off.

RIGHT BACK

Row 55(59): With RS facing, attach yarn with a sl st in same sc as last dc of Row 55(59) of front, rep Row 55(59) of left back.

Rows 56(60)–68(72): Rep Rows 56(60)–68(72) of left back.

All sizes

Join front to back at shoulders. Join edges at center back to within 6½" from neck edge.

BACK OPENING EDGING

Row 1: With RS facing, attach yarn with a sl st at neck edge of right back, ch 1, 64 sc evenly sp around back opening to left neck edge, ch 1, turn.

Row 2: Sl st in each sc across to last 8 sc, [ch 3, sl st in each of next 3 sc] twice, ch 3 (3 button lps made), sl st in each of last 2 sc, fasten off.

SLEEVE

Make 2

Row 1: Beg at lower edge, ch 76(88), work Foundation Row of Body Patt. (5, 6 shells + a partial shell at each edge)

Rows 2–12(16): Rep Rows 1–4 of Body Patt, ending with Row 3, fasten off at end of last row.

Join sleeve seam. Set in sleeve.

Edging

Rnd 1: With RS facing, attach yarn with a sl st in seam, ch 3 (counts as first dc), shell in each ch-5 sp of foundation ch around, join in 3rd ch of beg ch-3. (31, 36 sts)

Rnd 2: Ch 1, sc in each sc around, join in beg sc.

Rnd 3: Sl st in each st around, join in beg sl st, fasten off.

COLLAR

Rnd 1: Ch 66, sl st in 11th ch from hook, [ch 5, sk 4 chs, sl st in next ch] rep across, working in opposite side of foundation ch, ch 4 (counts as first tr), [4 tr, dc] in same sp, [[sc, dc, 5 tr, dc] in next sp] 10 times, [sc, dc, 10 tr, dc] in next sp, do not turn.

Row 2: Ch 1, [[sc, dc, 10 tr, dc] in next sp] 10 times, [sc, dc, 5 tr] in next sp, join in 4th ch of beg ch-4, do not turn.

Row 3: Ch 4 (counts as first dc, ch 1), *[dc, ch 1] in next tr, [dc, ch 1] 3 times in next tr **, [dc, ch 1] in each of next 2 tr, sk [dc, sc, dc], [dc, ch 1] in first tr of next group, rep from * 11 times, ending 11th rep at **, [dc, ch 1] in next tr, dc in next tr, ch 1, turn. (6 ch-1 sps for each pineapple)

Row 4: Sc in first sp, *[ch 3, sc in next sp] 5 times **, sl st in next sp, sc in next sp, rep from * across, ending last rep at **, ch 1, turn.

Row 5: Sc in first sp, *[ch 3, sc in next ch-3 sp] 4 times **, sc in next ch-3 sp, rep from * across, ending last rep at **, ch 1, turn.

Row 6: Sc in first sp, *[ch 3, sc in next ch-3 sp] 3 times **, sc in next ch-3 sp, rep from * across, ending last rep at **, ch 1, turn.

Row 7: Sc in first sp, ch 3, *[sc, ch 3, sc] in next sp **, ch 3, sc in each of next 2 sps, ch 3, rep from * across, ending last rep at **, ch 3, sc in last sp, fasten off.

Leaving Rnd 1 free, sew collar to neck edge, having opening in back.

FINISHING

Cut 1 yard of ecru ribbon; weave through ch-5 sps of Row 3 of body. Tie at 1 side.

Cut 2 (12") lengths of ecru ribbon; weave each length through Row 1 of sleeve, beg and ending opposite sleeve seam; tie in bow.

Tie rem ecru ribbon into bow at center front of collar.

Sew buttons onto left back opening edge to correspond with button lps.

—Designed by Ann E. Smith

Rainbow of Hearts

EXPERIENCE LEVEL
Advanced

SIZE
Approximately 36" x 40" excluding fringe

MATERIALS
- Lion Brand Jaime® pompadour yarn: 12¼ oz white #200 (MC), 3½ oz each light pink #201 (A), aqua #271 (B), pastel yellow #257 (C) and pastel blue #206 (D)
- Size F/5 crochet hook or size needed to obtain gauge

CHART A

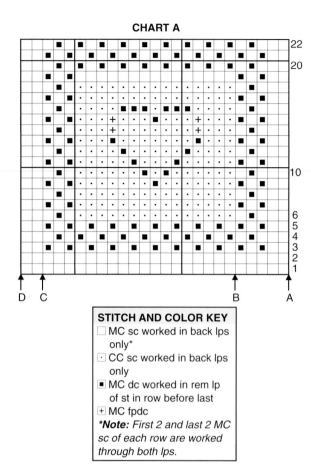

STITCH AND COLOR KEY
- ☐ MC sc worked in back lps only*
- ⋅ CC sc worked in back lps only
- ■ MC dc worked in rem lp of st in row before last
- ⊞ MC fpdc

Note: First 2 and last 2 MC sc of each row are worked through both lps.

GAUGE

15 sc sts worked in back lps only = 3¼"; 13 rows = 3½"

To save time, take time to check gauge.

PATTERN NOTES

All rows are worked on RS. Do not turn at end of each row; fasten off, leaving a 3" length of each color for fringe. Beg each row in first st of previous row.

All CC sc are worked in back lps only of previous row.

All MC sts are worked in back lps only of previous row, except for the first 2 and last 2 sts of each row, which are worked in both lps.

All dc are worked in rem lps of indicated sts of the row before last. Do not work into st on previous row that is directly behind a dc worked into rem lp of st of the row before last or directly behind a fpdc.

To beg a row when both MC and CC are used: Leaving a 3" length of each color for fringe, lay CC across MC at WS of work after joining MC in first st, carry CC loosely across WS of work, working over it with MC until it is needed, then carry MC across WS of work, working over it with CC until it is needed.

To change color, work last st before color change until last 2 lps before final yo rem on hook, drop working color to WS, yo with next color, draw through 2 lps on hook.

AFGHAN

Row 1 (RS): With MC, ch 170, sc in 2nd ch from hook and in each rem ch across, do not turn, fasten off, leaving 3" length. (169 sc)

Row 2: With RS facing, leaving 3" length, attach MC with a sl st through both lps of first sc, ch 1, sc in both lps of same st and in both lps of next st, working in back lps only, sc in each st across to last 2 sts, sc through both lps of each of last 2 sts, do not turn, fasten off, leaving 3" length. (169 sc)

Row 3: With RS facing, leaving 3" length, attach MC with a sl st through both lps of first st, ch 1, sc in both lps of same st and in both lps of next st, *dc in rem lp of next st on row before last **, sc in back lp only of next st on previous row, rep from * across to within last 2 sts, ending last rep at **, sc through both lps of each of last 2 sts, do not turn, fasten off, leaving 3" length. (169 sts)

Row 4: With RS facing, leaving a 3" length, attach MC with a sl st through both lps of first st, ch 1, sc in both lps of same st and in both lps of next st, *sc in back lp only of next st **, dc in rem lp of next st of row before last, rep from * across to within last 2 sts, ending last rep at **, sc in both lps of each of last 2 sts, do not turn, fasten off, leaving a 3" length. (169 sts)

Row 5: Rep Row 3.

Row 6: With RS facing, leaving a 3" length, attach MC with a sl st through both lps of first st, lay A across MC on WS of work, leaving a 3" length for fringe, ch 1 with MC, working over A, sc in both lps of same st and in both lps of next st, *sc in back lp only of next st, dc in rem lp of next st of row before last, sc in back lp only of next st **, changing to A, working over MC, sc in back lps only of each of next 15 sts, changing to MC in last st, rep from * across to within last 2 sts, ending last rep at **, with MC, sc in both lps of each of last 2 sts, working over A, do not turn, fasten off, leaving 3" length. (169 sts)

Rows 7–22: Following chart and reading all rows from right to left, [work {from A to C} once, {B to C} 8 times, {C to D} once] for each row.

[{Rep Rows 6–22} 4 times, with B as CC for first rep, then C, D and A] twice for a total of 9 blocks, then rep Row 2 once.

FRINGE

Working across top and bottom edges with 6" lengths of yarn, attach 1 strand in each st across in the following color sequence: alternate MC and A across width of first block, [alternate MC and B across next block, alternate MC and C across next block, alternate MC and D across next block, alternate MC and A across next block] twice. Trim ends evenly.

—Designed by Diana Owen for Monsanto's Designs for America Program

Precious Pink Roses

EXPERIENCE LEVEL
Advanced beginner

SIZE
Approximately 35" square including border

MATERIALS
- Coats & Clark Red Heart® Classic™ worsted weight yarn (3½ oz per skein): 3 skeins eggshell #111 and 1 oz each lily pink #719 and mist green #681
- Size J/10 crochet hook or size needed to obtain gauge
- Yarn needle

GAUGE
Motif = 7" square

To save time, take time to check gauge.

PATTERN NOTES
Join rnds with a sl st unless otherwise stated.

Join motifs in 4 rows of 4 squares each.

PATTERN STITCHES
Shell: [3 dc, ch 2, 3 dc] in indicated st.

Beg shell: [Ch 3, 2 dc, ch 2, 3 dc] in indicated st.

FIRST MOTIF
Rnd 1: With eggshell, ch 4, join to form a ring, ch 3 (counts as first dc throughout), 2 dc in ring, [ch 2, 3 dc in ring] 3 times, ch 2, join in 3rd ch of beg ch-3.

Rnd 2: Sl st to next ch-2 sp, beg shell in same sp, ch 1, [shell in next ch-2 sp, ch 1] rep around, join in 3rd ch of beg ch-3.

Rnd 3: Sl st to next ch-2 sp, beg shell in same ch-2 sp, *[ch 1, 3 dc, ch 1] in next ch-1 sp **, shell in ch-2 sp of next shell, rep from * around ending last rep at **, join in 3rd ch of beg ch-3.

Rnd 4: Ch 3, dc in each dc and ch-1 sp and shell in each shell sp around, join in 3rd ch of beg ch-3. (68 dc)

Rnd 5: Ch 1, sc in next st, *ch 4, sk 2 sts, sc in next st, ch 4, [sc, ch 6, sc] in corner ch-2 sp, ch 4, sk 1 st, sc in next st, ch 4, sk 2 sts, sc in next st, [ch 4, sk 3 sts, sc in next st] twice, rep from * around, join in beg sc, fasten off. (24 ch-4 sps; 4 ch-6 sps)

SECOND & SUBSEQUENT MOTIFS
Rnds 1–4: Rep Rnds 1–4 of first motif.

Joining
Rnd 5: Rep Rnd 5 of first motif, joining to previous motif as follows: For each ch-4 sp, ch 2, drop lp from hook, insert hook in corresponding ch-4 sp on previous motif, pick up dropped lp, draw through ch-4 sp, ch 2, sc in next indicated st on working motif.

For each corner ch-6 sp, ch 3, drop lp from hook, insert hook in ch-6 sp on previous motif, pick up dropped lp and draw through sp, ch 3, sc in same corner sp on working motif.

EDGING
Rnd 1: Attach mist green in any outer corner ch-6 sp, ch 1, 5 sc in same sp, *[ch 2, sc] in each of next 6 ch-4 sps, ch 2 **, sc in center of joined ch-6 sps, rep from * to next corner, ending last rep at **, 5 sc in corner ch-6 sp, rep from * around, join in beg sc, fasten off.

Rnd 2: Attach eggshell in first sc of corner 5-sc group, ch 1, beg in same st, [sc, ch 4] in each sc and ch-2 sp around, ending with ch 1, dc in beg sc to form last ch-4 sp.

Rnds 3–5: Ch 1, sc in dc, ch 4, [sc, ch 4] in each ch-4 sp around, ending with ch 1, dc in beg sc.

Rnds 6 & 7: Ch 1, sc in dc, ch 5, [sc, ch 5] in each ch sp around, ending with ch 2, dc in beg sc, fasten off at end of Rnd 7.

FINISHING
Roses (make 16)
Row 1 (WS): Beg at outer edge of rose with lily pink, ch 20, 7 dc in 3rd ch from hook, ch 1, sk 1 ch, sc in next ch, ch 1, [sk 1 ch, 6 dc in next ch, ch 1, sk 1 ch, sc in next ch, ch 1] twice, sk 1 ch, 5 dc in next ch, sk 1 ch, sc in next ch, ch 1, 4 dc in each of next 2 chs, ch 2, sl st in last ch, fasten off, leaving 18" length for sewing.

Beg at fastening-off point, roll Row 1 up back to starting point so RS is on outside, secure at base with a few sts, using 18" length of yarn and yarn needle; sew 1 rose in center of each motif.

Leaves (make 16)
With mist green, ch 9, sl st in first ch, ch 11, sl st in same ch, fasten off, leaving length for sewing.

With yarn needle and yarn length, sew 1 leaf to motif under rose, as shown in photo.

—Designed by Jo Ann Maxwell

Little Boy Blue Layette

EXPERIENCE LEVEL
Intermediate

SIZE
Afghan: 43" x 36"

Sweater, Cap & Booties: 3–6 months

FINISHED MEASUREMENTS
Chest: 19"

Length: 11"

MATERIALS
- Sport weight yarn: 25 oz baby blue, 3½ oz white
- Size F/5 crochet hook
- Size G/6 crochet hook or size needed to obtain gauge
- Size H/8 crochet hook or size needed to obtain gauge
- Yarn needle

- 2½"-wide piece cardboard

G A U G E

[2 sc, ch 1] 6 times = 5"; 4 rows = 1" in patt with size H hook

[2 sc, ch 1, sc] and 4 rows = 1" in patt with size G hook

To save time, take time to check gauge.

P A T T E R N   N O T E

Join rnds with a sl st unless otherwise stated.

• — •

Afghan

Row 1 (RS): With largest hook and baby blue, ch 120, sc in 2nd ch from hook and in next ch, [ch 1, sk 1 ch, sc in each of next 2 chs] rep across, ch 1, turn. (80 sc; 39 ch-1 sps)

Row 2: Sc in each of first 2 sc, [2 hdc in next ch-1 sp, sc in each of next 2 sc] rep across, ch 1, turn. (80 sc; 78 hdc)

Row 3: Sc in each of first 2 sc, pushing all hdc to RS of work, [ch 1, sk 2 hdc, sc in each of next 2 sc] rep across, ch 1, turn. (80 sc; 39 ch-1 sps)

Rows 4–11: Rep Rows 2 and 3.

Row 12: Sc in each of first 2 sc, [2 hdc in next ch-1 sp, sc in each of next 2 sc] 4 times, [ch 1, sk next ch-1 sp, sc in each of next 2 sc] 31 times, [2 hdc in next ch-1 sp, sc in each of next 2 sc] 4 times, ch 1, turn.

Row 13: Sc in each of first 2 sc, pushing all hdc to RS of work, [ch 1, sk next 2 hdc or next ch-1 sp, sc in each of next 2 sc] rep across, ch 1, turn.

Rows 14–55: Rep Rows 12 and 13 alternately.

Row 56: Sc in each of first 2 sc, [2 hdc in next ch-1 sp, sc in each of next 2 sc] 4 times, [ch 1, sk next ch-1 sp, sc in each of next 2 sc] 15 times, 2 hdc in next ch-1 sp, sc in each of next 2 sc, [ch 1, sc in each of next 2 sc] 15 times, [2 hdc in next ch-1 sp, sc in each of next 2 sc] 4 times, ch 1, turn.

Row 57: Rep Row 13.

Row 58: Sc in each of first 2 sc, [2 hdc in next ch-1 sp, sc in each of next 2 sc] 4 times, [ch 1, sk next ch-1 sp, sc in each of next 2 sc] 14 times, [2 hdc in next ch-1 sp, sc in each of next 2 sc] 3 times, [ch 1, sc in each of next 2 sc] 14 times, [2 hdc in next ch-1 sp, sc in each of next 2 sc] 4 times, ch 1, turn.

Row 59: Rep Row 13.

Row 60: Sc in each of first 2 sc, [2 hdc in next ch-1 sp, sc in each of next 2 sc] 4 times, [ch 1, sk next ch-1 sp, sc in each of next 2 sc] 13 times, [2 hdc in next ch-1 sp, sc in each of next 2 sc] 5 times, [ch 1, sc in each of next 2 sc] 13 times, [2 hdc in next ch-1 sp, sc in each of next 2 sc] 4 times, ch 1, turn.

Row 61: Rep Row 13.

Row 62: Sc in each of first 2 sc, [2 hdc in next ch-1 sp, sc in each of next 2 sc] 4 times, [ch 1, sk next ch-1 sp, sc in each of next 2 sc] 12 times, [2 hdc in next ch-1 sp, sc in each of next 2 sc] 7 times, [ch 1, sc in each of next 2 sc] 12 times, [2 hdc in next ch-1 sp, sc in each of next 2 sc] 4 times, ch 1, turn.

Row 63: Rep Row 13.

Row 64: Sc in each of first 2 sc, [2 hdc in next ch-1 sp, sc in each of next 2 sc] 4 times, [ch 1, sk next ch-1 sp, sc in each of next 2 sc] 11 times, [2 hdc in next ch-1 sp, sc in each of next 2 sc] 9 times, [ch 1, sc in each of next 2 sc] 11 times, [2 hdc in next ch-1 sp, sc in each of next 2 sc] 4 times, ch 1, turn.

Row 65: Rep Row 13.

Row 66: Sc in each of first 2 sc, [2 hdc in next ch-1 sp, sc in each of next 2 sc] 4 times, [ch 1, sk next ch-1 sp, sc in each of next 2 sc] 10 times, [2 hdc in next ch-1 sp, sc in each of next 2 sc] 11 times, [ch 1, sc in each of next 2 sc] 10 times, [2 hdc in next ch-1 sp, sc in each of next 2 sc] 4 times, ch 1, turn.

Row 67: Rep Row 13.

Row 68: Sc in each of first 2 sc, [2 hdc in next ch-1 sp, sc in each of next 2 sc] 4 times, [ch 1, sk next ch-1 sp, sc in each of next 2 sc] 9 times, [2 hdc in next ch-1 sp, sc in each of next 2 sc] 13 times, [ch 1, sc in each of next 2 sc] 9 times, [2 hdc in next ch-1 sp, sc in each of next 2 sc] 4 times, ch 1, turn.

Row 69: Rep Row 13.

Row 70: Sc in each of first 2 sc, [2 hdc in next ch-1 sp, sc in each of next 2 sc] 4 times, [ch 1, sk next ch-1 sp, sc in each of next 2 sc] 8 times, [2 hdc in next ch-1 sp, sc in each of next 2 sc] 15 times, [ch 1, sc in each of next 2 sc] 8 times, [2 hdc in next ch-1 sp, sc in each of next 2 sc] 4 times, ch 1, turn.

Row 71: Rep Row 13.

Row 72: Sc in each of first 2 sc, [2 hdc in next ch-1 sp, sc in each of next 2 sc] 4 times, [ch 1, sk next ch-1 sp, sc in each of next 2 sc] 7 times, [2 hdc in next ch-1 sp, sc in each of next 2 sc] 17 times, [ch 1, sc in each of next 2 sc] 7 times, [2 hdc in next ch-1 sp, sc in each of next 2 sc] 4 times, ch 1, turn.

Row 72 is center of afghan. Working in reverse order, rep Rows 71–2, then rep Row 3 once, do not fasten off, ch 1, turn.

B O R D E R

Rnd 1: Rep Row 2 across to corner, *working over row ends, 2 hdc over end of same row, [sc over ends of each of next 2 rows, 2 hdc over end of next row] rep to within last 2 rows, sc over end of next row, [sc, 2 hdc] over end of last row **, working in rem lps of foundation ch, rep Row 2 across bottom, rep from * to **, join in beg sc, ch 1, turn.

Rnd 2: Sc in same st as joining. [ch 1, sk 2 hdc, sc in each of next 2 sc] rep around, ending with sc in last sc, join in beg sc, fasten off.

Rnd 3: With RS facing, using largest hook, attach white with a sl st in any ch-1 sp, [ch 3, sl st in next ch-1 sp] rep around, ending last rep with ch 3, sl st in beg sl st, fasten off.

Weave in loose ends.

P O M P O N S

Make 4

Wrap white around cardboard 125 times. Remove from cardboard; tie in center.

Cut lps; trim into ball shape.

Tack 1 pompon in each corner of blanket.

Sweater

BODY

Row 1 (WS): Beg at bottom with middle size hook and baby blue, ch 72, sc in 2nd ch from hook and in next ch, [ch 1, sk 1 ch, sc in each of next 2 chs] rep across, ch 1, turn. (48 sc; 23 ch-1 sps)

Row 2: Sc in each of first 2 sc, [ch 1, sk next ch-1 sp, sc in each of next 2 sc] rep across, ch 1, turn.

Rows 3–24: Rep Row 2, do not fasten off at end of last row, ch 1, turn.

LEFT FRONT YOKE

Rows 25–34: Sc in each of first 2 sc, [ch 1, sk next ch-1 sp, sc in each of next 2 sc] 4 times, ch 1, turn, at end of Row 34 do not ch 1; turn.

Neck shaping

Row 35: Sl st in each of first 2 sc and ch-1 sp, ch 1, sc in each of next 2 sc, [ch 1, sk next ch-1 sp, sc in each of next 2 sc] 3 times, ch 1, turn.

Row 36: Sc in each of first 2 sc, [ch 1, sk next ch-1 sp, sc in each of next 2 sc] 3 times, turn.

Row 37: Sl st in each of first 2 sc and ch-1 sp, ch 1, sc in each of next 2 sc, [ch 1, sk next ch-1 sp, sc in each of next 2 sc] twice, ch 1, turn.

Rows 38 & 39: Sc in each of first 2 sc, [ch 1, sk next ch-1 sp, sc in each of next 2 sc] twice, ch 1, turn, do not ch 1 at end of Row 39, fasten off.

BACK

Row 25: With WS facing, sk next ch-1 sp, 2 sc and ch-1 sp of Row 24 of body, attach baby blue with a sl st in next sc, ch 1, sc in same st, sc in next sc, [ch 1, sk next ch-1 sp, sc in each of next 2 sc] 11 times, ch 1, turn.

Rows 26–39: Sc in each of first 2 sc, [ch 1, sk next ch-1 sp, sc in each of next 2 sc] rep across, ch 1, turn, do not ch 1 at end of last row, fasten off at end of Row 39.

RIGHT FRONT YOKE

Row 25: With WS facing, sk next ch-1 sp, 2 sc and ch-1 sp of Row 24 of body, attach baby blue with sl st in next sc, ch 1, sc in same st, sc in next sc, [ch 1, sk next ch-1 sp, sc in each of next 2 sc] 4 times, ch 1, turn.

Rows 26–34: Sc in each of first 2 sc, [ch 1, sk next ch-1 sp, sc in each of next 2 sc] 4 times, ch 1, turn.

Neck shaping

Rows 35 & 36: Sc in each of first 2 sc, [ch 1, sk next ch-1 sp, sc in each of next 2 sc] 3 times, ch 1, turn.

Rows 37–39: Sc in each of first 2 sc, [ch 1, sk next ch-1 sp, sc in each of next 2 sc] twice, ch 1, turn, do not ch 1 at end of last row, fasten off at end of Row 39.

Sew shoulder seams.

SLEEVE

Make 2

Rnd 1: With baby blue and middle size hook, ch 30, being careful not to twist, join to form a ring, ch 1, sc in same st and in next ch, ch 1, [sk next ch, sc in each of next 2 chs, ch 1] 9 times, join in beg sc, turn. (20 sc; 10 ch-1 sps)

Rnd 2: Sl st in ch-1 sp, ch 2 (counts as first hdc throughout), hdc in same ch-1 sp, sc in each of next 2 sc, [2 hdc in next ch-1 sp, sc in each of next 2 sc] rep around, join in 2nd ch of beg ch-2, turn.

Rnd 3: Sl st in next sc, ch 1, beg in same st, [sc in each of next 2 sc, ch 1, sk next 2 hdc] rep around, join in beg sc, ch 1, turn.

Rnd 4: Sc in same st, ch 1, [sc in each of next 2 sc, ch 1] 9 times, sc in next sc, join in beg sc, ch 1, turn.

Rnd 5: Sc in each of first 2 sc, ch 1, [sc in each of next 2 sc, ch 1] 9 times, join in beg sc, ch 1, turn.

Rnds 6–25: Rep Rnds 4 and 5 alternately, fasten off at end of Rnd 25.

Edging

With inside of sleeve facing and smallest hook, attach white with a sl st in first ch-1 sp of Rnd 1, [ch 3, sl st in next ch-1 sp] rep around, ending last rep with ch 3, join in beg sl st, fasten off.

Sew sleeves into armholes. Turn Rnds 1 and 2 to outside for cuffs.

FRONT & BOTTOM BORDER

Row 1: With WS facing and middle size hook, attach baby blue with sl st over end of Row 34 at right front neck, ch 1, working down right front opening, sc over same row end, [2 hdc over end of next row, sc over ends of each of next 2 rows] rep to bottom corner, ending with 2 hdc over end of same last row as last sc, working across bottom, [sc in each of next 2 sc, 2 hdc in next sp] rep across to next corner, ending with sc in each of last 2 sc, working up left front, [2 hdc, sc] over end of last row, sc over end of next row, [2 hdc over end of next row, sc over ends of each of next 2 rows] rep up to Row 34, ending with 2 hdc over end of next row, sc over end of Row 34, ch 1, turn.

Row 2: Sc in first sc, [ch 1, sk 2 hdc, sc in each of next 2 sc] rep across, ending with ch 1, sk 2 hdc, sc in last sc, fasten off.

NECKLINE EDGING

Row 1: With RS facing and smallest hook, attach white with a sl st at top right neckline edge, ch 1, 14 sc evenly sp to shoulder seam, 19 sc across back neckline, 14 sc evenly sp across left front neckline, ch 1, turn.

Row 2: Sc in each sc across, turn.

Row 3: Ch 35 (for right front tie), sl st in 2nd ch from hook and in each rem ch across to neckline, sc in each sc across neckline, ch 35 (for left front tie), sl st in 2nd ch from hook and in each ch across to neckline edge, fasten off.

FRONT & BOTTOM EDGING

With RS facing and smallest hook, attach white with a sl st in end of first row of neckline edging at top left edge, [ch 3, sl st in next ch-1 sp] rep down left front, around bottom and up right front edge, ending last rep with ch 3, sl st in end of first row of neckline edging, fasten off.

POMPON

Make 2

Wrap white 40 times around tines of a dinner fork. Remove from fork; tie in center.

Cut lps; trim into ball shape.

Tack 1 pompon to end of each tie.

Cap

Rnd 1: Beg at bottom with middle size hook and baby blue, ch 48, being careful not to twist ch, join to form a ring, ch 1, sc in same ch and in next ch, ch 1, sk 1 ch, [sc in each of next 2 chs, ch 1, sk 1 ch] 15 times, join in beg sc, turn. (32 sc; 16 ch-1 sps)

Rnd 2: Sl st in next ch-1 sp, ch 2, hdc in same ch-1 sp, sc in each of next 2 sc, [2 hdc in next ch-1 sp, sc in each of next 2 sc] rep around, join in 2nd ch of beg ch-2, turn.

Rnd 3: Sl st in next sc, ch 1, beg in same st, [sc in each of next 2 sc, ch 1, sk next 2 hdc] rep around, join in beg sc, ch 1, turn.

Rnd 4: Sc in same st as joining, ch 1, [sc in each of next 2 sc, ch 1] 15 times, sc in next sc, join in beg sc, ch 1, turn.

Rnd 5: Sc in same sc and in next sc, ch 1, [sc in each of next 2 sc, ch 1] 15 times, join in beg sc, ch 1, turn.

Rnds 6–26: Rep Rnds 4 and 5 alternately, ending with Rnd 4.

Rnd 27: Ch 1, sc in same sc and in next sc, [sk next ch-1 sp, sc in each of next 2 sc] rep around, join in beg sc, ch 1, turn. (32 sc)

Rnd 28: Beg in same st as joining, [sc dec] rep around, join in beg sc dec, fasten off, leaving length of yarn for sewing. (16 sts)
Sew rem sts tog.

EDGING

With inside of cap facing and smallest hook, attach white with a sl st in first ch-1 sp of Rnd 1, [ch 3, sl st in next ch-1 sp] rep around, ending last rep with ch 3, join in beg sl st, fasten off.

Turn Rnds 1 and 2 to outside for cuff.

POMPON

Make in same manner as for afghan. Tack pompon to center top of cap.

Booties

SOLE

Rnd 1: Beg at back with baby blue and middle size hook, ch 12, 3 hdc in 3rd ch from hook, hdc in each of next 5 chs, dc in each of next 3 chs, 7 dc in end ch, working on opposite side of foundation ch, dc in each of next 3 chs, hdc in each of next 5 chs, join in last ch of foundation ch, do not turn. (27 sts, counting last 2 chs of foundation ch as first hdc)

Rnd 2: Ch 1, 2 sc in same st as joining, 2 sc in each of next 3 sts, hdc in each of next 8 sts, 2 hdc in each of next 7 sts, hdc in each of next 8 sts, join in beg sc, do not turn. (38 sts)

SIDES

Rnd 1: Sl st in each of next 3 sts, ch 1, working in back lps

only this rnd, 2 sc in same st as last sl st, sc in each rem st around, join in beg sc, ch 1, turn. (39 sc)

Rnd 2: Sc in same st as joining, sc in next sc, [ch 1, sk next sc, sc in each of next 2 sc] rep around, ending with ch 1, sk last sc, join in beg sc, ch 1, turn. (26 sc; 13 ch-1 sps)

Rnd 3: Sc in same sc, 2 hdc in next ch-1 sp, [sc in each of next 2 sc, 2 hdc in next ch-1 sp] rep around, ending with sc in last sc, join in beg sc, ch 1, turn.

Rnd 4: Sc in same sc, sc in next sc, ch 1, [sk 2 hdc, sc in each of next 2 sc, ch 1] rep around, join in beg sc, fasten off.

INSTEP

With yarn needle, sew center front 18 sts tog to form instep.

CUFF

Rnd 1: With middle size hook and WS facing, attach baby blue with a sl st in first sc at center back, ch 2, 20 hdc around top edge, join in 2nd ch of beg ch-2, ch 1, turn. (21 hdc)

Rnd 2: Sc in same st and in next st, ch 1, [sk 1 st, sc in each of next 2 sts, ch 1] rep around, join in beg sc, ch 1, turn. (14 sc; 7 ch-1 sps)

Rnd 3: Sc in same sc, 2 hdc in next ch-1 sp, [sc in each of next 2 sc, 2 hdc in next ch-1 sp] rep around, ending with sc in last sc, join in beg sc, ch 1, turn.

Rnd 4: Sc in same sc and in next sc, ch 1, [sc in each of next 2 sc, ch 1] rep around, join in beg sc, ch 1, turn.

Rnds 5 & 6: Rep Rnds 3 and 4, fasten off at end of Rnd 6.

Edging

Rnd 1: With RS facing and smallest hook, attach white with a sl st in first ch-1 sp of Rnd 6, [ch 3, sl st in next ch-1 sp] rep around, ending last rep with ch 3, join in beg sl st, fasten off.

TIE

Make 2

With white, ch 6, sl st in 6th ch from hook, ch 66, sl st in 6th ch from hook, fasten off.

Weave through Rnd 1 of cuff; tie ends in bow at center front of bootie.

–Designed by Ruth Shepherd

Cream Lattice

EXPERIENCE LEVEL
Intermediate

SIZE
Approximately 38" x 40"

MATERIALS
- Coats & Clark Red Heart® Sport yarn (2.5 oz per skein): 6 skeins off-white #4
- Size G/6 crochet hook or size needed to obtain gauge

GAUGE

4 rows = 2¼"; 4 sps = 2½"

To save time, take time to check gauge.

PATTERN NOTE

Join rnds with a sl st unless otherwise stated.

PATTERN STITCHES

Picot: Ch 3, sl st in last sc made.

Beg popcorn (beg pc): Ch 3 (counts as first dc), 4 dc in indicated sp, remove hook from lp, insert in 3rd ch of beg ch-3, pick up dropped lp and draw through, pulling tightly to close.

Popcorn (pc): 5 dc in indicated sp, remove hook from lp, insert in top of first dc, pick up dropped lp and draw through, pulling tightly to close.

———————•———————

AFGHAN

Row 1: Ch 194, dc in 8th ch from hook, [ch 2, sk 2 chs, dc in next ch] rep across, turn. (63 sps)

Row 2: Ch 5 (counts as first dc, ch 2 throughout), sk ch-2 sp, dc in next dc, *[2 dc in next ch-2 sp, dc in next dc] twice, [ch 6, sk next dc, {sc, picot} in next dc] twice, ch 6, {sc, picot} in next dc, ch 6, sk next dc, {sc, picot} in next dc, ch 6, sk next dc, dc in next dc, [2 dc in next ch-2 sp, dc in next dc] twice **, [ch 2, dc in next dc] 11 times, rep from * across, ending last rep at **, ch 2, sk 2 chs, dc in next ch, turn.

Row 3: Ch 4 (counts as first tr throughout), sk ch-2 sp, dc in next dc, *ch 2, sk 2 dc, dc in each of next 4 dc, 3 dc in next ch-6 sp, [ch 6, {sc, picot} in next ch-6 sp] 3 times, ch 6, 3 dc in next ch-6 sp, dc in each of next 4 dc, ch 2, sk 2 dc, dc in next dc **, [ch 2, dc in next dc] 11 times, rep from * across, ending last rep at **, sk 2 chs, tr in next ch, turn.

Row 4: Ch 4, sk ch-2 sp, dc in next dc, *ch 2, sk 2 dc, dc in each of next 4 dc, 3 dc in next ch-6 sp, [ch 6, {sc, picot} in next ch-6 sp] twice, ch 6, 3 dc in next ch-6 sp, dc in each of next 4 dc, ch 2, sk 2 dc, dc in next dc **, [ch 2, dc in next dc] 13 times, rep from * across, ending last rep at **, sk 2 chs, tr in next dc, turn.

Row 5: Ch 4, sk ch-2 sp, dc in next dc, *ch 2, sk 2 dc, dc in each of next 4 dc, 3 dc in next ch-6 sp, ch 6, {sc, picot} in next ch-6 sp, ch 6, 3 dc in next ch-6 sp, dc in each of next 4 dc, ch 2, sk 2 dc, dc in next dc **, [ch 2, dc in next dc] 15 times, rep from * across, ending last rep at **, sk 2 chs, tr in next dc, turn.

Row 6: Ch 4, sk ch-2 sp, dc in next dc, *ch 2, sk 2 dc, dc in each of next 4 dc, 3 dc in next ch-6 sp, ch 2, 3 dc in next ch-6 sp, dc in each of next 4 dc, ch 2, sk 2 dc, dc in next dc **, [ch 2, dc in next dc] 17 times, rep from * across, ending last rep at **, sk 2 chs, tr in next dc, turn.

Row 7: Ch 4, sk ch-2 sp, dc in next dc, *ch 2, sk 2 dc, dc in each of next 4 dc, 2 dc in next ch-2 sp, dc in each of next 4 dc, ch 2, sk 2 dc, dc in next dc **, [ch 2, dc in next dc] 19 times, rep from * across, ending last rep at **, sk 2 chs, tr in next dc, turn.

Row 8: Sl st in last dc made, ch 5, dc in next dc, *[ch 2, sk 2 dc, dc in next dc] 3 times **, [ch 2, dc in next dc] 21 times, rep from * across, ending last rep at **, ch 2, dc in next dc, turn.

Row 9: Ch 6 (counts as first tr, ch 2 throughout), dc in same dc, ch 2, dc in next dc, *[2 dc in next ch-2 sp, dc in next dc] 3 times **, [ch 2, dc in next dc] 21 times, rep from * across, ending last rep at **, ch 2, sk 2 chs, [dc, ch 2, tr] in next ch, turn.

Row 10: Ch 6, dc in same tr, ch 2, dc in next dc, *2 dc in next ch-2 sp, dc in each of next 4 dc, ch 2, sk 2 dc, dc in each of next 4 dc, 2 dc in next ch-2 sp, dc in next dc **, [ch 2, dc in next dc] 19 times, rep from * across, ending last rep at **, ch 2, sk 2 chs, [dc, ch 2, tr] in next ch, turn.

Row 11: Ch 6, dc in same tr, ch 2, dc in next dc, *2 dc in next ch-2 sp, dc in each of next 4 dc, ch 6, {sc, picot} in next ch-2 sp, ch 6, sk 3 dc, dc in each of next 4 dc, 2 dc in next ch-2 sp, dc in next dc **, [ch 2, dc in next dc] 17 times, rep from * across, ending last rep at **, ch 2, sk 2 chs, [dc, ch 2, tr] in next ch, turn.

Row 12: Ch 6, dc in same tr, ch 2, dc in next dc, *2 dc in next ch-2 sp, dc in each of next 4 dc, [ch 6, {sc, picot} in next ch-6 sp] twice, ch 6, sk 3 dc, dc in each of next 4 dc, 2 dc in next ch-2 sp, dc in next dc **, [ch 2, dc in next dc] 15 times, rep from * across, ending last rep at **, ch 2, sk 2 chs, [dc, ch 2, tr] in next ch, turn.

Row 13: Ch 6, dc in same tr, ch 2, dc in next dc, *2 dc in next ch-2 sp, dc in each of next 4 dc, [ch 6, {sc, picot} in next ch-6 sp] 3 times, ch 6, sk 3 dc, dc in each of next 4 dc, 2 dc in next ch-2 sp, dc in next dc **, [ch 2, dc in next dc] 13 times, rep from * across, ending last rep at **, ch 2, sk 2 chs, [dc, ch 2, tr] in next ch, turn.

Row 14: Ch 5, sk ch-2 sp, dc in next dc, *2 dc in next ch-2 sp, dc in each of next 4 dc, [ch 6, {sc, picot} in next ch-6 sp] 4 times, ch 6, sk 3 dc, dc in each of next 4 dc, 2 dc in next ch-2 sp, dc in next dc **, [ch 2, dc in next dc] 11 times, rep from * across, ending last rep at **, ch 2, sk 2 chs, dc in next ch, turn.

Rows 15–73: Rep Rows 3–14, ending last rep with Row 13.

Row 74: Ch 5, sk ch-2 sp, dc in next dc, *2 dc in next ch-2 sp, dc in each of next 4 dc, [ch 5, dc in next ch-6 sp] twice, ch 2, dc in next ch-6 sp, ch 5, dc in next ch-6 sp, ch 5, sk 3 dc, dc in each of next 4 dc, 2 dc in next ch-2 sp, dc in next dc **, [ch 2, dc in next dc] 11 times, rep from * across, ending last rep at **, ch 2, sk 2 chs, dc in next ch, turn.

Row 75: Ch 5, dc in next dc, [ch 2, sk 2 sts, dc in next st] rep across, fasten off. (63 sps)

FLOWER MOTIF BORDER

Rnd 1: Ch 4, join to form a ring, beg pc in ring, [ch 3, pc in ring] twice, ch 3, join in top of beg pc.

Rnd 2: Ch 1, sc in same st, [ch 3, sc in next ch-3 sp, ch 3, sc in top of next pc] rep around, ending with ch 3, join in beg sc.

Rnd 3: Ch 1, sc in same st as joining, [hdc, dc, tr, dc, hdc] in next ch-3 sp, sc in next sc, [hdc, dc, tr] in next ch-3 sp, ch 5, sl st over end st of Row 12 at bottom right corner of afghan, working back over ch-5 sp, sc in first ch, dc in each of next 3 chs, sc in last ch, sl st in top of last tr made, [dc, hdc] in same ch-3 sp on motif to complete petal, *sc in next sc, [hdc, dc, tr] in next ch-3 sp, sk next row on afghan, sl st over end st of next row, sl st in last tr made, [dc, hdc] in same ch-3 sp to complete petal, rep from * twice, sc in sc, [hdc, dc, tr] in next ch-3 sp of motif, ch 5, sk next row on afghan, sl st over end st of next row, working back over ch-5, sc in first ch, dc in each of next 3 chs, sc in last ch, sl st in tr, [dc, hdc] in same ch-3 sp to complete petal, join in beg sc, fasten off.

Make and join over corresponding row ends 6 motifs on each of 2 longer sides of afghan.

EDGINGS

Working across shorter end of afghan, with RS facing, attach yarn with a sl st in corner sp, ch 1, beg in same sp, *[sc, hdc] in ch-2 sp, dc in next dc, 2 dc in next ch-2 sp, dc in next dc, [hdc, sc] in next ch-2 sp, sk next dc, rep from * across, ending with sl st in corner sp, fasten off.

Rep for opposite end.

—Designed by Lucille LaFlamme

Sherbet Stripes

EXPERIENCE LEVEL
Beginner

SIZE
Approximately 36" x 42" including border

MATERIALS
- Coats & Clark Red Heart® Classic™ worsted weight yarn: 12 oz white #1, 5 oz mist green #681 and 4 oz sea coral #246
- Size J/10 crochet hook or size needed to obtain gauge

GAUGE
7 dc = 2"; 3 dc rows = 1½"

To save time, take time to check gauge.

PATTERN NOTE
When changing color at end of row, work last dc until 2 lps rem on hook, yo with next color, draw through 2 lps on hook.

AFGHAN
Row 1 (RS): With white, ch 140, dc in 6th ch from hook, [ch 1, sk next ch, dc in next ch] rep across, turn. (68 ch-1 sps, counting last 4 chs of foundation ch as dc, ch 1)

Row 2: [Ch 5, sk next dc, sl st in next dc] rep across, ending with ch 5, sk last dc and next ch, sl st in next ch, ch 1, turn. (34 ch sps)

Row 3: [Sc, hdc, dc, hdc, sc] in next ch-5 lp, rep across, turn.

Row 4: Ch 3 (counts as first hdc, ch 1), sc in next dc, [ch 3, sc in next dc] rep across, ending with ch 1, hdc in last sc, turn.

Row 5: Ch 4 (counts as first dc, ch 1 throughout), dc in first sc, [ch 1, dc in 2nd ch of next ch-3 sp, ch 1, dc in next sc] rep across, ending with ch 1, sk next ch, dc in next ch of turning ch-3, changing to mist green, fasten off white, turn. (68 ch-1 sps)

Row 6: Ch 3 (counts as first dc), dc in each ch and each rem dc across, ending with dc in each of next 2 chs of turning ch-4, turn. (137 dc)

Row 7: Ch 3, dc in each rem dc across, turn. (137 dc)

Row 8: Rep Row 7, changing to white in last dc, turn.

Row 9: Ch 4, sk next st, dc in next st, [ch 1, sk next st, dc in next st] rep across, turn. (68 ch-1 sps)

Rows 10–93: Alternating mist green and sea coral for Rows 6–8, rep Rows 2–9, ending last rep after Row 5, do not change colors at end of Row 93, fasten off.

EDGING

Top

Row 1: With WS facing, working over ends of rows, attach white with a sl st in top of end st of last row, ch 5, sk same row and next row, [sl st over end of next row, ch 5, sk next row] rep across, ending with sl st in corner of last row, ch 1, turn. (46 ch-5 lps)

Rows 2–4: Rep Rows 3–5, do not change color in last row, fasten off. (92 ch-1 sps at end of last row)

Bottom

Rep as for top across ends of rows on opposite side.

Weave in loose ends.

—Designed by Darla J. Fanton

Lilac Lace

EXPERIENCE LEVEL
Intermediate

SIZE
Approximately 28" x 33" including border

MATERIALS
- Patons® Astra® sport weight yarn: 7 oz each country lilac #2216 and white #2751
- Size E/4 crochet hook or size needed to obtain gauge
- Yarn needle

GAUGE
2 shells = 2"

To save time, take time to check gauge.

PATTERN NOTE
Join rnds with a sl st unless otherwise stated.

PATTERN STITCH
Shell: [2 dc, ch 1, 2 dc] in indicated sp.

AFGHAN

Row 1: With country lilac, ch 125, sc in 2nd ch from hook and in each rem ch across, turn. (124 sc)

Row 2: Ch 2, [dc, ch 1, dc] in next sc, dc in next sc, *sk 2 sc, dc in next sc, [dc, ch 1, dc] in next sc, dc in next sc, rep from * across, leaving last sc unworked, remove hook, leaving lp to be worked later, do not turn. (25 shells)

Row 3: Attach white with a sl st over edge of beg ch-2, ch 1, sc in same sp, working in front of shells of last row, *ch 6, sk 1 shell, sc in first sc of 2 sk sc, rep from * across, ending last rep with ch 6, sc in last sc, turn. (25 lps)

Row 4: Ch 2, sl st in first dc of row before last, ch 2, *holding ch-6 sp behind shell, work shell in next ch-1 sp and ch-6 sp at same time, rep from * across, remove hook, leaving lp to be worked later, do not turn.

Row 5: Pick up dropped lp of country lilac, *ch 6, working in front of shells of last row, sc between next 2 shells of same color, rep from * across, ending last rep with ch 6, sk last shell, sc in beg ch-2 sp of same color, turn.

Row 6: With country lilac, rep Row 4.

Row 7: Pick up dropped white lp, rep Row 5.

Rep Rows 4–7 for patt until afghan meas approximately 31" or desired length, ending with Row 6, fasten off.

EDGING

Rnd 1: Attach white in first ch on opposite side of beg ch-125, ch 1, [sc, ch 1, sc] in same st, *sc in each of next 122 sts, [sc, ch 1, sc] in end st, sc evenly sp along side to next corner *, [sc, ch 1, sc] in corner st, rep from * to *, join in beg sc.

Rnds 2 & 3: Ch 1, sc in each sc around, working [sc, ch 1, sc] in each corner ch-1 sp, join in beg sc, fasten off at end of Rnd 3.

Rnd 4: Attach country lilac in any corner ch-1 sp, ch 1, sc in same st, *[sk 2 sc, 5 dc in next sc, sk 2 sc, sc in next sc] rep across to next corner, ending with sc in corner ch-1 sp, adjusting number of sts sk before corner sp if necessary so patt rep will come out even, rep from * around, join in beg sc, fasten off.

Rnd 5: Attach white with a sl st in back lp of any st, [sl st in back lp of next st] rep around, join in beg sl st, fasten off.

Weave in loose ends and block.

—Designed by Loa Ann Thaxton

Striped Ripple Jumpsuit, Cardigan & Hat

EXPERIENCE LEVEL
Intermediate

SIZE
Toddlers' 1(2)(3) Instructions are given for smallest size,

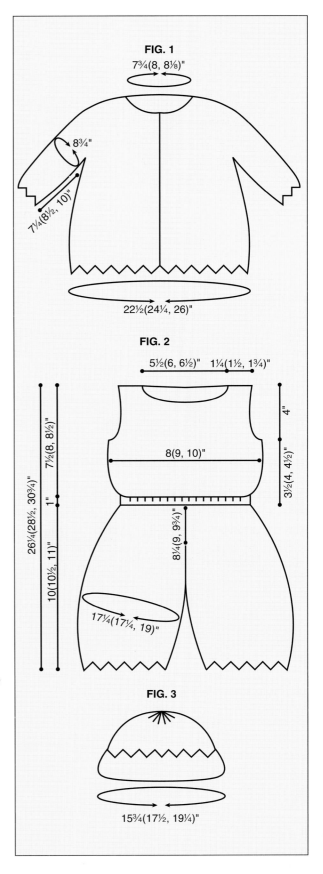

FIG. 1

7¾(8, 8⅛)"

8¾"

7¼(8½, 10)"

22½(24¼, 26)"

FIG. 2

5½(6, 6½)"   1¼(1½, 1¾)"

4"

8(9, 10)"

3½(4, 4½)"

26¼(28½, 30¾)"

7½(8, 8½)"

1"

10(10½, 11)"

8¼(9, 9¾)"

17¼(17¼, 19)"

FIG. 3

15¾(17½, 19¼)"

with larger sizes in parentheses. When only 1 number is given, it applies to all sizes.

MATERIALS

- Bernat® Handicrafter® 100 percent 4-ply cotton yarn (1¾ oz/50 grams per skein): 4(4)(5) skeins each pale peach #33 (A), baby pink #12 (B), mint #42 (C) and hyacinth #38 (D), and 5(5)(6) skeins ecru #4 (E)
- Size G/6 crochet hook or size needed to obtain gauge
- 1½ yds ⅝"-wide elastic
- 2 (1⅓") decorative heart buttons
- Tapestry needle

GAUGE

21 sts and 11 rows = 4" in striped ripple patt

18 sc = 5"; 14 sc rows = 4" worked in back lps only

To save time, take time to check gauge.

PATTERN NOTES

Work 2 rows each A, B, C, D and E throughout for stripe patt.

When changing colors in sc at end of row, insert hook in last st, yo with working color, draw up a lp, drop working color to WS, complete sc with next color.

Work all sts in back lps only throughout, unless otherwise stated.

Join rnds with a sl st unless otherwise stated.

PATTERN STITCH

Striped Ripple Pattern (multiple of 9 sts + 1)

Row 1 (RS): 2 sc in 2nd ch from hook, *sc in each of next 3 chs, sk 2 chs, sc in each of next 3 chs, 3 sc in next ch, rep from * across to last ch, 2 sc in last ch, ch 1, turn.

Row 2: Working in back lps only, 2 sc in first st, *sc in each of next 3 sc, sk 2 sc, sc in each of next 3 sc, 3 sc in next sc, rep from * across to last sc, 2 sc in last sc, ch 1, turn.

Rep Row 2 for patt.

———————————•———————————

Hat

With A, ch 83(92)(101), work in Striped Ripple Patt on 82(91)(100) sc for 20 rows, ending with E, do not fasten off, do not change color.

Next Row: With E, working in both lps this row only, insert hook in first sc, draw lp through, [insert hook in center sc of next 3-sc group, draw lp through] rep across, yo and draw through all lps on hook, ch 1 to secure, fasten off, leaving length for sewing.

Sew seam; fold cuff up.

Weave in loose ends.

Cardigan

BODY

Beg with A(E)(D), ch 119(128)(137), work in Striped Ripple

Patt on 118(127)(136) sc for 20(22)(24) rows, ending with E, do not change color at end of last row, ch 1, turn.

Next Row: With E, sc in each of first 4 sc, [sk next 2 sc, sc in each of next 7 sc] rep across, ending with sk next 2 sc, sc in each of last 4 sc, fasten off, set aside. (92, 99, 106 sc)

SLEEVES

Make 2

With A(D)(B), ch 47, work in Striped Ripple Patt for 20(24)(28) rows, ending with E, do not change color at end of last row, ch 1, turn.

Next Row: With E, sc in each of first 4 sc, [sk 2 sc, sc in each of next 7 sc] rep across, ending with sk 2 sc, sc in each of last 4 sc, fasten off, set aside. (36 sc)

YOKE

Row 1: With WS facing, attach E in back lp of first sc of body, ch 1, sc in first sc, sc in each of next 18(19)(21) sc, sk first 4 sc of sleeve, sc in each of next 28 sc of sleeve, sk 8(9)(9) sc of body, sc in each of next 38(41)(44) sc of body, sk next 4 sc of 2nd sleeve, sc in each of next 28 sc of sleeve, sk 8(9)(9) sc of body, sc in each of rem 19(20)(22) sc of body, ch 1, turn. (132, 137, 144 sc)

Row 2: Sc in each of first 2(7)(4) sc, [sc dec, sc in each of next 8 sc] rep across, ch 1, turn. (119, 124, 130 sts)

Row 3 and all WS rows: Sc in each st across, ch 1, turn.

Row 4: Sc in each of first 2(7)(4) sc, [sc dec, sc in each of next 7 sc] rep across, ch 1, turn. (106, 111, 116 sts)

Row 6: Sc in each of first 2(7)(4) sc, [sc dec, sc in each of next 6 sc] rep across, ch 1, turn. (93, 98, 102 sts)

Row 8: Sc in each of first 2(0)(4) sc, [sc dec, sc in each of next 5 sc] rep across, ch 1, turn. (80, 84, 88 sts)

Row 10: Sc in each of first 2(0)(4) sc, [sc dec, sc in each of next 4 sc] rep across, ch 1, turn. (67, 70, 74 sts)

Row 12: Sc in each of first 2(0)(4) sc, [sc dec, sc in each of next 3 sc] rep across, ch 1, turn. (54, 56, 60 sts)

Row 14: Sc in each of first 2(0)(0) sc, [sc dec, sc in each of next 2 sc] rep across, ch 1, turn. (41, 42, 45 sc)

Row 15: Rep Row 3, fasten off for size 1 only, for sizes 2 and 3, ch 1, turn.

Size 2 only

Row 16: Sc in each st across, fasten off.

Size 3 only

Row 16: Sc dec, sc in each st across to last 2 sc, sc dec, ch 1, turn. (43 sts)

Row 17: Sc in each st across, fasten off.

Sew sleeve seams; sew underarm.

FRONT EDGINGS

Row 1: With RS facing, working over row ends, sc evenly sp across either front opening, ch 1, turn.

Row 2: Working through both lps, sc in each sc across, fasten off.

Rep for opposite front opening.

TIE

With E, ch 54, with RS facing, working in both lps for this row and next row only, sc across neck, working 5(4)(3) sc dec evenly sp, ch 55, turn.

Beg in 2nd ch from hook, work Row 1 of Striped Ripple Patt over next 19 chs, sc in each of next 35 chs, sc in each sc across neck, sc in each of next 35 chs, work Striped Ripple Patt over rem 19 chs, fasten off.

Weave in loose ends.

Jumpsuit

LEGS

Make 2

Beg with A, ch 92(92)(101), work in Striped Ripple Patt on 91(91)(100) sts until 10(10½)(11)" from beg.

Shape crotch

Work to within 9 sts of end of next 2 rows, continue on 73(73)(82) sc until 17¾(19)(20¼)" from beg, ending with a WS row, fasten off.

Sew inseams of legs. Join legs at crotch; sew tog.

WAISTBAND RIBBING

Rnd 1: With RS facing, attach E at center back seam, ch 1, work 32(36)(40) sc evenly sp around to center front seam, 32(36)(40) sc evenly sp around to beg of rnd, join in both lps of beg sc. (64, 72, 80 sc)

Rnd 2: Ch 3 (counts as first dc), working in both lps this rnd only, dc in each sc around, join in 3rd ch of beg ch-3. (64, 72, 80 dc)

Rnd 3: Ch 3, [bpdc over next dc, fpdc over next dc] rep around, ending with bpdc over last dc, join in 3rd ch of beg ch-3, fasten off E.

BODICE

Rnd 1: With RS facing, attach next color in stripe pattern sequence after last leg row, ch 1, sc in each sc around, join in beg sc, ch 1, turn.

Rnd 2: Sc in each sc around, changing to next color of est color stripe patt in last sc, ch 1, turn.

Work even in sc on 64(72)(80) sts in est color stripe patt until 3½(4)(4½)" from top of waistband ribbing, ending with a WS rnd, fasten off.

BACK YOKE

Row 1: With RS facing, continuing in est color stripe patt, attach next color in 13th(15th)(17th) sc to right of back seam, ch 1, sc in same st as joining, sc in each of next 25(29)(33) sc, ch 1, turn. (26, 30, 34 sc)

Rows 2, 4, 6, 8, 10: Sc in each sc across, changing to next color in last st, ch 1, turn.

Rows 3, 5 & 7: Sc dec, sc across to last 2 sts, sc dec, ch 1, turn. (20, 24, 28 sts at end of Row 7)

Rows 9 & 11: Sc in each sc across, ch 1, turn.

Row 12: Sc in each of first 5(6)(7) sc, sl st in each of next 10(12)(14) sc, sc in each of last 5(6)(7) sc, changing to next color in last sc, ch 1, turn.

Rows 13 & 14: Sc in each of first 5(6)(7) sc, ch 1, turn, fasten off at end of Row 14.

With RS facing, sk 10(12)(14) sl sts of Row 12, attach yarn in next sc, ch 1, beg in same st as joining, rep Rows 13 and 14.

FRONT YOKE

Row 1: With RS facing, sk next 6 sc on last complete rnd of bodice for underarm, continuing in est color stripe patt, attach next color in next sc, ch 1, beg in same st as joining, sc in each of next 26(30)(34) sc, ch 1, turn.

Rows 2–8: Rep Rows 2–8 of back yoke.

Left neck

Row 9: Sc in each of first 7(8)(9) sc, ch 1, turn.

Row 10: Sc dec, sc in each of next 5(6)(7) sc, changing to next color in last sc, ch 1, turn.

Row 11: Sc in each of next 4(5)(6) sc, sc dec, ch 1, turn.

Row 12: Sc in each st across, changing to next color in last sc, ch 1, turn. (5, 6, 7 sc)

Rows 13 & 14: Sc in each sc across, ch 1, turn, at end of Row 14 do not ch 1; turn.

Button loop

Row 15: Ch 4(5)(5), sk first 4(5)(6) sc, sl st in last sc, fasten off.

Right neck

With RS facing, sk next 6(8)(10) sc on Row 8 of yoke, attach yarn in next sc, ch 1, work as for left neck, reversing shaping.

Sew buttons to yoke back to correspond with button lps.

ELASTIC CASINGS

Waist

Turn jumpsuit inside out, attach E with a sl st at top of waistband ribbing at seam, *ch 4, sk approximately ½", sl st on bottom of waistband ribbing into back of st, ch 4, sk approximately ½", sl st to top of waistband ribbing, rep from * around, creating a ch that zigzags across ribbing, join to first st, fasten off.

Cut elastic 20(21)(22)" long, or waist-size length; thread through zigzag ch. Sew ends tog at center back.

Legs

Work zigzag ch around each ankle on inside of leg, placing lower points of zigzags 1 row above bottom of leg.

Thread 8(8½)(9)" length of elastic through each zigzag ch; sew ends tog.

Weave in loose ends.

—Designed by Maureen Egan Emlet

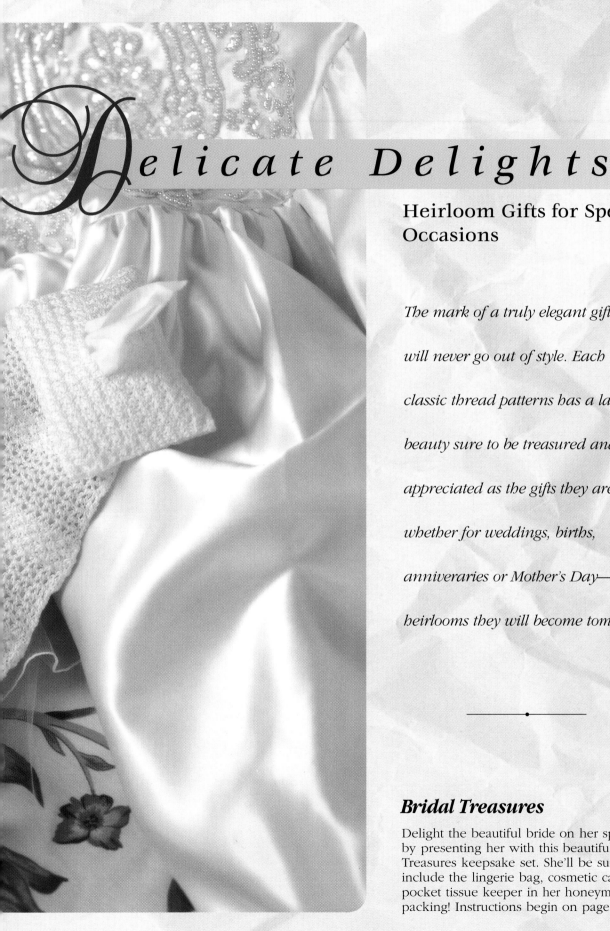

Delicate Delights

Heirloom Gifts for Special Occasions

The mark of a truly elegant gift is that it will never go out of style. Each of these classic thread patterns has a lasting beauty sure to be treasured and appreciated as the gifts they are today— whether for weddings, births, anniveraries or Mother's Day—and the heirlooms they will become tomorrow.

———————•———————

Bridal Treasures

Delight the beautiful bride on her special day by presenting her with this beautiful Bridal Treasures keepsake set. She'll be sure to include the lingerie bag, cosmetic case and pocket tissue keeper in her honeymoon packing! Instructions begin on page 90.

Sweetness & Light Doily

Pretty and delicate, this enchanting Sweetness & Light Doily (above), makes a wonderful housewarming gift for the young and elderly alike. Its versatile design makes it the perfect accent for any room in the house! Instructions begin on page 92.

Bride's Hankie & Bridal Garter

Delight the bride-to-be at her shower with a special crocheted Bridal Garter and Bride's Hankie (left). Both items will be treasured for years to come as she looks back on her special day. Instructions begin on pages 91 and 92.

White Pineapples

White Pineapples (right) stitched in pure white cotton has a simple elegance that makes this pineapple pattern a treasure. Instructions begin on page 94.

Donegal Doily

Celebrate a lifetime of love by giving an exquisite doily as a 25th or 50th anniversary gift! Donegal Doily (below) has a unique look reminiscent of Irish crochet. Instructions begin on page 93.

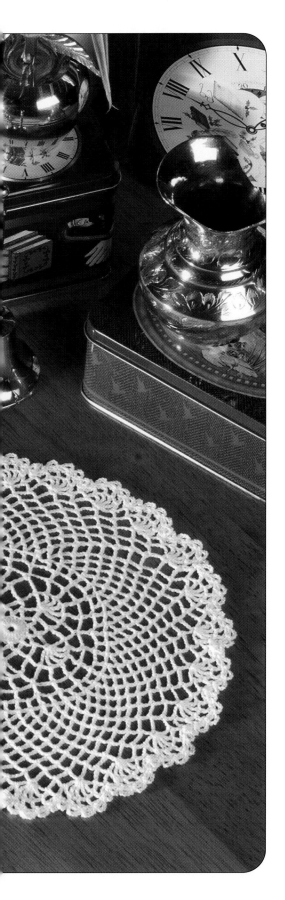

Daisy Edging & Narrow Edging

Give family and friends visiting your home an extra-special welcome by adding pretty edgings and accents to their guest towels. Daisy Edging and Narrow Edging will also add a simple, yet classy, look to napkins, tablecloths, handkerchiefs or pillowcases. Instructions begin on page 96.

One-Day Doilies

Enjoy the satisfaction of seeing a completed doily the same day you begin! Each of these pretty One-Day Doilies (left) takes between eight to 10 hours to crochet, making either a perfect last-minute gift! Instructions begin on page 95.

Delicate Napkin Edgings

Give your elegant dinner a sparkling touch by adding a metallic edging to your napkins! Delicate Napkin Edgings (left) include five eye-catching patterns, three of which are accented with metallic thread and two with classic crochet cotton. Instructions begin on page 97.

Pineapple Garden

Round upon round of perfect pineapples form the edge of this charming Pineapple Garden doily. Doily lovers will find it a delight to crochet and display! Instructions begin on page 99.

Whirls & Rows Purse & Tiny Coin Purse

Two quick-to-stitch purses, the larger Whirls & Rows Purse (above) and smaller Tiny Coin purse (right), are just the right size for carrying on an evening out on the town. Crochet them in colors to match your favorite dinner dress! Instructions begin on page 101.

Lover's Knot Tablecloth

The perfect gift for a newlywed couple, this Lover's Knot Tablecloth (left) will add grace to the most special dinners and last throughout the years. Instructions begin on page 100.

Bridal Treasures

Lingerie Bag

EXPERIENCE LEVEL
Beginner

SIZE
9¾" x 9"

MATERIALS
- DMC® Cebelia® crochet cotton size 10 (50 grams per ball): 2 balls white #10
- Size 7 steel crochet hook or size needed to obtain gauge
- Sewing needle and white thread
- 30" ¼"-wide white satin ribbon

GAUGE
Rows 1–10 = 2" x 9¾"

To save time, take time to check gauge.

FIRST SIDE

Row 1: Ch 89, sc in 2nd ch from hook and in each rem ch across, ch 1, turn. (88 sc)

Row 2: [Sc, 2 dc] in first sc, *sk 2 sts, [sc, 2 dc] in next sc, rep from * across to last 3 sts, sk 2 sts, sc in last sc, ch 1, turn. (88 sts)

Row 3: Rep Row 2, do not ch 1; turn.

Row 4: Ch 3 (counts as first dc throughout), dc in same sc, [dc, ch 1, dc] in each sc across, ending with 2 dc in last sc, turn.

Rows 5–10: Ch 3, dc in next dc, [dc, ch 1, dc] in each ch-1 sp across, ending with dc in each of last 2 sts, turn, at end of Row 10, ch 1, turn.

Row 11: [Sc, 2 dc] in first dc, *[sc, 2 dc] in next ch-1 sp, rep from * across, sc in 3rd ch of turning ch-3, ch 1, turn. (88 sts)

Rows 12–15: Rep Row 2, do not ch 1 at end of Row 15; turn.

Rows 16–42: Rep Rows 4–15 alternately, ending with Row 6, turn.

Edging

Row 1 (RS): Ch 3, dc in next dc, ch 1, 3 tr in next ch-1 sp, ch 4, sl st in last tr (picot), 3 tr in same ch-1 sp, *[ch 3, sc in next ch-1 sp] twice, ch 3, [3 tr, picot, 3 tr] in next ch-1 sp, rep from * across, ending with ch 1, dc in each of last 2 sts, fasten off.

SECOND SIDE

Row 1: With RS facing, attach thread with a sl st in first ch of foundation ch, ch 1, sc in same st, sc in each ch across, ch 1, turn.

Rows 2–42: Rep Rows 2–42 of first side.

Edging

Row 1: Rep Row 1 of edging for first side.

FINISHING
Fold sides, WS tog, so edgings are at top. With sewing needle and white thread, stitch sides.

Weave white satin ribbon through 3rd row below edging, beg and ending at center front. To close bag, draw ribbon tight and tie in bow.

Pocket Tissue Case

EXPERIENCE LEVEL
Beginner

SIZE
3½" x 5¼"

MATERIALS
- DMC® Cebelia® crochet cotton size 10 (50 grams per ball): 1 ball white #10
- Size 7 steel crochet hook or size needed to obtain gauge
- Sewing needle and white thread

GAUGE
Rows 1–12 = 2" x 5¼"

To save time, take time to check gauge.

FIRST SIDE

Row 1: Ch 47, sc in 2nd ch from hook and in each rem ch across, ch 1, turn. (46 sc)

Row 2: [Sc, 2 dc] in first sc, *sk 2 sts, [sc, 2 dc] in next sc, rep from * across to last 3 sts, sk 2 sts, sc in last sc, ch 1, turn. (46 sts)

Rep Row 2 until piece meas 3½", at end of last row, fasten off.

SECOND SIDE

Row 1: Working in foundation ch, attach thread with a sl st in first st, ch 1, [sc, 2 dc] in same st, *sk 2 sts, [sc, 2 dc] in next st, rep from * across to last 3 sts, sk 2 sts, sc in last st, ch 1, turn.

Rep Row 2 of first side until second side meas 3½", fasten off.

FINISHING
Fold so foundation ch sts are at center back of pack and 2 ends meet at center front. With sewing needle and white thread, sew center front 1¾" from each end, leaving center opening unstitched to pull tissues through.

Sew 1 end closed, leaving 1 end open to replace pack.

Cosmetic Case

EXPERIENCE LEVEL
Advanced beginner

SIZE
9¼" x 5"

MATERIALS
- DMC® Cebelia® crochet cotton size 10 (50 grams per ball): 1 ball white #10
- Size 7 steel crochet hook or size needed to obtain gauge
- Sewing needle and white thread
- ¾" gold metallic button

GAUGE

Rows 1–7 = 1" x 9¼"

To save time, take time to check gauge.

FRONT & BACK

Row 1: Ch 80, sc in 2nd ch from hook and in each rem ch across, ch 1, turn. (79 sc)

Row 2: [Sc, 2 dc] in first sc, *sk 2 sts, [sc, 2 dc] in next sc, rep from * across to last 3 sts, sk 2 sts, sc in last sc, ch 1, turn. (79 sts)

Rep Row 2 until piece meas 10", do not fasten off, turn.

FLAP

Row 1: Ch 3 (counts as first dc throughout), sk 2 dc, dc in next sc, [ch 2, dc in next sc] 24 times, dc in beg sc, turn. (24 ch-2 sps)

Row 2 (RS): Ch 3, sk next ch-2 sp, *dc in next dc, [ch 1, {dc, ch 1} twice in next ch-2 sp, dc in next dc] twice **, sc in next dc, rep from * across, ending last rep at **, dc in last dc, turn.

Row 3: Ch 4 (counts as first tr throughout), *sk 3 ch-1 sps, [dc, ch 2, dc, ch 2, dc] in next dc **, ch 3, [sc, ch 5, sc] in next sc, ch 3, rep from * across, ending last rep at **, tr in 3rd ch of turning ch-3, turn.

Row 4: Sl st to 2nd dc, *ch 3, dc in next ch-5 lp, [ch 2, dc] 3 times in same ch-5 lp **, ch 3, sk next dc, sc in next dc, rep from * across, ending last rep at **, sk next dc, dc in next dc, turn.

Row 5: Sl st to 2nd ch-2 sp, sl st in same ch-2 sp, ch 4, [7 dc in next sc, ch 3, sk next ch-3 sp and next ch-2 sp, 3 sc in next ch-2 sp, ch 3] 3 times, 7 dc in next sc, sk next ch-3 sp and next ch-2 sp, tr in next ch-2 sp, turn.

Row 6: Sl st to 4th dc, ch 1, sc in same dc, [ch 2, 3 dc in each of next 3 sc, ch 2, sc in 4th dc of next 7-dc group] rep across, turn.

Row 7: Ch 5, sc in 5th dc of next 9-dc group, ch 5, [dc, ch 2, dc] in next sc, ch 3, [tr, ch 7, tr] in 5th dc of next 9-dc group, ch 3, [dc, ch 2, dc] in next sc, ch 5, sc in 5th dc of next 9-dc group, ch 5, sl st in beg sc, fasten off.

EDGING

Row 1: With RS facing, attach thread with a sl st in sp created by end st of Row 1 of flap, ch 1, 3 sc in same sp, sc evenly across edge of flap, fasten off.

FINISHING

With WS tog, fold piece in half to bottom of flap. With sewing needle and thread, st sides tog.

Fold flap over front; mark place for button through center lp of flap. Sew button in place.

—Designed by Lucille LaFlamme

Bride's Hankie

"Here is a special gift to carry

As you and your groom prepare to marry.

Fold and stitch and store away

For your daughter's christening day.

Then, in time, when she is married,

'Twill be unstitched and once more carried."

EXPERIENCE LEVEL

Beginner

SIZE

13" square

MATERIALS

- Crochet cotton size 20: 25 grams white
- Size 10 steel crochet hook or size needed to obtain gauge
- 12" square cotton hankie

GAUGE

Edging = 1" wide

To save time, take time to check gauge.

PATTERN NOTE

Join rnds with a sl st unless otherwise stated.

EDGING

Rnd 1: With RS of hankie facing, beg 1" to the left of any corner, insert hook into hankie below line of hemstitching, being careful to go between the threads and not break them, 91 sc evenly sp to first corner, drawing each lp up full length of hem, [sc in corner, 100 sc evenly sp along next edge] 3 times, sc in next corner, 9 sc along first edge, join in beg sc. (404 sc)

Rnds 2 & 3: Ch 1, sc in each sc around, working 3 sc in each corner sc, join in beg sc. (420 sc at end of Rnd 3)

Rnd 4: Ch 1, sc in first sc, *[ch 3, sk 2 sc, sc in next sc, ch 5, sk 3 sc, sc in next sc, ch 3, sk 2 sc, sc in next sc] rep to within 1 st of corner 3-sc, ch 7, sk next sc and corner 3-sc, sc in next sc, rep from * 3 times, rep between [] once, join in beg sc.

Rnd 5: Sl st to center of next ch-3 sp, ch 1, sc in same sp, *7 dc in next ch-5 sp, sc in next ch-3 sp, ch 3 **, sc in next ch-3 sp, rep from * to corner, ending last rep at **, [sc, 11 dc, sc] in next ch-7 sp, ch 3, sc in next ch-3 sp, rep from * around, join in beg sc.

Rnd 6: Ch 4 (counts as first dc, ch 1), [dc in next dc, ch 1] 7 times, dc in next sc, *sk next ch-3 sp, dc in next sc, [ch 1, dc in next dc] 7 times, ch 1, dc in next sc, rep from * around, working [ch 1, dc in next dc] 11 times in each corner, join in 3rd ch of beg ch-4.

Rnd 7: Sl st in ch-1 sp, ch 1, sc in same sp, *[ch 3, sc in next ch-1 sp] 7 times, sc in next ch-1 sp, rep from * around, working [ch 3, sc in next ch-1 sp] 11 times in each corner, join in beg sc, fasten off.

Weave in loose ends; press.

FOLDING INSTRUCTIONS
Fold hankie in half with RS tog.

Fold top layer of hankie back so lace edging extends beyond first fold (this is the front of the bonnet).

Fold short ends of hankie up 1" (not including lace); fold lace back down to be even with fold.

Using your fist to simulate shape of baby's head, drape hankie over your arm (Fig. 1). Allow center back of hankie to fall over the end of your fist so that corners form triangles extending on both sides. Fold triangles to center over bonnet back, overlapping corners. Tack corners in place.

Fig. 1

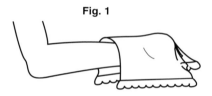

Insert crochet hook through all layers of lace at front corner, work 1 sc around posts to hold layers tog, ch 75 (for tie), fasten off.

Rep on opposite side.

Present to bride with verse (page 91) and instructions for folding.

—Designed by Maureen Egan Emlet

Bridal Garter

EXPERIENCE LEVEL
Beginner

ACTUAL MEASUREMENTS
12¾" in diameter, stretching to 16½"

MATERIALS
- J. & P. Coats Knit-Cro-Sheen® crochet cotton size 10: 60 yds white #1
- Size 7 steel crochet hook or size needed to obtain gauge
- 13" ¼"-wide soft elastic
- 3 (⅜") pink heart buttons
- 3 (12") lengths ⅜"-wide white satin ribbon
- Sewing needle and white thread

GAUGE
10 sc = 1"

To save time, take time to check gauge.

PATTERN NOTE
Join rnds with a sl st unless otherwise stated.

GARTER
Overlap ends of elastic ½"; sew in place to form ring.

Top edge

Rnd 1: Ch 120, join to form a ring, ch 1, beg in same st as joining, sc in each ch around, join in beg sc. (120 sc)

Rnd 2: Ch 2, working over elastic ring and beg in same st as joining, *insert hook in next sc, yo, draw up a lp to top of elastic, yo, complete sc in usual manner, rep from * around, join in beg sc. (120 sc)

Rnd 3: Ch 1, sc in each sc around, join in beg sc.

Rnd 4: Ch 1, sc in first sc, [ch 3, sk 1 sc, sc in next sc] rep around, ending with ch 3, sk last sc, join in beg sc.

Rnd 5: Ch 1, working behind ch-3 sps of Rnd 4, sc in first sk sc of Rnd 4, [ch 3, sc in next sk sc of Rnd 4] rep around, ending with ch 3, join in beg sc, fasten off.

Bottom edge

Attach thread in rem lp of first ch of beg ch-120, ch 1, rep Rnds 4 and 5, working in chs and sk chs instead of sc.

Weave in and sew down ends on WS.

Sew buttons evenly sp at center around garter.

Tie ribbon lengths into bows over 1 st, centered between buttons.

—Designed by Katherine Eng

Sweetness & Light Doily

EXPERIENCE LEVEL
Advanced beginner

SIZE
17" in diameter

MATERIALS
- South Maid® crochet cotton size 10: 1 (400-yd) ball white #1 and 1 (350-yd) ball French rose #493
- Size 7 steel crochet hook or size needed to obtain gauge
- Fabric stiffener

GAUGE
First 4 rnds = 3½" in diameter

To save time, take time to check gauge.

PATTERN NOTE
Join rnds with a sl st unless otherwise stated.

PATTERN STITCH
Beg 3-tr cl: Ch 3, holding back on hook last lp of each st, 2 tr in same sp, yo and draw through all 3 lps on hook.

3-tr cl: Holding back on hook last lp of each st, 3 tr in indicated sp, yo and draw through all 4 lps on hook.

Beg 5-tr cl: Work as for beg 3-tr cl until 4 tr are worked, yo, draw through all 5 lps on hook.

5-tr cl: Work as for 3-tr cl until 5 tr are worked, yo and draw through all 6 lps on hook.

Beg V-st: Ch 4 (counts as first dc, ch 1), dc in same st.

V-st: [Dc, ch 1, dc] in indicated st.

DOILY

Rnd 1: With French rose, ch 8, join to form a ring, beg 3-tr cl in ring, ch 5, [3-tr cl in ring, ch 5] 7 times, join in top of beg 3-tr cl. (8 3-tr cls)

Rnd 2: Sl st to center of next ch-5 sp, beg 3-tr cl in same sp, [ch 7, 3-tr cl in next ch-5 sp] rep around, ending with ch 7, join in top of beg 3-tr cl.

Rnd 3: Ch 1, sc in same st as joining, [9 sc in next ch-7 sp, sc in top of next 3-tr cl] rep around, ending with 9 sc in last ch-7 sp, join in beg sc. (80 sc)

Rnd 4: Ch 5 (counts as first dc, ch 2), [sk next st, dc in next st, ch 2] rep around, join in 3rd ch of beg ch-5. (40 ch-2 sps)

Rnds 5 & 6: Sl st in next sp, beg 3-tr cl in same sp, [ch 3, 3-tr cl in next sp] rep around, ending with ch 3, join in top of beg 3-tr cl. (40 3-tr cls)

Rnd 7: Sl st in next ch-3 sp, beg 3-tr cl in same sp, [ch 6, sc in next ch-3 sp, ch 6, 3-tr cl in next ch-3 sp] rep around, ending with ch 6, join in top of beg 3-tr cl. (20 3-tr cls)

Rnd 8: Ch 1, sc in same st as joining, ch 11, [sc in top of next 3-tr cl, ch 11] rep around, join in beg sc. (20 ch-11 sps)

Rnd 9: Ch 1, sc in same st as joining, *[7 sc, ch 3, 7 sc] in next ch-11 sp, sc in next sc, rep from * around, join in beg sc, fasten off.

Rnd 10: Attach white with a sl st in any ch-3 sp, ch 1, sc in same sp, [ch 13, sc in next ch-3 sp] rep around, join in beg sc.

Rnd 11: Ch 1, sc in same st as joining, [ch 5, sc] twice in next sp, ch 5 **, sc in next sc, rep from * around, ending last rep at **, join in beg sc.

Rnd 12: Sl st to center of next ch-5 sp, ch 1, sc in same sp, *ch 5, [3-tr cl, ch 3, 3-tr cl, ch 3, 3-tr cl] in next ch-5 sp, [ch 5, sc in next sp] twice, rep from * around, join in beg sc.

Rnd 13: Sl st across next ch-5 sp and next cl, sl st in first ch-3 sp, beg 3-tr cl in same sp, *ch 3, 3-tr cl in next ch-3 sp, ch 7, holding back on hook last lp of each st, tr in each of next 3 ch-5 sps, yo and draw through all 4 lps on hook, ch 7 **, 3-tr cl in next ch-3 sp, rep from * around, ending last rep at **, join in top of beg 3-tr cl.

Rnd 14: Sl st in next ch-3 sp, beg 5-tr cl in same sp, *[ch 7, sc in next sp] twice, ch 7 **, 5-tr cl in next ch-3 sp, rep from * around, ending last rep at **, join in top of beg 5-tr cl.

Rnd 15: Sl st to center of next ch-7 sp, ch 1, sc in same sp, [ch 8, sc in next ch-7 sp] rep around, ending with ch 4, tr in beg sc. (60 ch-8 sps)

Rnd 16: Ch 1, sc in sp just formed, [ch 8, sc in next sp] rep around, ending with ch 4, tr in beg sc.

Rnd 17: Beg V-st in sp just formed, [ch 7, V-st in next ch-8 sp] rep around, ending with ch 7, join in 3rd ch of beg ch-4. (60 V-sts)

Rnds 18 & 19: Sl st in next ch-1 sp and next dc, sl st to center of next ch-7 sp, beg V-st in same sp, [ch 7, V-st in next ch-7 sp] rep around, ending with ch 7, join in 3rd ch of beg ch-4.

Rnd 20: Sl st in next ch-1 sp, ch 1, sc in same sp, *[5 sc, ch 3, 5 sc] in next ch-7 sp **, sc in next ch-1 sp, rep from * around, ending last rep at **, join in beg sc, fasten off.

Stiffen according to manufacturer's instructions.

—Designed by Emma Willey

Donegal Doily

EXPERIENCE LEVEL
Intermediate

SIZE
Approximately 12½" in diameter

MATERIALS
- J. & P. Coats Knit-Cro-Sheen® crochet cotton size 10 (325 yds per ball): 1 ball cream #42
- Size 7 steel crochet hook or size needed to obtain gauge
- Spray starch

GAUGE
First 3 rnds = 2¾" in diameter
To save time, take time to check gauge.

PATTERN NOTE
Join rnds with a sl st unless otherwise stated.

PATTERN STITCHES
2-dc cl: Holding back on hook last lp of each st, work 2 dc in indicated sp, yo and draw through all rem lps on hook.

3-dc cl: Work as for 2-dc cl with 3 dc.

2-tr cl: Work as for 2-dc cl with 2 tr.

3-tr cl: Work as for 2-dc cl with 3 tr.

3-dtr cl: Work as for 2-dc cl with 3 dtr.

4-dtr cl: Work as for 2-dc cl with 4 dtr.

DOILY

Rnd 1: [Ch 5, sc in 5th ch from hook] 12 times, join in first ch of beg ch-5 to form a ring. (12 ch-5 lps)

Rnd 2: Sl st in first ch-5 sp, ch 2, 2-dc cl in same ch-5 sp, [ch 5, 3-dc cl in same ch-5 sp, ch 1, 3-dc cl in next ch-5 sp] rep around, ending with ch 1, join in top of first 2-dc cl.

Rnd 3: Sl st to 3rd ch of next ch-5 sp, ch 1, sc in same ch-5 sp, ch 3, sl st in last sc made (picot), *ch 7, [sc, picot] in 3rd ch of next ch-5 sp, rep from * around, ending with [ch 3, tr] in beg sc to form last ch-7 sp. (12 ch-7 sps)

Rnd 4: Ch 8 (counts as first dc, ch 5), dc in top of last tr, *ch 5, [dc, ch 5, dc] in 4th ch of next ch-7 sp, rep from * around, ending with ch 5, join in 3rd ch of beg ch-8.

Rnd 5: Sl st in next ch-5 sp, ch 3, 2-tr cl in same ch-5 sp, [ch 4, 3-tr cl] twice in same ch-5 sp, ch 4, *sk next ch-5 sp, [3-tr cl, ch 4] 3 times in next ch-5 sp, rep from * around, ending with sk last ch-5 sp, join in top of first 2-tr cl.

Rnd 6: Sl st to center of next ch-4 sp, ch 8 (counts as first dc, ch 5), dc in same ch-4 sp, *[dc, ch 5, dc] in next ch-4 sp, rep from * around, join in 3rd ch of beg ch-8. (36 ch-5 sps)

Rnd 7: Sl st to center of next ch-5 sp, ch 1, sc in same ch-5 sp, [ch 5, sc in next sp] rep around, ending with ch 2, dc in beg sc. (36 ch-5 sps)

Rnd 8: Ch 1, sc in lp just formed, [ch 6, sc in next ch-5 sp] rep around, ending with ch 3, dc in beg sc. (36 ch-6 sps)

Rnd 9: Ch 1, 4 sc over post of dc just made, *[3 sc, picot, 3 sc] in next ch-6 sp, 3 sc in next ch-6 sp, ch 15, drop lp from hook, sk last 12 sc made, insert hook in next sc, draw lp through, ch 1, 24 sc over ch-15 sp, sc in same ch-6 sp as last 3-sc group, [ch 6, sc in next ch-6 sp] 4 times, 3 sc in same ch-6 sp as last sc, rep from * around, ending with ch 6, join in beg sc.

Rnd 10: Sl st in first sc of 24-sc group, ch 3 (counts as first dc), dc in each of next 23 sc, *sc in next ch-6 sp, [ch 6, sc in next ch-6 sp] 3 times **, dc in each of next 24 sc, rep from * around, ending last rep at **, join in 3rd ch of beg ch-3.

Rnd 11: Ch 4 (counts as first dc, ch 1), [dc, ch 1] in each of next 23 dc, *sc in next ch-6 sp, [ch 6, sc in next ch-6 sp] twice, ch 1 **, [dc, ch 1] in each of next 24 dc, rep from * around, ending last rep at **, join in 3rd ch of beg ch-4.

Rnd 12: Ch 6 (counts as first dc, ch 3), *sk next dc, dc in next dc, ch 3] 11 times, dc in last dc, ch 2, 3 sc in next ch-6 sp, picot, 3 sc in next ch-6 sp, ch 2 **, dc in next dc, ch 3, rep from * around, ending last rep at **, join in 3rd ch of beg ch-6.

Rnd 13: Sl st to next ch-3 sp, ch 4, 3-dtr cl in same ch-3 sp, *[ch 5, 4-dtr cl in next ch-3 sp] 11 times, ch 1, 4-dtr cl in next ch-3 sp, rep from * around, ending with ch 1, join in top of first 3-dtr cl.

Rnd 14: [3 sc, picot, 3 sc] in next ch-5 sp, *[3 sc, picot, 3 sc] in next ch-5 sp, ch 12, drop lp from hook, sk last 5 sc made, insert hook in next sc, draw lp through, ch 1, 6 sc in ch-12 sp, [ch 5, sl st, ch 7, sl st, ch 5, sl st] in last sc made, 6 sc in same ch-12 sp *, rep from * to * 8 times, **[3 sc, picot, 3 sc] in next ch-5 sp] twice, rep from * to * 9 times, rep from ** around, ending with [3 sc, picot, 3 sc] in last ch-5 sp, join in beg sc, fasten off.

Weave in loose ends; lightly spray-starch and press.

—*Designed by Dot Drake*

White Pineapples

E X P E R I E N C E   L E V E L
Beginner

S I Z E
15" in diameter

M A T E R I A L S
• J. & P. Coats Knit-Cro-Sheen® crochet cotton size 10 (225 yds per ball): 1 ball white #1
• Size 6 steel crochet hook or size needed to obtain gauge

G A U G E
First 2 rnds = 1½" in diameter
To save time, take time to check gauge.

P A T T E R N   N O T E
Join rnds with a sl st unless otherwise stated.

P A T T E R N   S T I T C H E S
Dtr: Yo 3 times, insert hook in next st, yo and draw up a lp, [yo and draw through 2 lps on hook] 4 times.

Beg 3-tr cl: Ch 3, holding back on hook last lp of each st, 2 tr in same sp, yo and draw through all 3 lps on hook.

3-tr cl: Holding back on hook last lp of each st, work 3 tr in indicated sp, yo and draw through all 4 lps on hook.

Beg shell: [Ch 3, dc, ch 3, 2 dc] in indicated st.

Shell: [2 dc, ch 3, 2 dc] in indicated st.

D O I L Y
Rnd 1: Ch 8, join to form a ring, ch 3 (counts as first dc throughout), 23 dc in ring, join in 3rd ch of beg ch-3. (24 dc)

Rnd 2: Ch 5 (counts as first dc, ch 2), sk next dc, dc in next dc, [ch 2, sk next dc, dc in next dc] rep around, ending with ch 2, join in 3rd ch of beg ch-5. (12 ch-2 sps)

Rnd 3: Sl st in next ch-2 sp, [beg 3-tr cl, ch 3, 3-tr cl] in same sp, *ch 5, sc in next ch-2 sp, ch 5 **, [3-tr cl, ch 3, 3-tr cl] in next ch-2 sp, rep from * around, ending last rep at **, join in top of beg 3-tr cl. (12 3-tr cls)

Rnd 4: Sl st in next ch-3 sp, beg 3-tr cl in same sp, *ch 5, sc in next ch-5 sp, ch 3, sc in next ch-5 sp, ch 5 **, 3-tr cl in next ch-3 sp, rep from * around, ending last rep at **, join in top of beg 3-tr cl. (6 3-tr cls)

Rnd 5: Ch 1, sc in same st as joining, *ch 7, dtr in next ch-3 sp, ch 7 **, sc in top of next 3-tr cl, rep from * around, ending last rep at **, join in beg sc. (12 ch-7 sps)

Rnd 6: Ch 1, sc in same st as joining, *[ch 5, {sc, ch 5, sc} in next ch-7 sp] twice **, ch 5, sc in next sc, rep from * around, ending last rep at **, ch 2, dc in beg sc to form last ch-5 sp. (30 ch-5 sps)

Rnds 7 & 8: Ch 1, sc in sp just formed, [ch 5, sc in next sp] rep around, ending with ch 2, dc in beg sc. (30 ch-5 sps)

Rnd 9: Ch 1, sc in sp just formed, *[ch 5, sc in next ch-5 sp] 3 times, ch 3, 9 dc in next ch-5 sp, ch 3, sc in next ch-5 sp, rep from * around, join in beg sc.

Rnd 10: Sl st to 3rd ch of next ch-5 sp, ch 1, sc in same sp, *[ch 5, sc in next ch-3 sp] twice, ch 3, sk next ch-5 sp, [dc in next dc, ch 1] 8 times, dc in next dc, ch 3, sk next ch-3 sp, sc in next ch-5 sp, rep from * around, join in beg sc.

Rnd 11: Sl st to 3rd ch of next ch-5 sp, ch 1, sc in same sp, ch 5, sc in next ch-5 sp, *ch 5, sk next ch-3 sp, sc in next dc, [ch 4, sc in next dc] 8 times, sk next ch-3 sp **, [ch 5, sc in next ch-5 sp] twice, rep from * around, ending last rep at **, ch 2, dc in beg sc.

Rnd 12: Ch 1, sc in sp just formed, *[ch 5, sc in next ch-5 sp] twice, ch 3, sc in next ch-4 sp, [ch 4, sc in next ch-4 sp] 7 times, ch 3, sc in next ch-5 sp, rep from * around, join in beg sc.

Rnd 13: Sl st to 3rd ch of next ch-5 sp, ch 1, sc in same sp, *ch 5, sc in next ch-5 sp, ch 3, sk next ch-3 sp, sc in next ch-4 sp, [ch 4, sc in next ch-4 sp] 6 times, ch 3, sk next ch-3 sp, sc in next ch-5 sp, rep from * around, join in beg sc.

Rnd 14: Sl st to 3rd st of next ch-5 sp, beg shell in same sp, *ch 5, sk next ch-3 sp, sc in next ch-4 sp, [ch 4, sc in next ch-4 sp] 5 times, ch 5, sk next ch-3 sp **, shell in next ch-5 sp, rep from * around, ending last rep at **, join in 3rd ch of beg ch-3.

Rnd 15: Sl st to center of shell, beg shell in same shell, *ch 5, sk next ch-5 sp, sc in next ch-4 sp, [ch 4, sc in next ch-4 sp] 4 times, ch 5, sk next ch-5 sp **, shell in center sp of next shell (shell in shell made), rep from * around, ending last rep at **, join in 3rd ch of beg ch-3.

Rnd 16: Sl st to center of shell, beg shell in same shell, *ch 7, sk next ch-5 sp, sc in next ch-4 sp, [ch 4, sc in next ch-4 sp] 3 times, ch 7, sk next ch-5 sp **, shell in next shell, rep from * around, ending last rep at **, join in 3rd ch of beg ch-3.

Rnd 17: Sl st to center of shell, beg shell in same shell, *ch 6, dc in next ch-7 sp, ch 6, sc in next ch-4 sp, [ch 4, sc in next ch-4 sp] twice, ch 6, dc in next ch-7 sp, ch 6 **, shell in next shell, rep from * around, ending last rep at **, join in 3rd ch of beg ch-3.

Rnd 18: Sl st to center of shell, beg shell in same shell, *[ch 6, dc in next ch-6 sp] twice, ch 6, sc in next ch-4 sp, ch 4, sc in next ch-4 sp, [ch 6, dc in next ch-4 sp] twice, ch 6 **, shell in next shell, rep from * around, ending last rep at **, join in 3rd ch of beg ch-3.

Rnd 19: Sl st to center sp of shell, ch 1, *sc in center sp of shell, [ch 6, sc in next ch-6 sp] 3 times, ch 6, dc in next ch-4 sp, [ch 6, sc in next ch-6 sp] 3 times **, ch 6, rep from * around, ending last rep at **, ch 3, dc in beg sc.

Rnds 20 & 21: Ch 1, sc in sp just formed, [ch 7, sc in next ch sp] rep around, ending with ch 3, tr in beg sc.

Rnd 22: Ch 1, sc in sp just formed, *ch 5, [3-tr cl, ch 3, 3-tr cl, ch 3, 3-tr cl] in next ch-7 sp **, ch 5, sc in next ch-7 sp, rep from * around, ending last rep at **, ch 2, dc in beg sc.

Rnd 23: Ch 1, sc in sp just formed, ch 5, sc in next ch-5 sp, ch 5, *3-tr cl in next ch-3 sp, ch 3, 3-tr cl in next ch-3 sp **,

[ch 5, sc in next ch-5 sp] twice, ch 5, rep from * around, ending last rep at **, ch 2, dc in beg sc.

Rnd 24: Ch 1, sc in sp just formed, [ch 5, sc in next ch-5 sp] twice, ch 5, *3-tr cl in next ch-3 sp, ch 3, sl st in top of 3-tr cl just made **, [ch 5, sc in next ch-5 sp] 3 times, ch 5, rep from * around, ending last rep at **, ch 5, join in beg sc, fasten off.

—Designed by Emma L. Willey

One-Day Doilies

EXPERIENCE LEVEL
Intermediate

SIZE
White Doily: 10" in diameter

Cream Doily: 14" in diameter

MATERIALS
- South Maid® crochet cotton size 10: 1 (400-yd) ball white #1 and 1 (350-yd) ball cream #430
- Size 7 steel crochet hook or size needed to obtain gauge
- Tapestry needle
- Fabric stiffener

GAUGE
White Doily: Rnds 1–3 = 1⅝" in diameter

Cream Doily: Rnds 1–3 = 2¾" in diameter

To save time, take time to check gauge.

PATTERN NOTE
Join rnds with a sl st unless otherwise stated.

PATTERN STITCHES
Beg 3-dc cl: Ch 3, holding back on hook last lp of each dc, 2 dc in indicated st, yo, draw through 3 lps on hook.

3-dc cl: Holding back on hook last lp of each dc, 3 dc in indicated st, yo, draw through 4 lps on hook.

Beg 3-tr cl: Ch 4, holding back on hook last lp of each tr, 2 tr in indicated st, yo, draw through 3 lps on hook.

3-tr cl: Holding back on hook last st of each tr, 3 tr in indicated st, yo, draw through 4 lps on hook.

White Doily

Rnd 1: With white, ch 8, join to form a ring, ch 3 (counts as first dc), 19 dc in ring, join in 3rd ch of beg ch-3. (20 dc)

Rnd 2: Ch 1, sc in same st, [ch 5, sk 1 dc, sc in next dc] rep around, ending with ch 2, dc in beg sc to form last ch-5 sp. (10 ch-5 sps)

Rnd 3: Ch 1, sc in sp just formed, [ch 7, sc in next ch-5 sp] rep around, ending with ch 3, tr in beg sc to form last ch-7 sp.

Rnd 4: Ch 1, sc in sp just formed, [ch 9, sc in next ch-7 sp] rep around, ending with ch 4, dtr in beg sc to form last ch-9 sp.

Rnd 5: Ch 1, sc in sp just formed, *ch 2, [[dtr, ch 2] 4 times] in next sc, sc in next ch-9 sp **, ch 7, sc in next ch-9 sp, rep from * around, ending last rep at **, ch 3, tr in beg sc to form last ch-7 sp.

Rnd 6: Ch 1, sc in sp just formed, *[ch 4, tr in next dtr] 4 times, ch 4, sc in next ch-7 sp, rep from * around, ending with ch 4, join in beg sc.

Rnd 7: Ch 8 (counts as first dc, ch 5), *[dc in next tr, ch 5] 4 times **, dc in next sc, ch 5, rep from * around, ending last rep at **, join in 3rd ch of beg ch-8. (25 ch-5 sps)

Rnd 8: Ch 6 (counts as first dc, ch 3), *dc in next ch-5 sp, ch 3 **, dc in next dc, ch 3, rep from * around, ending last rep at **, join in 3rd ch of beg ch-6. (50 ch-3 sps)

Rnd 9: Ch 1, sc in same st, [ch 5, sc in next dc] rep around, ending with ch 2, dc in beg sc to form last ch-5 sp.

Rnds 10–13: Ch 1, sc in sp just formed, [ch 5, sc in next sp] rep around, ending with ch 2, dc in beg sc to form last ch-5 sp.

Rnds 14–16: Ch 1, sc in sp just formed, [ch 6, sc in next sp] rep around, ending with ch 3, dc in beg sc to form last ch-6 sp.

Rnds 17 & 18: Ch 1, sc in sp just formed, [ch 7, sc in next sp] rep around, ending with ch 3, tr in beg sc to form last ch-7 sp.

Rnd 19: Ch 1, sc in sp just formed, *ch 2, [[tr, ch 2] 4 times] in next sc, sc in next ch-7 sp **, ch 5, sc in next ch-7 sp, rep from * around, ending last rep at **, ch 2, dc in beg sc to form last ch-5 sp.

Rnd 20: Ch 1, sc in sp just formed, *[ch 3, dc in next tr] 4 times, ch 3, sc in next ch-5 sp, rep from * around, ending with ch 3, join in beg sc.

Rnd 21: *[Ch 5, dc in same st, sl st in next dc] 4 times, ch 5, dc in same st **, sl st in next sc, rep from * around, ending last rep at **, join at base of beg ch-5, fasten off.

Weave in loose ends; stiffen and block to measurements.

Cream Doily

Rnd 1: Ch 4, holding back on hook last lp of each dc, 2 dc in 4th ch from hook, yo, draw through 3 lps on hook, [beg 3-dc cl in top of cl just made] 7 times, join at base of first cl made. (8 cls)

Rnd 2: *Beg 3-dc cl in same sp, [beg 3-dc cl in top of cl just made] twice (3-cl ch made), sl st between next 2 cls of previous rnd, rep from * around, sl st at base of first cl made. (8 3-cl chs)

Rnd 3: Sl st in each of first 3 chs of first cl, sl st in sp between this cl and next cl, *ch 9, sl st between 2nd and 3rd cls on same 3-cl ch **, ch 9, sl st between first and 2nd cls of next 3-cl ch, rep from * around, ending last rep at **, ch 4, dtr at base of beg ch-9 to form last ch-9 sp. (16 ch-9 sps)

Rnds 4 & 5: Ch 1, sc in sp just formed, *ch 9, sc in next ch-9 sp, rep from * around, ch 4, dtr in beg sc.

Rnd 6: [3-cl ch, ch 1, sl st in next ch-9 sp] rep around, join at base of first 3-cl ch.

Rnd 7: Rep Rnd 3. (32 ch-9 sps)

Rnds 8–10: Rep Rnd 4.

Rnd 11: Rep Rnd 6.

Rnd 12: Rep Rnd 3. (64 ch-9 sps)

Rnds 13–16: Rep Rnd 4.

Rnd 17: [Beg 3-tr cl in same sp, ch 1, sl st in next ch-9 sp] rep around, join at base of first 3-tr cl.

Rnd 18: Rep Rnd 2, fasten off.

Weave in loose ends; stiffen and block to measurements.

—Designed by Linda Gustafson

Daisy Edging

EXPERIENCE LEVEL
Beginner

SIZE
15½" x 3"

MATERIALS
• DMC® Cebelia® crochet cotton size 20 (50 grams per skein): 1 skein white
• Size 8 steel crochet hook
• 16" x 25" rose-colored hand towel
• Sewing needle
• White sewing thread

GAUGE
12 dc = 1"
To save time, take time to check gauge.

SPECIAL ABBREVIATIONS
Block (bl): Dc in each of next 2 sts.
Sp: Ch 1, sk next st, dc in next dc.

PATTERN STITCH
Row 1: Ch 44, dc in 6th ch from hook (first space), [ch 1, sk next ch, dc in next ch] 19 times, turn. (20 spaces)

CHART A

Row 20

Row 15

Row 10

Row 5

Row 1

STITCH KEY
● Block
□ Space

Rows 2–4: Ch 4 (counts as first dc, ch 1 throughout), [dc in next dc, ch 1] rep across, ending with sk 1 ch, dc in next ch, turn.

---•---

EDGING

Rows 1–4: Work Rows 1–4 of Pattern Stitch.

Rep Chart A 3 times.

Last 4 Rows: [Rep Row 2 of Pattern Stitch] 4 times, fasten off. Stitch edging to towel.

—Designed by Nazanin S. Fard

Narrow Edging

---•---

EXPERIENCE LEVEL
Beginner

SIZE
16" x ¾"

MATERIALS
- DMC® Cebelia® crochet cotton size 20 (50 grams per skein): 1 skein white
- Size 8 steel crochet hook
- 16" x 25" rose-colored hand towel
- Sewing needle
- White sewing thread

GAUGE
13 dc = 1"

To save time, take time to check gauge.

---•---

EDGING
Make 2

Multiple of 4 chs + 3 turning chs

Row 1: Ch 171, dc in 4th ch from hook and in each ch across, turn. (169 dc, counting last 3 chs of foundation ch as first dc)

Row 2: Ch 3 (counts as first dc), sk next st, *[2 dc, ch 3, sl st in first ch (picot), 2 dc] in next dc**, ch 2, sk next 3 dc, rep from * across to last 2 sts, ending last rep at **, sk next dc, dc in last ch of foundation ch, turn.

Row 3: [Ch 7, sl st in next ch sp] rep across, ending with sl st in 3rd ch of turning ch-3, turn.

Row 4: [Ch 5, sl st in next ch sp] rep across, ending with sl st in last dc of Row 2, fasten off.

Stitch 1 edging at bottom edge of towel; stitch 2nd edging 3" higher than first.

—Designed by Nazanin S. Fard

Delicate Napkin Edgings

---•---

Blue-Trimmed White Ruffle

EXPERIENCE LEVEL
Beginner

SIZE
To fit 16"-square napkin

MATERIALS
- Crochet cotton size 20 (50 grams per ball): 1 ball white
- Kreinik® Fine (#8) Braid (11 yds per spool): 3 spools blue #006
- Size 10 steel crochet hook

GAUGE
Work evenly and consistently

PATTERN NOTE
Join rnds with a sl st unless otherwise stated.

---•---

EDGE
Rnd 1: With cotton, insert hook under hemmed sts of napkin, ch 1, [sc, ch 3, sk ⅛"] rep evenly around, working [sc, ch 3] twice in each corner st, ending with an even total number of ch-3 lps, join in beg sc.

Rnd 2: Ch 1, sc in same lp, *[ch 5, sc in next lp] twice, ch 5, sc in same lp, rep from * around, ending with [ch 5, sc] in same lp as beg sc, join in beg sc.

Rnd 3: Sl st in first ch-5 lp, ch 1, sc in same lp, [ch 5, sc in next lp] rep around, ch 5, join in beg sc.

Rnd 4: Rep Rnd 3, fasten off.

Rnd 5: Join braid with a sl st in ch-5 lp, ch 1, sc in same lp, [ch 5, sc in next lp] rep around, ch 5, join in beg sc, fasten off.

Filet Edge

EXPERIENCE LEVEL
Beginner

SIZE
To fit 16"-square napkin

MATERIALS
- Crochet cotton size 20 (50 grams per ball): 1 ball white
- Size 10 steel crochet hook or size needed to obtain gauge

GAUGE
12 dc = 1"

To save time, take time to check gauge.

PATTERN NOTES
When stitching into napkin hem sts, strive for a square format. Different napkins have different st lengths; you may need to sk more to make the patt square.

Join rnds with a sl st unless otherwise stated.

EDGE

Rnd 1: Inserting hook under hemmed sts of napkin, ch 3 (counts as first dc throughout), dc in each of next 2 sts, [ch 3, sk 3 sts, dc in each of next 3 sts] rep around napkin, working [ch 3, 3 dc] in each corner st, ending with ch 3, join in 3rd ch of beg ch-3.

Rnd 2: Sl st to first ch-3 sp, ch 3, 2 dc in same sp, [ch 3, 3 dc in next ch-3 sp] rep around, working [3 dc in ch-3 sp, dc in next dc, 3 dc in 2nd dc, dc in next dc, 3 dc in ch-3 sp] at each corner, join in 3rd ch of beg ch-3.

Rnd 3: Rep Row 2, working corners as follows: 3 dc in ch-3 sp, ch 3, sk 3 dc, [dc in next dc] twice, 3 dc in corner, [dc in next dc] twice, ch 3, sk 3 dc, 3 dc in ch-3 sp, fasten off.

Scalloped Edge

EXPERIENCE LEVEL
Intermediate

SIZE
To fit 16"-square napkin

MATERIALS
- Crochet cotton size 30 (50 grams per ball): 1 ball white
- Size 10 steel crochet hook or size needed to obtain gauge

GAUGE
4 scallops = 1½"

To save time, take time to check gauge.

PATTERN NOTES
Be careful not to work initial (sc, ch 3) sts too closely or scallops will not lie flat.

Join rnds with a sl st unless otherwise stated.

***

EDGE

Rnd 1: Insert hook under hemmed st of napkin at any corner, ch 1, [sc, ch 3, sc] in same sp, ch 3, sk ⅛", [sc, ch 3, sk ⅛"] rep around, working [sc, ch 3] twice in each corner, ending with an even total number of ch-3 lps, with an odd number of lps along each side between corner lps, join in beg sc.

Rnd 2: Sl st in first ch-3 lp, ch 1, [sc, ch 3, sc] in same lp, [ch 3, sc in next lp] rep around, working [[ch 3, sc] twice in corner lp, ch 3, sc in next lp] at each corner, join in beg sc.

Rnd 3: Ch 4 (counts as first tr), tr in same sc, ch 5, 2 tr in next sc, *sk 1 sc, [2 tr, ch 3, 2 tr] in next sc, rep from * around, working [3 tr in first of 2 corner sc, ch 5, 3 tr in next corner sc] in corners, join in 4th ch of beg ch-4.

Rnd 4: Sl st to first ch-5 lp, ch 3, 10 dc in same lp, sc in sp between same tr group and next tr group, [7 dc in next ch-3 lp, sc in sp between tr groups] rep around, working 11 dc in ch-5 corner lps, join in 3rd ch of beg ch-3, fasten off.

Mauve-Trimmed Strawberry Edge

EXPERIENCE LEVEL
Intermediate

SIZE
To fit 16"-square napkin

MATERIALS
- Crochet cotton size 30 (50 grams per ball): 1 ball white
- Kreinik® Fine (#8) Braid (11 yds per spool): 2 spools confetti fuchsia #042
- Size 10 steel crochet hook or size needed to obtain gauge

GAUGE
4 strawberries and 3-dc groups = 3"

To save time, take time to check gauge.

PATTERN NOTES
When stitching into napkin hem sts, strive for a square format. Different napkins have different st lengths; you may need to sk more to make the patt square.

Join rnds with a sl st unless otherwise stated.

***

EDGE

Rnd 1: Insert hook under hemmed sts of napkin at any corner, ch 1, beg in same sp, [sc, ch 3, sk ⅛"] rep around, working [sc, ch 3] twice in each corner st, ending [sc, ch 3] in same sp as beg sc, join in beg sc. (Total number of ch-3 lps = multiple of 4 with an odd number of ch-3 lps along each side between corner sps)

Rnd 2: Sl st in first ch-3 lp, ch 3 (counts as first dc), 4 dc in same lp, [ch 3, sc in next lp, ch 3, 5 dc in next lp] rep around, working [[ch 3, sc] in corner lp, ch 3, sc in same lp, ch 3, 5 dc in next lp] in each corner, ending with ch 3, join in 3rd ch of beg ch-3.

Rnd 3: *Sc between first 2 dc, [ch 3, sc between next 2 dc] 3 times, ch 1, 3 dc in next sc, ch 1, rep from * around, working [ch 3, {2 dc, ch 3, 2 dc} in ch-3 lp of corner ch-3, ch 3] at corners, join in beg sc.

Rnd 4: [Sc in ch-3 lp, {ch 3, sc in next lp} twice, ch 2, 3 dc in 2nd dc, ch 2] rep around, working [ch 4, {2 dc, ch 3, 2 dc} in ch-3 sp, ch 4] at corners, join in beg sc.

Rnd 5: [Sc in ch-3 lp, ch 3, sc in next lp, ch 3, 3 dc in 2nd dc, ch 3] rep around, working [ch 5, {2 dc, ch 3, 2 dc} in ch-3 sp, ch 5] at corners, join in beg sc, fasten off.

Rnd 6: Attach braid with a sl st in first dc of any 3-dc group, ch 1, sc in same st, sc in each of next 2 dc, [ch 5, sc in top of strawberry (ch-3 lp), ch 5, sc in each of next 3 dc] rep around, working [ch 5, sc in ch-5 sp, ch 5, sc in ch-3 sp, ch 5, sc in ch-5 sp] at corners, ending with ch 5, sc in ch-3 lp, ch 5, join in beg sc.

Clover Edge

EXPERIENCE LEVEL
Advanced

SIZE
To fit 16"-square napkin

- Crochet cotton size 30 (50 grams per ball): 1 ball white
- Kreinik® Fine (#8) Braid (11 yds per spool): 2 spools confetti blue #044
- Size 10 steel crochet hook

GAUGE
Work evenly and consistently

PATTERN NOTE
Join rnds with a sl st unless otherwise stated.

PATTERN STITCH
Clover cluster (cvc): *[Yo, insert hook in indicated st, yo, draw lp through loosely] twice (5 lps on hook) *, yo, draw through 4 lps on hook, yo, draw through rem 2 lps on hook.

Joint cvc (jt cvc): Work cvc from * to * in indicated st for first leg, rep from * to * in next indicated st for 2nd leg (9 lps on hook), yo, draw through 8 lps on hook, yo, draw through rem 2 lps on hook.

————————•————————

EDGE
Rnd 1: Insert hook under hemmed sts of napkin at any corner, ch 1, [sc, ch 3, sc] in same sp, ch 3, sk ⅛", [sc, ch 3, sk ⅛"] rep around, working [sc, ch 3] twice in each corner st, having a multiple of 6 + 1 ch-3 lps along each side between corner lps, join in beg sc.

Rnd 2: Sl st in first ch-3 lp, ch 1, sc in same lp, [5 dc in next lp, sc in next lp] rep around, join in beg sc.

Rnd 3: Ch 1, [sc, ch 5, sc] in same st, ch 1, *cvc in next dc, [ch 2, jt cvc in same st as previous cvc or 2nd leg of previous jt cvc for first leg and in next dc for 2nd leg] 4 times, ch 2, work cvc in same st as 2nd leg of previous jt cvc, ch 1 **, sk 1 sc and 2 dc, sc in next dc, ch 5, sk 2 dc, 1 sc and 2 dc, sc in next dc, ch 1, sk 2 dc and 1 sc, rep from * across to corner, ending last rep at **, [sc, ch 5, sc] in corner sc, ch 1, rep from * around, join in beg sc.

Rnd 4: Sl st in each of next 3 chs of ch-5 lp, ch 1, sc in same ch-5 lp, *work cvc in top of next cvc, [ch 2, jt cvc in same st as previous cvc or 2nd leg of previous jt cvc for first leg and in top of next jt cvc for 2nd leg] 5 times, ch 2, cvc in same st as 2nd leg of previous jt cvc, sc in next ch-5 lp, rep from * around, join in beg sc, fasten off.

Rnd 5: Attach braid with sl st in ch-2 sp, ch 1, *[sc, ch 1, sc, ch 1, sc] in each ch-2 sp, sc in sc between fans, rep around, join in beg sc.

—Designed by Debby Caldwell

Pineapple Garden Doily
————————•————————

EXPERIENCE LEVEL
Advanced

SIZE
13" in diameter

MATERIALS
- Crochet cotton size 10 (250 yds per ball): 1 ball white
- Size 7 steel crochet hook or size needed to obtain gauge

GAUGE
Rnds 1–4 = 2½"

To save time, take time to check gauge.

PATTERN NOTE
Join rnds with a sl st unless otherwise stated.

PATTERN STITCHES
Beg 3-dc cl: Ch 2, holding back on hook last lp of each st, dc in each of next 2 sts, yo, draw through all 3 lps on hook.

3-dc cl: Holding back on hook last lp of each st, dc in each of next 3 sts, yo, draw through all 4 lps on hook.

Beg 4-dc cl: Ch 2, holding back on hook last lp of each st, dc in each of next 3 sts, yo, draw through all 4 lps on hook.

4-dc cl Holding back on hook last lp of each st, dc in each of next 4 sts, yo, draw through all 5 lps on hook.

Joint dc (jt dc): Holding back on hook last lp of each st, dc in each of next 2 indicated sts, yo, draw through all 3 lps on hook.

————————•————————

DOILY
Rnd 1: Ch 6, join to form a ring, ch 3 (counts as first dc throughout), dc in ring, [ch 1, 2 dc in ring] 8 times, ch 1, join in 3rd ch of beg ch-3. (9 ch-1 sps)

Rnd 2: Ch 3, dc in next dc, [ch 2, dc in each of next 2 dc] 8 times, ch 2, join in 3rd ch of beg ch-3.

Rnd 3: Ch 3, dc in next dc, [ch 3, dc in each of next 2 dc] 8 times, ch 3, join in 3rd ch of beg ch-3.

Rnd 4: Ch 3, [2 dc, ch 1, dc] in same dc, *[dc, ch 1, 3 dc] in next dc, sk ch-3 sp **, [3 dc, ch 1, dc] in next dc, rep from * around, ending last rep at **, join in 3rd ch of beg ch-3.

Rnd 5: Beg 3-dc cl, *ch 2, dc in each of next 2 dc, ch 2, 3-dc cl over next 3 dc, ch 2 **, 3-dc cl over next 3 dc, rep from * around, ending last rep at **, join in top of beg 3-dc cl.

Rnd 6: Sl st in next 2 chs and in first dc, ch 3, [2 dc, ch 2, dc] in same dc, *[dc, ch 2, 3 dc] in next dc, ch 3, sk next 2 3-dc cls **, [3 dc, ch 2, dc] in next dc, rep from * around, ending last rep at **, join in 3rd ch of beg ch-3.

Rnd 7: Beg 3-dc cl, *ch 3, sk next ch-2 sp, dc in each of next 2 dc, ch 3, sk next ch-2 sp, 3-dc cl over next 3 dc, ch 3, sk next ch-3 sp **, 3-dc cl over next 3 dc, rep from * around, ending last rep at **, join in top of beg 3-dc cl.

Rnd 8: Sl st in next 3 chs and in first dc, ch 3, [3 dc, ch 2, dc] in same dc, *[dc, ch 2, 4 dc] in next dc, ch 5, sk next 2 3-dc cls **, [4 dc, ch 2, dc] in next dc, rep from * around, ending last rep at **, join in 3rd ch of beg ch-3.

Rnd 9: Beg 4-dc cl, *ch 4, sk next ch-2 sp, dc in each of next 2 dc, ch 4, sk next ch-2 sp, 4-dc cl over next 4 dc, ch 6, sk next ch-5 sp **, 4-dc cl over next 4 dc, rep from * around, ending last rep at **, join in top of beg 4-dc cl.

Rnd 10: Sl st in next 4 chs and in first dc, ch 3, [3 dc, ch 2, dc] in same dc, *[dc, ch 2, 4 dc] in next dc, ch 4, sk next ch-4 sp and 4-dc cl, dc in 3rd and 4th chs of next ch-6 sp, ch 4, sk next 4-dc cl and ch-4 sp **, [4 dc, ch 2, dc] in next dc, rep from * around, ending last rep at **, join in 3rd ch of beg ch-3.

Rnd 11: Beg 4-dc cl, *ch 4, sk next ch-2 sp, dc in each of next 2 dc, ch 4, sk next ch-2 sp, 4-dc cl over next 4 dc, ch 5, sk next ch-4 sp, dc in each of next 2 dc, ch 5, sk next ch-4 sp **, 4-dc cl over next 4 dc, rep from * around, ending last rep at **, join in top of beg 4-dc cl.

Rnd 12: Sl st in next 4 chs and in first dc, ch 3, [3 dc, ch 2, dc] in same dc, *[dc, ch 2, 4 dc] in next dc, ch 3, sk next [ch-4 sp, 4-dc cl and ch-5 sp], [4 dc, ch 2, dc] in next dc, [dc, ch 2, 4 dc] in next dc, ch 3, sk next [ch-5 sp, 4-dc cl and ch-4 sp] **, [4 dc, ch 2, dc] in next dc, rep from * around, ending last rep at **, join in 3rd ch of beg ch-3.

Rnd 13: Beg 4-dc cl, *ch 3, sk next ch-2 sp, dc in each of next 2 dc, ch 3, sk next ch-2 sp, 4-dc cl over next 4 dc, ch 3, sk next ch-3 sp **, 4-dc cl over next 4 dc, rep from * around, ending last rep at **, join in top of beg 4-dc cl.

Rnd 14: Sl st in next 3 chs and in first dc, ch 3, 5 dc in same dc, 6 dc in next dc, *ch 3, sk next ch-3 sp and 4-dc cl, sc in next ch-3 sp, ch 3, sk next 4-dc cl and ch-3 sp **, [6 dc in next dc] twice, rep from * around, ending last rep at **, join in 3rd ch of beg ch-3.

Rnd 15: Ch 4, dc in next dc, [ch 1, dc in next dc] 10 times, *sc in next sc, [dc in next dc, ch 1] 11 times, dc in next dc, rep from * around, ending with sc in last sc, join in 3rd ch of beg ch-4.

Rnd 16: Sl st in next ch and in next dc, ch 4, dc in next dc, [ch 2, dc in next dc] 7 times, ch 2, jt dc over next dc and 2nd dc of next 12-dc group, [ch 2, dc in next dc] 8 times, rep from * around, ending with ch 2, dc in next dc until 2 lps rem on hook, insert hook in 2nd ch of beg ch-4, yo, draw through st on hook, yo, draw through all 3 lps on hook, fasten off.

Pineapple points (make 9)

Row 1: With RS facing, join thread with a sl st in first dc after jt dc, ch 1, sc in same st as joining, [ch 4, sc in next dc] 7 times, turn. (7 ch-4 sps)

Row 2: Sl st in ch-4 sp, ch 1, sc in same sp, [ch 4, sc in next ch-4 sp] 6 times, turn.

Row 3: Sl st in ch-4 sp, ch 1, sc in same sp, [ch 4, sc in next ch-4 sp] 5 times, turn.

Row 4: Sl st in ch-4 sp, ch 1, sc in same sp, [ch 4, sc in next ch-4 sp] 4 times, turn.

Row 5: Sl st in ch-4 sp, ch 1, sc in same sp, [ch 4, sc in next ch-4 sp] 3 times, turn.

Row 6: Sl st in ch-4 sp, ch 1, sc in same ch-4 sp, [ch 4, sc in next ch-4 sp] twice, turn.

Row 7: Sl st in next ch-4 sp, ch 1, sc in same sp, ch 4, sc in next ch-4 sp, fasten off.

Rep around in every other [dc, ch-2] area.

EDGING

With RS facing, attach thread with a sl st in first jt dc to the right between any pineapple and [dc, ch-2] area, ch 1, sc in joining, *[ch 4, sl st in first ch (picot), sc in next dc] 8 times, picot, sc in jt dc, working in ch sps up side of pineapple, [picot, sc] in each end sp to tip, [picot, sc] twice in tip, working in ch sps down opposite side, [picot, sc] in each end sp to base, [picot, sc] in next jt dc, rep from * around, ending last rep with picot, join in beg sc.

Weave in loose ends; block and starch.

—Designed by Rhonda Semonis

Lover's Knot Tablecloth

EXPERIENCE LEVEL
Intermediate

SIZE
51" x 65"

MATERIALS
- South Maid® crochet cotton size 10 (400 yds per ball): 15 balls white #1
- Size 7 steel crochet hook or size needed to obtain gauge
- Tapestry needle
- Fabric stiffener

GAUGE
Motif = approximately 3½" square before blocking
To save time, take time to check gauge.

PATTERN NOTE
Join rnds with a sl st unless otherwise stated.

PATTERN STITCHES
Lover's Knot (LK): Draw up lp on hook to ½", yo, draw through lp, insert hook between lp and long single strand, yo, draw up lp, complete sc.

Double LK (DLK): [LK] twice.

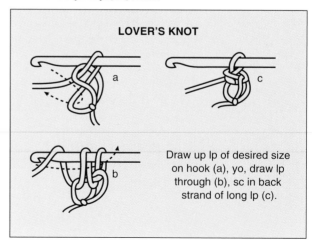

LOVER'S KNOT

Draw up lp of desired size on hook (a), yo, draw lp through (b), sc in back strand of long lp (c).

FIRST MOTIF

Rnd 1: Ch 1 (center ch), [ch 9, sl st in center ch (petal made)] 7 times, ch 4, dtr in center ch to form last petal. (8 petals)

Rnd 2: Sl st in petal just made, [ch 3, sl st in next petal] rep around, join in beg sl st.

Rnd 3: [DLK, sl st in next sl st] rep around, join at base of first DLK. (8 DLKs)

Rnd 4: Ch 3, sl st in sc at center of first DLK, [DLK, sl st in sc at center of next DLK] rep around, sl st in beg sl st.

Rnd 5: Ch 1, sc in same st as joining, *ch 9, sc in sc at center of next DLK **, ch 9, sc in next sl st, rep from * around, ending last rep at **, ch 4, dtr in beg sc to form last ch-9 sp. (16 ch-9 sps)

Rnd 6: Ch 1, sc in sp just formed, [ch 5, sc in next ch-9 sp], rep around, join in beg sc.

Rnd 7: Ch 1, sc in same st, *ch 11, sc in next sp (corner made), ch 9, sc in next sc, ch 7, sc in next sp, ch 5, sc in next sc, ch 5, sc in next sp, ch 5, sc in next sc, ch 7, sc in next sp, ch 9, sc in next sc, rep from * around, join in beg sc, fasten off.

SECOND MOTIF

Rnds 1–6: Rep Rnds 1–6 of first motif, do not fasten off at end of Rnd 6.

Joining

Rnd 7: Ch 5, sl st in center of corresponding corner ch-11 sp on previous motif, ch 5, sc in next sp of working motif, ch 4, sl st in center of corresponding ch-9 sp on previous motif, ch 4, sc in next sc on working motif, ch 3, sl st in center of corresponding ch-7 sp on previous motif, ch 3, sc in next sp of working motif, ch 2, sl st in center of corresponding ch-5 sp, ch 2, sc in next sc of working motif, ch 2, sl st in center of corresponding ch-5 sp, ch 2, sc in next sp of working motif, ch 2, sl st in center of corresponding ch-5 lp of previous motif, ch 2, sc in next sc of working motif, ch 3, sl st in center of corresponding ch-7 sp, ch 3, sc in next lp of working motif, ch 4, sl st in center of corresponding ch-9 sp on previous motif, ch 4, sc in next sc on working motif, ch 5, sl st in center of corresponding corner ch-11 sp on previous motif, ch 5, sc in next sp of working motif (first adjacent side joined), continue around in est patt as for first motif, join in beg sc, fasten off.

Make and join a total of 285 motifs, having 19 rows of 15 motifs each. On subsequent motifs, join as many adjacent sides as are required in the same manner as for second motif, always ending joining portion by joining corner ch-11 sps.

BORDER

Rnd 1: Attach thread with a sl st in any of 4 corner ch-11 sps, *[LK, sl st in next sp] 7 times, LK, dc in joining of next 2 ch-11 sps, rep from * to last joining before next corner, [LK, sl st in next sp] 8 times, rep from * around, join at base of first LK, fasten off.

Weave in loose ends. Stiffen lightly and block to measurements.

—Designed by Linda Gustafson

Whirls & Rows Purse

EXPERIENCE LEVEL
Intermediate

SIZE
Approximately 6½" tall x 5¾" wide without handles

MATERIALS
- Halcyon® 3/2 pearl cotton: 1½ oz medium forest green #136 (MC)
- J. & P. Coats Luster Sheen® sport weight yarn: ½ oz purple #590 (CC)
- Size D/3 crochet hook or size needed to obtain gauge

GAUGE
[Shell, 3 sc, shell] = 2½" in patt st

To save time, take time to check gauge.

PATTERN NOTE
Join rnds with a sl st unless otherwise stated.

PATTERN STITCHES
Dc dec: Holding back on hook last lp of each st, dc in each of next 2 sts, yo, draw through all 3 lps on hook.

Cl: Holding back on hook last lp of each st, dc in each st indicated for number of sts specified, yo, draw through all rem lps on hook.

Shell: 7 dc in indicated sp.

PURSE

Rnd 1: Beg at top of purse with MC, ch 84, join to form a ring, being careful not to twist foundation ch, ch 1, beg in same st as joining, sc in each ch around, join in beg sc. (84 sc)

Rnd 2: Ch 3 (counts as first dc throughout), dc in each sc around, join in 3rd ch of beg ch-3. (84 dc)

Rnd 3: Ch 3, dc in each of next 18 dc, dc dec, [dc in each of next 19 dc, dc dec] 3 times, join in 3rd ch of beg ch-3. (80 sts)

Rnd 4: Ch 1, sc in same st, sc in next st, [sk 3 dc, shell in next dc, sk 3 dc, sc in each of next 3 dc] rep around, ending with sk 3 dc, shell in next dc, sk 3 dc, sc in last dc, join in beg sc. (8 shells)

Rnd 5: Ch 1, sc in same st, sc in next st, *ch 3, 7-dc cl over next 7 dc, ch 3, sc in each of next 3 sc, rep from * around, ending with ch 3, sc in last sc, join in beg sc.

Rnd 6: Ch 1, sc in same st, sc in next st, *shell in top of next 7-dc cl, sc in each of next 3 sc, rep from * around, ending with sc in last sc, join in beg sc with CC, do not fasten off MC.

Rnd 7: With CC, ch 3 (counts as first dc), 3-dc cl over next 3 sts, [ch 3, sc in each of next 3 sts, ch 3, 7-dc cl over next 7 sts] rep around to last 3 sts, holding back on hook last lp of each st, dc in each of last 3 sts, insert hook into top of next 3-dc cl, yo, draw through all lps on hook, pull to tighten.

Rnd 8: Ch 3 (counts as first dc), 3 dc in st just made, sc in each of next 3 sc, [shell in top of next 7-dc cl, sc in each of next 3 sc] rep around, ending with 3 dc in same st as beg ch-3, insert hook in top of beg ch-3, drop CC, pick up MC and draw through to complete sl st, fasten off CC.

Rnd 9: Ch 1, sc in same st, sc in next st, [ch 3, 7-dc cl over next 7 sts, ch 3, sc in each of next 3 sts] rep around, ending with ch 3, sc in last st, join in beg sc.

Working in MC only for rem of purse, rep Rnds 6–9 until piece meas approximately 6½", ending after Rnd 7, do not fasten off.

Purse bottom

Rnd 1: Ch 1, hdc around, sk tops of cl sts and working 1 hdc in each sc and 2 hdc in each ch-3 sp, join in top of first hdc. (56 hdc)

Rnds 2 & 3: Ch 2 (counts as first hdc throughout), working in back lps only these 2 rnds, hdc in each rem st around, join in 2nd ch of beg ch-2. (56 hdc)

Rnds 4 & 5: Ch 2, hdc in each rem hdc around, join in 2nd ch of beg ch-2. (56 hdc)

Row 6: Turn purse inside out; holding bottom edges tog, sc through both thicknesses across base of purse, fasten off.

PURSE HANDLES

Make 1 purple & 1 medium forest green

Make ch 24" long, sc in 2nd ch from hook and in each rem ch across, fasten off.

Sew ends of each handle to inside of purse at sides.

BUTTON

Make 3

With CC, ch 3, join to form a ring, ch 1, 12 sc in ring, join in beg sc, fasten off, leaving length for sewing.

Weave end through tops of sts; pull to tighten.

FINISHING

On inside of purse, position button within first patt row of clusters opposite ch-3 sps (buttonholes). Sew firmly to inside, making certain that sts do not show on outside of purse.

Bottom trim

With top of purse pointing down, working through both thicknesses of last rnd of purse body and first rnd of purse bottom, attach CC with a sl st in first sc of any 3-sc group, ch 2, hdc around, sk top of cl sts and working 3 hdc in each ch-3 sp and 1 hdc in each sc, join in 2nd ch of beg ch-2, fasten off. (72 hdc)

—Designed by Shirley Guess

Tiny Coin Purse

EXPERIENCE LEVEL
Intermediate

SIZE
Approximately 3" wide x 3½" tall without drawstring

MATERIALS
- Pearl cotton #5: 50 yds each dark blue (MC) and dark rose (CC)
- Metallic crochet thread size 10 (cotton) or 5 (pearl): small amount silver
- Size 7 crochet hook or size needed to obtain gauge

GAUGE
First 2 rnds = 1" in diameter

To save time, take time to check gauge.

PATTERN NOTE
Join rnds with a sl st unless otherwise stated.

PATTERN STITCHES
2-sc dec: [Draw up lp in next st] 3 times, yo, draw through all 4 lps on hook.

3-dc cl: Holding back on hook last lp of each st, dc in each of next 3 sts, yo, draw through all 4 lps on hook.

3-tr cl: Work as for 3-dc cl with 3 tr.

PURSE

Rnd 1: Beg at base with MC, ch 4, join to form a ring, ch 2 (counts as first hdc throughout), 13 hdc in ring, join in 2nd ch of beg ch-2. (14 hdc)

Rnd 2: Ch 2, hdc in same st, 2 hdc in each rem hdc around, join in 2nd ch of beg ch-2. (28 hdc)

Rnd 3: Ch 2, hdc in same st, [hdc in next hdc, 2 hdc in next hdc] rep around, ending with hdc in last st, join in 2nd ch of beg ch-2. (42 hdc)

Rnd 4: Ch 2, hdc in each hdc around, join in 2nd ch of beg ch-2. (42 hdc)

Rnd 5: Ch 2, hdc in same st, [hdc in each of next 5 hdc, 2 hdc in next hdc] rep around, ending with hdc in each of last 5 hdc, join in 2nd ch of beg ch-2. (49 hdc)

Rnd 6: Ch 3 (counts as first dc throughout), working through back lps only this rnd, dc in same st, dc in each of next 6 hdc, [2 dc in next hdc, dc in each of next 6 hdc] rep around, join in 3rd ch of beg ch-3. (56 dc)

Rnd 7: Ch 3, working in back lps only this rnd, dc in each dc around, join in 3rd ch of beg ch-3. (56 dc)

Rnd 8: Ch 3, *3 tr in next st, dc in next st, hdc in next st, sc in next st, sk next st, hdc in next st **, dc in next st, rep from * around, ending last rep at **, join in 3rd ch of beg ch-3 with metallic thread, fasten off MC. (64 sts)

Rnd 9: Sc in same st as joining, sc in next st, *3 sc in next st, sc in each of next 2 sts, 2-sc dec over next 3 sts **, sc in each of next 2 sts, rep from * around, ending last rep at **, join in beg sc. (64 sts)

Rnd 10: Sl st in next sc, ch 1, sc in same st, sc in next st, rep Rnd 9 from * around, join in beg sc, sl st in next sc with CC, fasten off metallic thread.

Rnd 11: Ch 3, *hdc in next st, sc in next st, hdc in next st, dc in next st, ch 1, 3-tr cl in next 3 sts, ch 1 **, dc in next st, rep from * around, ending last rep at **, join in 3rd ch of beg ch-3.

Rnd 12: Ch 1, sc in each st and ch-1 sp around, sk tops of 3-tr cls, join in beg sc. (56 sts)

Rnd 13: Ch 1, sc in same st and in each rem st around, join in beg sc with MC, fasten off CC. (56 sts)

Rnds 14 & 15: Rep Rnds 8 and 9.

Rnd 16: Sl st in next st, ch 1, sc in same st, sc in next st, *2 sc in next st, sc in each of next 2 sts, 3-dc cl over next 3 sts **, sc in each of next 2 sts, rep from * around, ending last rep at **, join in beg sc with CC, fasten off metallic thread. (56 sts)

Rnd 17: Ch 1, sc in same st as joining and in each rem st around, join in beg sc, do not fasten off. (56 sc)

Border

Rnd 1: Ch 5 (counts as tr, ch 1), *sk next st, tr in next st, ch 1, rep from * around, join in 4th ch of beg ch-5, fasten off.

Drawstring

Holding 1 strand of dark blue, dark rose and metallic thread tog, make ch approximately 16" long, fasten off.

Weave through border of purse; pull tight to close.

Knot each end of drawstring; knot ends of drawstring tog.

—Designed by Shirley Guess

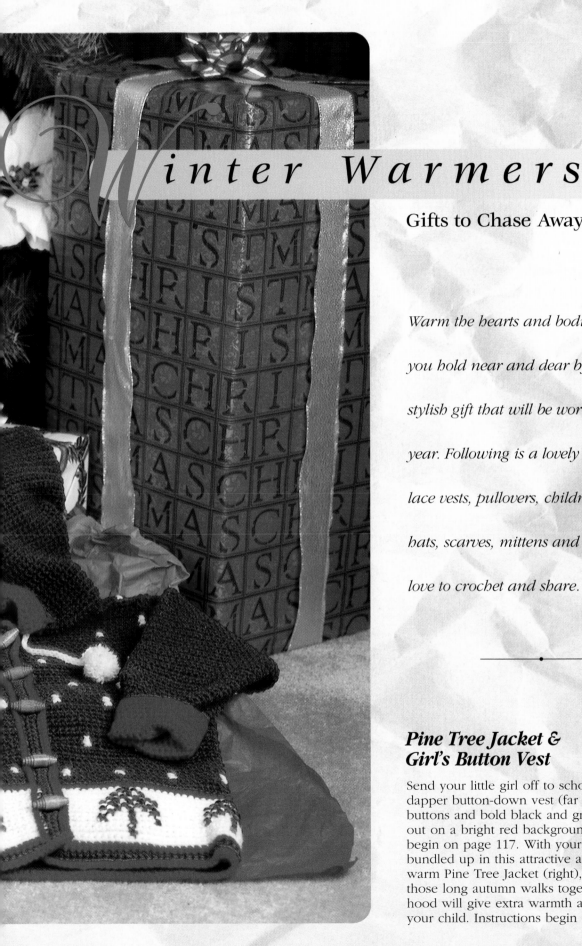

Winter Warmers

Gifts to Chase Away the Chills

Warm the hearts and bodies of those

you hold near and dear by crocheting a

stylish gift that will be worn year after

year. Following is a lovely collection of

lace vests, pullovers, children's sweaters,

hats, scarves, mittens and slippers you'll

love to crochet and share.

Pine Tree Jacket & Girl's Button Vest

Send your little girl off to school in this dapper button-down vest (far left). Rustic buttons and bold black and gray stripes stand out on a bright red background. Instructions begin on page 117. With your youngster bundled up in this attractive and snuggly warm Pine Tree Jacket (right), you'll enjoy those long autumn walks together! A large hood will give extra warmth and comfort to your child. Instructions begin on page 115.

Basket-Weave Pullover

Dress up with a silk blouse or dress down with a cotton turtleneck and this gorgeous Basket-Weave Pullover (above)! Mohair yarn with just a touch of sparkle makes this garment elegant and warm. Instructions begin on page 118.

Beaded Fringe Vest

Crochet this unique Beaded Fringe Vest (right) with a folksy look! Wooden buttons, beaded fringe and spruce crochet cotton make an eye-catching combination you'll wear again and again! Instructions begin on page 120.

Geometric Stripes

This attractive Geometric Stripes sweater (below) is one that will actually please that hard-to-please young man. Interesting geometric shapes are cool enough to suit him, while the good-looking style and fit will please Mom! Instructions begin on page 122.

Tapestry Scarf & Hat

Richly colored ombre yarn makes this lovely Tapestry Scarf & Hat set (above) look more difficult to crochet than it really is. With all the wonderful ombre yarns available today, you're sure to find just the right color combination to suit your taste and style. Instructions begin on page 125.

Pineapple Lace Vest

Classy, beautiful and elegant describe this enchanting tunic-style Pineapple Lace Vest (left). A pretty shell pattern forms the body while lacy pineapples at the bottom give a slightly flared look. Instructions begin on page 123.

Peachy Keen Top

Soft peach cotton is the ideal fiber for this pretty
Peachy Keen Top (above), giving it a delicate,
feminine look. An easy-to-crochet rosebud at
the neck adds the perfect finishing touch.
Instructions begin on page 126.

Classic Shells Pullover

Inspired by a vintage pattern for lace edging,
this exceptionally pretty Classic Shells Pullover
(right) can be worn at the office or on that
weekend getaway. Worked in vibrant pink
cotton, its beautfiul pattern stands out when
worn over a white blouse. Instructions begin
on page 128.

Toddler's Hooded Scarf

Keep your little one warm during those winter trips with this handy hooded scarf (right). And, Mom will love the ease with which the scarf can be put on. Soft ombre yarn in pretty pastel colors give just the right look to this sweet winter warmer. Instructions begin on page 132.

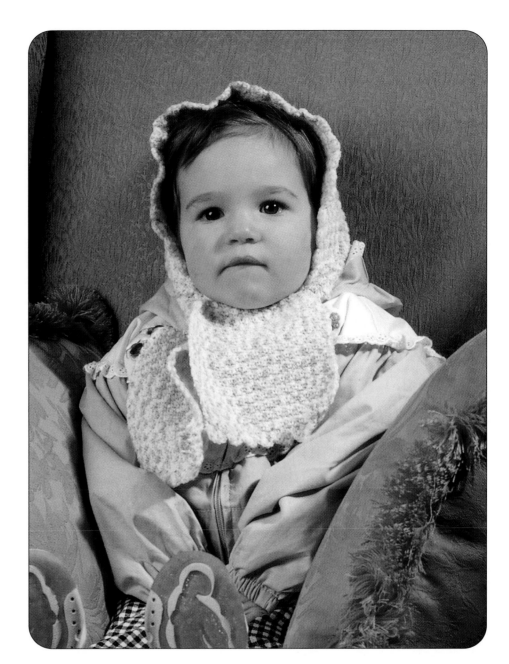

Raspberry Winter Ensemble

Stay warm this winter without losing your fashionable look by crocheting this lovely women's hooded scarf with coordinating mittens (left). A delicate lace pattern on the scarf and around the mittens' cuffs gives an elegant look to this delightful set. Instructions begin on page 130.

Striped Slippers

The perfect gift for a man or woman of any age, these warm Striped Slippers (above) are a breeze to crochet, and have a very comfortable fit. Crochet them in the recipient's favorite colors for a special gift to chase away those winter blues! Instructions begin on page 132.

Pine Tree Jacket

EXPERIENCE LEVEL
Intermediate

SIZE

Toddler size 2(4)(6) Instructions are given for smallest size, with larger sizes in parentheses. When only 1 number is given, it applies to all sizes.

FINISHED MEASUREMENTS

Chest: 28(30)(32)"

Length: 16½(18½)(20½)"

MATERIALS

- Brunswick® Fore 'N Aft Sport® 100 percent Monsanto acrylic yarn (175 yds/50 grams per skein): 5(5)(6) skeins bottle green #60022, 1(1)(2) skeins ecru #6000 and 1(2)(2) skeins red #6024
- Size F/5 crochet hook or size needed to obtain gauge
- Tapestry needle
- 5 (1¼") wooden toggle buttons

GAUGE

16 sc = 4"; 14 sc rows = 3"

To save time, take time to check gauge.

PATTERN NOTES

Jacket is worked in 1 piece to the underarm. Pine trees and snowflakes are added with cross-stitches after crocheting has been completed.

Join rnds with a sl st unless otherwise stated.

BODY

Row 1 (RS): Beg at lower edge with ecru, ch 110(118)(126), sc in 2nd ch from hook and in each ch across, ch 1, turn. (109, 117, 125 sts)

Row 2: Sc in each sc across, ch 1, turn.

Rows 3–13: Rep Row 2, do not ch 1 at end of Row 13, fasten off.

Row 14: With RS facing, attach red with a sl st in first sc at right edge, ch 1, sc in each sc across, ch 1, turn.

Row 15: Sc in each sc across, fasten off.

Row 16: With RS facing, attach bottle green with a sl st in first sc at right edge, sc in each sc across, ch 1, turn.

Rep Row 2 until piece meas 8(9½)(11)" from beg, ending with a WS row.

RIGHT FRONT

Next Row: Sc in each of first 27(29)(31) sts, ch 1, turn.

Rep until piece meas 12½(14½)(16½)" from beg, ending with a RS row.

Neck shaping

Next Row: Sc in each of first 19(21)(23) sts, sc dec, leave rem 6 sts unworked, ch 1, turn. (20, 22, 24 sts)

Continuing in sc, [dec 1 st at neck edge] every other row 5 times.

Work even on 15(17)(19) sc until piece meas 15(17)(19)" from beg, do not ch 1 at end of last row, fasten off.

BACK

Next Row: With RS facing, attach bottle green with a sl st in next unworked sc on last row of body, ch 1, sc in same st as joining and in each of next 54(58)(62) sc, ch 1, turn. (55, 59, 63 sc)

Next Row: Sc in each sc across, ch 1, turn.

Rep last row until piece meas 15(17)(19)", fasten off.

LEFT FRONT

Next Row: With RS facing, attach bottle green with a sl st in next unworked sc on last row of body, ch 1, sc in same st and in each rem st across, ch 1, turn. (27, 29, 31 sc)

Work as for right front, reversing neck shaping.

SLEEVE

Make 2

Row 1: Beg at lower edge above cuff with bottle green, ch 37(39)(41), sc in 2nd ch from hook and in each rem ch across, ch 1, turn. (36, 38, 40 sts)

Row 2: Sc in first sc, 2 sc in next sc, sc in each rem sc across to last 2 sts, 2 sc in next sc, sc in last sc, ch 1, turn. (38, 40, 42 sc)

Continuing in sc, [inc 1 st each edge of every 4th row] 6(3)(3) times, then [inc 1 st each edge every 6th row] 0(4)(5) times. (50, 54, 58 sc at end of last inc row)

Next Row: Sc in each sc across, ch 1, turn.

Rep last row until piece meas 7½(9½)(11½)" from beg, fasten off.

Join sleeve seam.

Cuff

Rnd 1: With RS facing, attach red with a sl st in foundation ch at seam, ch 1, 28(30)(32) sc evenly sp around, join in beg sc.

Rnd 2: Ch 1, beg in same st as joining, sc in each sc around, join in beg sc.

Rep Rnd 2 until cuff meas 3" long, fasten off.

Join shoulder seams; set in sleeves.

HOOD

Row 1: With bottle green, ch 33, sc in 2nd ch from hook and in each rem ch across, ch 1, turn. (32 sts)

Row 2: Sc in each sc across, ch 1, turn.

Rep Row 2 until piece meas 21(22)(23)" from beg, fasten off at end of last row.

Fold fabric in half lengthwise with RS tog, matching row ends along 1 side, sew center back seam.

Cuff

Row 1: With WS facing, attach red with a sl st in bottom front corner of hood, beg in same st, ch 1, work 82(86)(90) sc evenly sp around front edge, ch 1, turn.

Row 2: Sc in each of first 20 sc, hdc in next sc, dc in each of next 40(44)(48) sc, hdc in next sc, sc in each of last 20 sc, ch 1, turn.

Row 3: Sc in each of first 25 sts, hdc in next st, dc in each of next 30(34)(38) sts, hdc in next st, sc in each of last 25 sts, ch 1, turn.

Row 4: Sc in each of first 30 sts, hdc in next st, dc in each of next 20(24)(28) sts, hdc in next st, sc in each of last 30 sts, ch 1, turn.

Rows 5–13: Sc in each st across, ch 1, turn, do not ch 1 at end of Row 13, turn.

Row 14: Sl st in each sc across, fasten off.

Fold cuff back over RS of hood. Tack to hood at center top and both neck corners, leaving opening so tie can be inserted.

Place markers ½" from each front neck edge; pin hood to jacket between markers, easing to fit. Sew in place, leaving bottom of hood cuff open at both neck edges.

EMBROIDERY

Pine trees

Using a double strand of bottle green and tapestry needle, beg in 11th(7th)(11th) st from right edge of ecru border on Row 2, cross-st first tree, following Chart A.

Work 6(7)(7) more trees around ecru border, spacing 7 sts apart, fasten off.

Snowflakes

With RS facing, using double strand of ecru and tapestry needle, beg in 6th green row in 3rd st from right edge, work 1 cross-st in every 8th st across. Rep for next row directly above cross-sts just made. Sk 8 rows.

Beg in 7th st from right edge, work 1 cross-st in every 8th st across. Rep for next row directly above cross-sts just made. Sk 8 rows.

Continue in est pattern to shoulder seams, fasten off.

BORDER

Row 1: With RS facing, attach red with a sl st at first st at bottom left edge, ch 1, sc in each ch across foundation ch, ch 1, turn.

Row 2: Sc in each sc across, fasten off.

Row 3: With RS facing, attach green with a sl st in corner of left front neck edge, ch 1, 53(61)(69) sc evenly sp down left front edge, 3 sc in corner st, sc in each sc across lower edge, 3 sc in next corner st, 53(61)(69) sc up right front edge, ch 1, turn.

Row 4: Sc in first sc, [ch 3, sk 3 sc, sc in each of next 8(10)(12) sc] 4 times, ch 3, sk 3 sc, sc in next sc (5 button-holes made), sc in each rem sc around, working 3 sc in each corner sc, ch 1, turn.

Row 5: Sc in each sc around, working 3 sc in each corner and in each ch-3 sp, fasten off.

Row 6: With RS facing, attach red with a sl st at upper left front

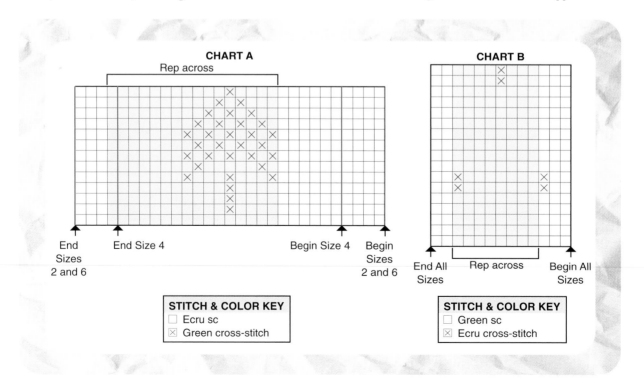

CHART A
Rep across

End Sizes 2 and 6   End Size 4   Begin Size 4   Begin Sizes 2 and 6

STITCH & COLOR KEY
☐ Ecru sc
☒ Green cross-stitch

CHART B
Rep across

End All Sizes   Begin All Sizes

STITCH & COLOR KEY
☐ Green sc
☒ Ecru cross-stitch

in st next to hood cuff, ch 1, sc evenly sp across to corner, 3 sc in corner, sc in each rem sc around to upper right front, working 3 sc in each corner, sc evenly sp to hood cuff, fasten off.

Row 7: With RS facing, attach red with a sl st in first sc of Row 6, ch 1, sl st in each st around, working [sl st, ch 1] in center sc at each corner, fasten off.

FINISHING

On right front only, with RS facing, ch st in each row between body and right front border, beg in first red border row at lower edge of ecru band and ending at neck edge, fasten off.

With RS facing, attach red in back lp of first ch st, sl st in back lp of each ch st across, fasten off.

Sew buttons opposite buttonholes.

Tie

With ecru, ch 150(175)(200), sl st in 2nd ch from hook and in each ch across, fasten off.

Make 2 small ecru pompons; attach 1 to each end of tie. Thread through hood cuff.

—Designed by Ann E. Smith
for Monsanto's Designs for America Program

Girl's Button Vest

EXPERIENCE LEVEL
Intermediate

SIZE
Girls' size 8(10)(12) Instructions are given for smallest size, with larger sizes in parentheses. When only 1 number is given, it applies to all sizes.

FINISHED MEASUREMENTS
Chest: 31½(33½)(35¾)"
Length: 16½(18¼)(20)"

MATERIALS
- Brunswick® Fore 'N Aft Sport® 100 percent Monsanto acrylic yarn (175 yds/50 grams per skein): 2(2)(3) skeins red #6024 and 1 skein each black #6013 and gray #60622
- Size F/5 crochet hook or size needed to obtain gauge
- 5 (⅝") black buttons
- 5 (⅝") square wooden buttons
- 4 (½") round wooden buttons
- Small tapestry needle

GAUGE
13 sts and 7 rows = 4" in Body Patt
To save time, take time to check gauge.

PATTERN NOTES
Join rnds with a sl st unless otherwise stated.

Vest is worked in 1 piece to underarms.

PATTERN STITCHES
Beg joint dc (beg jt dc): Ch 2, dc in next ch-1 sp.

Joint dc (jt dc): Holding back on hook last lp of each st, dc in each of next 2 indicated sts or sps, yo, draw through all 3 lps on hook.

BODY PATTERN
Row 1: Ch 3, dc between first and 2nd dc, [dc between next 2 dc] rep across, turn.

Rep Row 1 for patt.

———————●———————

STRIPED BORDER
Row 1 (RS): Beg at lower edge with black, ch 122(130)(142), sc in 2nd ch from hook and in each rem ch across, ch 1, turn. (121, 129, 141 sts)

Rows 2 & 3: Sc in each sc across, ch 1, turn, fasten off at end of Row 3, do not turn.

Row 4: With RS facing, attach red with a sl st in first sc of Row 3, ch 1, sc in same sc, [ch 1, sk 1 sc, sc in next sc] rep across, fasten off, do not turn.

Row 5: With RS facing, attach gray with a sl st in first sc of previous row, beg jt dc, ch 1, [jt dc in same sp as 2nd leg of last jt dc and in next ch-1 sp, ch 1] rep across, ending with jt dc over last ch-1 sp and last sc, fasten off, do not turn.

Row 6: With RS facing, attach black with a sl st in top of beg jt dc, ch 1, sc in same st, [sc in next ch-1 sp, ch 1] rep across, ending with sc in last ch-1 sp, sc in last jt dc, fasten off, do not turn.

Row 7: With RS facing, attach red with a sl st in beg sc of previous row, ch 3 (counts as first dc), jt dc over same sc and next ch-1 sp, ch 1, [jt dc in same sp as 2nd leg of last jt dc and in next ch-1 sp, ch 1] rep across, ending with jt dc over last ch-1 sp and last sc, dc in last sc, fasten off, do not turn.

Row 8: With RS facing, attach gray with a sl st in 3rd ch of beg ch-3, ch 1, sc in same st, [ch 1, sc in next ch-1 sp] rep across, ending with ch 1, sc in last sc, fasten off, do not turn.

Rows 9–16: Rep Rows 5–8, working in the following color sequence: [1 row black, 1 row red, 1 row gray] twice, 1 row black, 1 row red.

BODY
Row 17: With RS facing, attach red with a sl st in first sc of Row 16, ch 3 (counts as first dc throughout), work 98(104)(112) more dc in ch-1 sps evenly sp across, turn. (99, 105, 113 dc)

Rows 18–24(26)(28): Work in Body Patt on 99(105)(113) sts.

RIGHT FRONT
Row 25(27)(29): Ch 3, continuing in Body Patt, dc dec, [dc between next 2 dc] 15(16)(18) times, dc dec, sk next dc, dc in top of next dc, leave rem sts unworked, turn. (19, 20, 22 sts)

Rows 26(28)(30)–37(39)(41): Continuing in Body Patt, [dec 1 st at neck edge every row] 12 times, at the same time, [dec 1 st at armhole edge every other row] 2(2)(3) more times, fasten off. (5, 6, 7 sts at end of last row)

LEFT FRONT

With WS facing, attach red in first dc at left front edge, work as for right front.

BACK

Row 25(27)(29): With RS facing, sk next 12 dc on Row 24(26)(28), continuing in Body Patt, attach red with a sl st in next dc, ch 3, [dc between next 2 dc] 32(36)(40) times, turn. (33, 37, 41 sts)

Rows 26(28)(30)–31(33)(37): Continuing in Body Patt, dec 1 st at each edge every other row, turn. (27, 31, 33 sts at end of last row)

Rows 32(34)(38)–36(38)(40): Work even in Body Patt on 27(31)(33) sts.

Row 37(39)(41): Ch 3, dc between first and 2nd dc, [dc between next 2 dc] 3(4)(5) times, [hdc between next 2 dc] rep across to last 6(7)(8) dc, [dc between next 2 dc] 5(6)(7) times, fasten off.

Join front to back at shoulders.

With RS facing, attach red with a sl st at center of underarm, sl st evenly sp around armhole, join in beg sl st, fasten off.

Rep for 2nd armhole.

EDGING

Row 1: With RS facing, attach red with a sl st at lower right front corner, ch 1, 38(42)(46) sc evenly sp to first dec row, 3 sc in next st (corner), 21 sc evenly sp across neckline to shoulder seam, 18(20)(22) sc across neck to opposite shoulder seam, 21 sc evenly sp to first dec row at left front edge, 3 sc in next st (corner), 38(42)(46) sc evenly sp to lower left front corner, ch 1, turn.

Row 2: Sc in each sc across, working 3 sc in center sc of each corner, ch 1, turn.

Buttonholes

Row 3: Sc in each of first 2 sc, *ch 2, sk 2 sc **, sc in each of next 7(8)(9) sc, rep from * 4 times, ending 4th rep at **, 3 sc in next corner sc, sc in each rem sc across, working 3 sc in 2nd corner, ch 1, turn.

Row 4: Sc in each sc across, working 3 sc in each corner and 2 sc in each ch-2 sp, turn.

Row 5: Sl st in each sc across, working [sl st, ch 1] in each corner st, fasten off.

FINISHING

With tapestry needle and black yarn, sew black buttons to left front edge to correspond with buttonholes.

Beg with square button placed approximately 1" from black button at neck edge, alternating rem round and square buttons approximately 1½" apart around neck edge, sew wooden buttons on as follows: With tapestry needle and black yarn, bring needle from WS through vest and first hole in button, leaving end at WS for tying. Make French knot; insert needle through 2nd hole in button to WS of vest. Cut yarn, leaving end for tying; tie ends securely.

—Designed by Ann E. Smith
for Monsanto's Designs for America Program

Basket-Weave Pullover

EXPERIENCE LEVEL

Advanced

SIZE

Ladies small/medium(large/extra-large) Unless stated otherwise, instructions are given for smaller size, with larger size in parentheses. When only 1 number is given, it applies to both sizes.

FINISHED MEASUREMENTS

Chest: 37(40)"

Length: 20½(22)"

MATERIALS

- Schaefer Yarns Danya 78 percent mohair/13 percent wool/9 percent nylon yarn: 15 oz/900 yds
- Metallic/rayon blend filler fiber
- Size J/10 crochet hook
- Size J/10 (14") afghan hook
- Size K/10½ (14") afghan hook or size needed to obtain gauge
- Blunt tapestry needle

GAUGE

15 sts and 13 rows = 5" in center panel basket-weave patt using larger afghan hook

To save time, take time to check gauge.

PATTERN NOTES

Each row consists of 2 parts: Working from right to left, retaining all lps on hook, pick up sts as indicated (first part), do not turn; working from left to right, cast off sts (2nd part).

Lp that rems on hook at end of 2nd part of each row counts as first st of next row; therefore, beg each row in 2nd st of last row.

Metallic/rayon blend filler fiber is very fine and adds just a hint of glitter. Any filler fiber that is about the size of sewing thread may be used without affecting gauge.

Join rnds with a sl st unless otherwise stated.

PATTERN STITCHES

Afghan Knit St (AKS): Retaining all lps on hook, [holding yarn at back of work, insert hook from front to back between front and back lps of next vertical bar, draw up a lp] rep across number of sts indicated.

Afghan Purl St (APS): Retaining all lps on hook, [holding yarn in front of work below working row, insert hook under next vertical bar from right to left, draw up a lp] rep across number of sts indicated.

Cast off (CO): Yo, draw through first lp on hook, [yo, draw through 2 lps on hook] rep across to end of row (1 lp rems on hook).

Bind off in patt (BO): [Insert hook into next vertical bar as for patt st of previous row, yo, draw through bar and lp on hook (sl st made; 1 lp rem on hook)] rep across as indicated, fasten off.

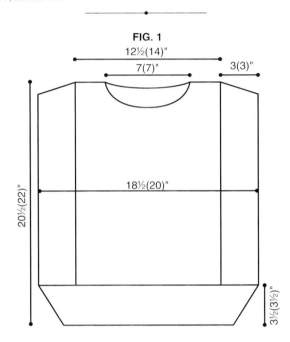

FIG. 1

BACK PANEL

Foundation Row: With larger afghan hook, ch 37(42), retaining all lps on hook, draw up lp in 2nd ch from hook and in each rem ch across (37, 42 lps on hook), CO.

Rows 1–5(6): [AKS over next 7(8) sts, APS over next 7(8) sts] twice, AKS over next 8(9) sts (37, 42 lps on hook), CO.

Rows 6(7)–10(12): [APS over next 7(8) sts, AKS over next 7(8) sts] twice, APS over next 7(8) sts, AKS over next st (37, 42 lps on hook), CO.

Rows 11(13)–40(44): Rep Rows 1–10(12) for basket-weave patt, ending with Row 10(8).

Right side back neck shaping

Row 41(45): Work in patt over next 8(11) sts (9, 12 lps on hook), yo, draw through first 2 lps on hook (mid-row dec made), CO.

Row 42(46): Work in patt over next 7(10) sts (8, 11 lps on hook), CO.

Row 43(47): Work in patt over next 7(10) sts (8, 11 lps on hook), mid-row dec, CO.

Row 44(48): Work in patt over next 6(9) sts (7, 10 lps on hook), CO, fasten off, leaving 4 yds for finishing.

Left side back neck shaping

Row 41(45): Sk next 19(18) sts on Row 40(44), work in patt over rem 9(12) sts, CO until 3 lps rem on hook, yo, draw through all 3 lps (end-of-row dec made). (1 lp on hook)

Row 42(46): Work in patt over next 7(10) sts (8, 11 lps on hook), CO.

Row 43(47): Work in patt over next 7(10) sts (8, 11 lps on hook), CO, working end-of-row dec on last 3 lps. (1 lp on hook)

Row 44(48): Work in patt over next 6(9) sts (7, 10 lps on hook), CO, fasten off.

Finishing

Return to right neck edge, pick up unworked lp, BO across right shoulder, around neck edge and across left shoulder, fasten off.

Weave in loose ends.

FRONT PANEL

Foundation Row: Work as for back panel.

Rows 1–36(40): Rep Rows 1–36(40) of back panel, ending with Row 6(4).

Left side front neck shaping

Row 37(41): Work in patt over next 10(13) sts (11, 14 lps on hook), mid-row dec, CO.

Row 38(42): Work in patt over next 9(12) sts (10, 13 lps on hook), CO.

Row 39(43): Work in patt over next 9(12) sts (10, 13 lps on hook), mid-row dec, CO.

Row 40(44): Work in patt over next 8(11) sts (9, 12 lps on hook), CO.

Row 41(45): Work in patt over next 8(11) sts (9, 12 lps on hook), mid-row dec, CO.

Row 42(46): Work in patt over next 7(10) sts (8, 11 lps on hook), CO.

Row 43(47): Work in patt over next 7(10) sts (8, 11 lps on hook), mid-row dec, CO.

Row 44(48): Work in patt over next 6(9) sts (7, 10 lps on hook), CO, fasten off, leaving 4 yds for finishing.

Right side front neck shaping

Row 37(41): Sk next 15(14) sts on Row 36(40), work in patt over rem 11(14) sts, CO, working end-of-row dec on last 3 lps. (1 lp on hook)

Row 38(42): Work in patt over next 9(12) sts (10, 13 lps on hook), CO.

Row 39(43): Work in patt over next 9(12) sts, CO, working end-of-row dec on last 3 lps. (1 lp on hook)

Row 40(44): Work in patt over next 8(11) sts (9, 12 lps on hook), CO.

Row 41(45): Work in patt over next 8(11) sts (9, 12 lps on hook), CO, working end-of-row dec on last 3 lps. (1 lp on hook)

Row 42(46): Work in patt over next 7(10) sts (8, 11 lps on hook), CO.

Row 43(47): Work in patt over next 7(10) sts (8, 11 lps on hook), CO, working end-of-row dec on last 3 lps. (1 lp on hook)

Row 44(48): Work in patt over next 6(9) sts, CO, fasten off.

Finishing

Return to left neck edge, pick up unworked lp, BO across left shoulder, around neck edge and across right shoulder, fasten off.

Weave in loose ends.

SIDE PANELS

Row 1: With larger afghan hook, RS facing, pull up a lp in end st of each row, including foundation row, along either side edge of front panel (45, 49 lps on hook), CO.

Row 2: AKS over next 44(48) sts (45, 49 lps on hook), CO, working mid-row or end-of-row dec as appropriate at shoulder edge.

Row 3: AKS over next 43(47) sts (44, 48 lps on hook), CO.

Row 4: AKS over next 43(47) sts (44, 48 lps on hook), CO, working dec at shoulder edge as in Row 2.

Row 5: AKS over next 42(46) sts (43, 47 lps on hook), CO.

Row 6: AKS over next 42(46) sts, (43, 47 lps on hook), CO, working dec at shoulder edge as in Row 2.

Row 7: AKS in each of next 41(45) sts (42, 46 lps on hook), CO.

Row 8: Changing to smaller afghan hook, APS in each of next 41(45) sts (42, 46 lps on hook), CO, fasten off.

Rep Rows 1–8 on opposite side edge of front panel and both side edges of back panel.

JOINING SHOULDER SEAMS

Note: *Needle must pass through 2 lps of yarn from each st to avoid forming holes. Do not lace too tightly or too loosely. Have edges just touching so that stitching forms a seam line that mimics purl st created in crochet.*

Lay front and back garment pieces side by side on flat surface, shoulder to shoulder, with RS facing up.

Beg at outside shoulder edge, with blunt yarn needle and same yarn used in pattern, beg lacing shoulder edges tog as you would a pair of shoes, alternating sts from 1 edge to the other, inserting needle from RS to WS.

Rep for opposite shoulder seam.

JOINING SIDE SEAMS

Note: *It is important to insert hook into sp between lps of APS and carry both the top threads of the APS into the seam. Do not pull too tightly, but keep the edges just touching as you work.*

Lay garment RS up on flat surface with side seams meeting.

Beg at bottom edge with crochet hook, attach yarn with a sl st in first APS of side panel on your right.

Insert hook from RS to WS of corresponding st on left side panel, hook yarn from underneath and draw up through fabric and through lp on hook (sl st made).

Work another sl st in same manner back to same st on right side panel.

Continue in same manner, working only 1 sl st in each APS st and alternating sl sts from 1 edge to the other until approximately 15 APS are joined.

Rep for opposite side seam.

NECK EDGE

Rnd 1: With RS facing and crochet hook, attach yarn with a sl st near 1 shoulder seam, ch 1, sc in same sp, 63 more sc evenly sp around neck edge, join in beg sc, do not turn. (64 sc)

Rnd 2: Ch 2 (counts as first hdc), hdc in each rem sc around, join in 2nd ch of beg ch-2, ch 1, do not turn. (64 hdc)

Rnd 3: Sc in each hdc around, join in beg sc, ch 1, do not turn. (64 sc)

Rnd 4: Sc in each sc around, join in beg sc, ch 1, turn. (64 sc)

Rnd 5: Sl st in each sc around, join in beg sl st, fasten off.

BOTTOM EDGE

Rnd 1: With RS facing and crochet hook, attach yarn with a sl st near 1 side seam, ch 1, sc in same sp, [sc dec, sc in next sc] rep around, join in beg sc, ch 1, do not turn.

Rnd 2: Sc in each sc around, join in beg sc, do not turn.

Rnd 3: Ch 2, hdc in each sc around, join in 2nd ch of beg ch-2, ch 1, do not turn.

Rnds 4–10: Rep Rnds 2 and 3 alternately, ending with Rnd 2, at end of last rnd, ch 1, turn.

Rnd 11: Sl st in each sc around, join in beg sc, fasten off.

—Designed by Bobbi Hayward

Beaded Fringe Vest

EXPERIENCE LEVEL
Intermediate

SIZE
Women's size small

FINISHED MEASUREMENTS
Chest: 33½"

Length: 20" including fringe

MATERIALS
- South Maid® crochet cotton size 10 (350 yds per ball): 3 balls spruce #479
- Size D/3 crochet hook or size needed to obtain gauge
- 432 tan pony beads
- 3 (¾") wooden buttons
- Long tapestry needle
- 1 yd 1"-wide jute braid trim

GAUGE

33 dc = 5"; [1 dc row, 1 sc row] 6 times = 2½"

To save time, take time to check gauge.

PATTERN NOTE

Join rnds with a sl st unless otherwise stated.

———————•———————

BACK

Row 1: Beg at bottom, ch 80, dc in 4th ch from hook and in each rem ch across, ch 1, turn. (78 dc, counting last 3 chs of foundation ch as first dc)

Row 2: Sc in each dc across, turn. (78 sc)

Row 3: Ch 3 (counts as first dc throughout), dc in next sc, 2 dc in next sc, dc in each sc across to last 3 sc, 2 dc in next sc, dc in each of last 2 sc, ch 1, turn. (80 dc)

Rows 4–34: Rep Rows 2 and 3 alternately, ending with Row 2. (Piece meas approximately 7¼" from beg; 110 sts on Rows 33 and 34)

Armhole shaping

Row 35: Ch 3, dc in next sc, [dc dec] 3 times, dc in each rem sc across to last 8 sc, [dc dec] 3 times, dc in each of last 2 sc, ch 1, turn. (104 sts)

Row 36: Sc in each st across, turn.

Rows 37–44: Rep Rows 35 and 36 alternately. (80 sts on Rows 43 and 44)

Row 45: Ch 3, dc in next sc, dc dec, dc in each rem sc across to last 4 sts, dc dec, dc in each of last 2 sc, ch 1, turn. (78 sts)

Row 46: Rep Row 36. (78 sc)

Row 47: Ch 3, dc in each rem sc across, ch 1, turn. (78 dc)

Rows 48–78: Rep Rows 46 and 47 alternately, ending with Row 46.

Neck shaping

Row 79: Ch 3, dc in each of next 15 sc, tr in each of next 9 sc, ch 1, turn. (25 sts)

Row 80: Sc in each st across, turn. (25 sc)

Row 81: Ch 3, dc in each of next 8 sc, [dc dec] 3 times, tr in each of next 10 sc, ch 1, turn. (22 sts)

Row 82: Sc in each st across, fasten off. (22 sc)

Beg at outer edge of Row 78, rep Rows 79–82 for opposite side.

RIGHT FRONT

Row 1: Beg at bottom, ch 44, dc in 4th ch from hook and in each ch across, ch 1, turn. (42 dc, counting last 3 chs of foundation ch as first dc)

Row 2: Sc in each dc across, turn. (42 sc)

Row 3: Ch 3, dc in next st, 2 dc in next st, dc in each rem st across, ch 1, turn. (43 dc)

Rows 4–13: Rep Rows 2 and 3 alternately, ending with Row 3. (48 dc at end of Row 13)

Row 14 (buttonhole): Sc in each of first 4 dc, ch 5, sk 5 dc, sc in each rem dc across, turn. (48 sts)

Rows 15–27: Rep Row 3, then rep Rows 2 and 3 alternately. (55 dc at end of Row 27)

Row 28 (buttonhole): Rep Row 14. (55 sts)

Rows 29–34: Rep Row 3, then rep Rows 2 and 3 alternately, ending with Row 2. (58 sts on Rows 33 and 34)

Armhole shaping

Row 35: Ch 3, dc in next st, [dc dec] 3 times, dc in each rem st across, ch 1, turn. (55 sts)

Row 36: Sc in each st across, turn. (55 sc)

Rows 37–41: Rep Rows 35 and 36 twice, then rep Row 35. (46 sts on Row 41)

Row 42 (buttonhole): Rep Row 14. (46 sts)

Rows 43 & 44: Rep Rows 35 and 36. (43 sts)

Row 45: Ch 3, dc in next st, dc dec, dc in each rem st across, ch 1, turn. (42 sts)

Row 46: Rep Row 36. (42 sc)

Neck shaping

Row 47: Ch 3, dc in each rem st across to last 8 sts, [dc dec] 3 times, dc in each of last 2 sts, ch 1, turn. (39 sts)

Rows 48–58: Rep Rows 46 and 47 alternately, ending with Row 46. (24 sts on Rows 57 and 58)

Row 59: Ch 3, dc in each rem st across to last 6 sts, [dc dec] twice, dc in each of last 2 sts, ch 1, turn. (22 sts)

Row 60: Rep Row 36. (22 sc)

Row 61: Ch 3, dc in each rem st across, ch 1, turn. (22 dc)

Rows 62–78: Rep Rows 60 and 61 alternately, ending with Row 60.

Row 79: Ch 3, dc in each of next 11 sts, tr in each of next 10 sts, ch 1, turn. (22 sts)

Row 80: Rep Row 60. (22 sc)

Rows 81 & 82: Rep Rows 79 and 80, fasten off at end of Row 82.

LEFT FRONT

Row 1: Rep Row 1 of right front.

Row 2: Sc in each st across, ch 1, turn. (42 sc)

Row 3: Ch 3, dc in each rem st across to last 3 sts, 2 dc in next st, dc in each of next 2 sts, ch 1, turn. (43 dc)

Rows 4–34: Rep Rows 2 and 3 alternately, ending with Row 2. (58 sts on Rows 33 and 34)

Rows 35–41: Rep Rows 35–41 of right front, reversing shaping.

Row 42: Rep Row 2 of right front. (48 sc)

Rows 43–82: Rep Rows 43–82 of right front, reversing shaping, beg Rows 79 and 81 with ch 4 for first tr.

Sew shoulder and side seams.

FINISHING

Armhole edging

Rnd 1: Attach thread at armhole with a sl st, ch 1, sc evenly around, join in beg sc, ch 1, do not turn.

Rnd 2: Rev sc in each sc around, join in beg rev sc, fasten off. Rep for rem armhole.

Button band

Row 1: With RS facing, attach thread on left front where neck shaping beg, ch 1, sc evenly sp down front, ch 1, turn.

Rows 2–4: Sc in each sc across, ch 1, turn, do not fasten off at end of Row 4, ch 1, turn.

Outer edging

Sc down left front, sc across bottom edge, sc evenly sp up right front and around neckline, working 3 sc in each corner, join in beg sc, do not turn, ch 1.

Rev sc in each sc around, join in beg rev sc, fasten off.

Pony beads

With long tapestry needle, beg at either bottom corner, sew 54 (8-bead) strands of beads evenly sp across bottom.

Buttons

Mark button placement; sew buttons on with crochet cotton and tapestry needle.

Trim

With tapestry needle and crochet cotton, sew jute braid trim around bottom over Rows 3–8.

—Designed by Jo Ann Burrington

Geometric Stripes

EXPERIENCE LEVEL
Intermediate

SIZE
Boy's size 6–8(8–10)(12)(14) Instructions are given for smallest size, with larger sizes in parentheses. When only 1 number is given, it applies to all sizes.

FINISHED MEASUREMENTS
Chest: 30(33)(36)(39)"

Length: 16(18)(20)(22)"

MATERIALS
- Brunswick® Fore 'N Aft Sport® 100 percent Monsanto acrylic yarn (175 yds/50 grams per skein): 3(4)(4)(4) skeins beige heather #6028 (MC), 1(1)(2)(2) skein(s) teal #6051 (CC), 1(1)(2)(2) skein(s) green #6044 (CC) and 1 skein black #6013 (CC)
- Size F/5 crochet hook or size needed to obtain gauge
- Crochet hook 3 sizes smaller than hook used for gauge

GAUGE
31 sts = 8"; Rows 3–13 = 4" in Stripe Patt with larger hook

To save time, take time to check gauge.

PATTERN NOTES
Join rnds with a sl st unless otherwise stated.

To change color in dc, work last dc before color change until 2 lps rem on hook, drop working color to WS, yo with next color, complete dc.

Carry MC loosely across WS when not in use, working over it with CC.

Carry CC loosely across WS when not in use; do not work over it with MC.

PATTERN STITCH

Stripe Pattern

Row 1 (RS): With MC, ch 3 (counts as first dc throughout), *dc in each of next 3 sts, changing to indicated CC in 3rd st, dc in each of next 3 sts, changing to MC in 3rd st, rep from * across, ending with dc in each of last 4 sts with MC, turn.

Row 2: Ch 3, dc in each of next 4 sts, changing to indicated CC in 4th st, *dc in next st, changing to MC, dc in each of next 5 sts, changing to indicated CC in 5th st, rep from * across, ending with dc in each of last 5 sts with MC, fasten off CC, ch 1, turn.

Row 3: Sc in each dc across, fasten off, do not turn.

Row 4: With RS facing, attach indicated CC with a sl st in first sc, ch 1, sc in same sc and in each rem sc across, fasten off CC, attach MC in last sc, ch 1, turn.

Row 5: Sc in each sc across, turn.

Rep Rows 1–5 for patt, alternating stripes in following CC sequence for each 5-row rep: teal, black, teal, green.

BACK

Foundation Row (WS): Beg above ribbing at lower edge, with larger hook and MC, ch 60(66)(72)(78), sc in 2nd ch from hook and in each rem ch across, turn. (59, 65, 71, 77 sc)

Rows 1–39(44)(49)(54): Work Rows 1–5 of Stripe Patt 7(8)(9)(10) times, then rep Rows 1–4 once, ending with green(teal)(black)(teal) as CC on last row, fasten off. (8, 9, 10, 11 stripes)

FRONT

Work as for back through Row 35(40)(45)(50).

Left shoulder

Row 36(41)(46)(51): With RS facing, continuing in Stripe Patt, ch 3, dc in each of next 20(22)(25)(27) sts, hdc in next st, sc in next st, ch 1, turn. (23, 25, 28, 30 sts)

Row 37(42)(47)(52): Continuing in Stripe Patt, sk sc, sc in next hdc, hdc in next dc, dc in each rem dc across, changing to MC in last dc, ch 1, turn. (22, 24, 27, 29 sts)

Row 38(43)(48)(53): With MC, sc in each of first 20(22)(25)(27) dc, changing to appropriate CC in last dc, ch 1, turn.

Row 39(44)(49)(54): Sc in each sc across, fasten off.

Right shoulder

Row 36(41)(46)(51): Sk next 13(15)(15)(17) unworked sts of Row 35(40)(45)(50), with RS facing, continuing in Stripe Patt, attach appropriate CC with a sl st in next st, ch 1, sc in same st as joining, hdc in next st, dc in each of last 21(23)(26)(28) sts, turn. (23, 25, 28, 30 sts)

Row 37(42)(47)(52): Continuing in Stripe Patt, ch 3 (counts as first dc), dc in each of next 19(21)(24)(26) sts, hdc in next st, sc in next st, changing to MC, ch 1, turn. (22, 24, 27, 29 sts)

Rows 38(43)(48)(53) & 39(44)(49)(54): Rep Rows 38(43)(48)(53) and 39(44)(49)(54) of left shoulder.

Join front to back at shoulder seams.

NECK BAND

Rnd 1: With RS facing, using larger hook, attach black with a sl st at right shoulder seam, ch 1, beg in same st, work 64(68)(68)(72) sc evenly sp around neck, join in beg sc, fasten off.

Rnd 2: With RS facing and smaller hook, attach green with a sl st in first sc, ch 3 (counts as first dc throughout), dc in each sc around, join in 3rd ch of beg ch-3.

Rnd 3: Ch 3, *fpdc in next dc, bpdc in next dc, rep from * around, ending with fpdc in last dc, join in 3rd ch of beg ch-3, fasten off.

SLEEVE

Make 2

Foundation Row (WS): Beg above cuff at lower edge, with larger hook and MC, ch 38(40)(40)(40), sc in 2nd ch from hook and in each rem ch across, turn. (37, 39, 39, 39 sc)

Row 1 (RS): Ch 3 (counts as first dc), dc in each of next 4(5)(5)(5) sts, changing to teal in 4th(5th)(5th)(5th) st, *dc in each of next 3 sts, changing to MC in 3rd st **, dc in each of next 3 sts, changing to teal in 3rd st, rep from * across, ending last rep at **, dc in each of last 5(6)(6)(6) sts with MC, turn.

Rows 2–24(29)(34)(39): Continuing in Stripe Patt, inc 1 st each edge on every MC sc row, ending with Row 4, fasten off at end of last row. (55, 61, 65, 69 sts; 5, 6, 7, 8 stripes)

Place markers 8(8½)(9)(9½)" from each shoulder seam. Set in sleeves between markers.

Join underarm and side seams.

Cuff

Rnd 1: With RS facing, using larger hook, attach black with a sl st in seam, ch 1, beg in same st, work 34(36)(36)(36) sc evenly sp around, join in front lp only of beg sc.

Rnd 2: Ch 1, sl st in front lp of each sc around, fasten off.

Rnd 3: With RS facing, using smaller hook, attach green with a sl st in rem back lp of Rnd 1, ch 3 (counts as first dc), working in back lps only, 27(29)(29)(31) dc evenly sp around, join in 3rd ch of beg ch-3. (28, 30, 30, 32 dc)

Rnd 4: Rep Rnd 3 of neck band.

LOWER RIBBING

Rnd 1: With RS facing, using smaller hook, attach green with a sl st in either side seam, ch 3 (counts as first dc throughout), working along rem foundation chs, dc in each ch around, join in 3rd ch of beg ch-3. (118, 130, 142, 154 dc)

Rnd 2: Rep Rnd 3 of neck band, do not fasten off.

Rnd 3: Ch 3, [fpdc over fpdc, bpdc over bpdc] rep around, ending with fpdc over fpdc, join in 3rd ch of beg ch-3, fasten off.

—Designed by Ann E. Smith
for Monsanto's Designs for America Program

Pineapple Lace Vest

EXPERIENCE LEVEL
Intermediate

SIZE
Ladies' small(medium)(large) Instructions are given for smallest size, with larger sizes in parentheses. When only 1 number is given, it applies to all sizes.

FINISHED MEASUREMENTS
Chest: 38(42)(46)"

MATERIALS
- J. & P. Coats Luster Sheen® sport weight yarn (1¾ oz/50 grams per ball): 10(12)(14) balls vanilla #007
- Size C/2(D/3)(E/4) crochet hook or size needed to obtain gauge
- 3 (1)" toggle buttons
- Tapestry needle

GAUGE
28(26)(24) sts = 4" in Body Patt

To save time, take time to check gauge.

PATTERN NOTE
Vest is begun at waist, working fronts and back separately in Pineapple Patt downward to bottom hem. Pieces are then joined as sts are worked into rem lps of foundation ch, and top of vest is worked from waist upward.

PATTERN STITCHES
Shell: [2 dc, ch 2, 2 dc] in indicated st.

V-st: [Dc, ch 1, dc] in indicated st.

Pineapple Pattern (multiple of 24 sts + 2)

Row 1 (RS): Sc in 2nd ch from hook, ch 4, sk next ch, sc in next ch, *ch 3, sk next 5 chs, shell in next ch, ch 2, sk next 2 chs, dc in each of next 3 chs, ch 2, sk next 2 chs, shell in next ch, ch 3, sk next 5 chs **, [sc in next ch, ch 4, sk next ch] twice, sc in next ch, rep from * across, ending last rep at **, sc in next ch, ch 4, sk next ch, sc in last ch, turn.

Row 2: Ch 6 (counts as first tr, ch-2 throughout), *sc in next ch-4 sp, ch 3, shell in ch-2 sp of next shell (shell in shell

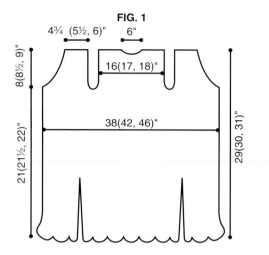

FIG. 1

4¾ (5½, 6)"   6"

16(17, 18)"

8(8½, 9)"

38(42, 46)"

21(21½, 22)"

29(30, 31)"

made), ch 2, 2 dc in next ch-2 sp, dc in each of next 3 dc, 2 dc in next ch-2 sp, ch 2, shell in next shell, ch 3, sc in next ch-4 sp, ch 4, rep from * across to last ch-4 sp, sc in last ch-4 sp, ch 2, tr in last sc, ch 1, turn.

Row 3: Sc in tr, *ch 3, shell in next shell, ch 2, 2 dc in next ch-2 sp, dc in each of next 7 dc, 2 dc in next ch-2 sp, ch 2, shell in next shell, ch 3, sk ch-3 sp, sc in next ch-4 sp, rep from * across, ending with sc in 4th of turning ch-6, turn.

Row 4: Ch 4 (counts as first tr), *shell in next shell, ch 3, sk next ch-2 sp, [sc in next dc, ch 4, sk next dc] 5 times, sc in next dc, ch 3, shell in next shell, ch 2, rep from * across, ending with shell in last shell, tr in last sc, turn.

Row 5: Ch 3 (counts as first dc throughout), *shell in next shell, ch 3, sk next ch-3 sp, [sc in next ch-4 sp, ch 4] 4 times, sc in next ch-4 sp, ch 3, shell in next shell, ch 2, rep from * across, ending with shell in last shell, dc in 4th ch of turning ch-4, turn.

Row 6: Ch 4 (counts as first dc, ch-1), *shell in next shell, ch 3, sk next ch-3 sp, [sc in next ch-4 sp, ch 4] 3 times, sc in next ch-4 sp, ch 3, shell in next shell, ch 3, rep from * across, ending with shell in last shell, ch 1, dc in 3rd ch of turning ch-3, turn.

Row 7: Ch 3, dc in same st, *ch 2, shell in next shell, ch 3, sk next ch-3 sp, [sc in next ch-4 sp, ch 4] twice, sc in next ch-4 sp, ch 3, shell in next shell, ch 2, 3 dc in next ch-3 sp, rep from * across, ending with shell in last shell, ch 2, 2 dc in 3rd ch of turning ch-4, turn.

Row 8: Ch 3, dc in next dc, *2 dc in next ch-2 sp, ch 2, shell in next shell, ch 3, sk next ch-3 sp, sc in next ch-4 sp, ch 4, sc in next ch-4 sp, ch 3, shell in next shell, ch 2, 2 dc in next ch-2 sp **, dc in each of next 3 dc, rep from * across, ending last rep at **, dc in each of last 2 sts, turn.

Row 9: Ch 3, dc in each of next 3 dc, *2 dc in next ch-2 sp, ch 2, shell in next shell, ch 3, sk next ch-3 sp, sc in next ch-4 sp, ch 3, shell in next shell, ch 2, 2 dc in next ch-2 sp **, dc in each of next 7 dc, rep from * across, ending last rep at **, dc in each of next 4 dc, turn.

Row 10: Ch 4 (counts as first hdc, ch-2), [sc in next dc, ch 4, sk next dc] twice, *sc in next dc, ch 3, shell in next shell, ch 2, shell in next shell, ch 3, sk next ch-2 sp **, [sc in next dc, ch 4, sk next dc] 5 times, rep from * across, ending last rep at **, sc in next dc, [ch 4, sk next dc, sc in next dc] twice, ch 2, hdc in last st, ch 1, turn.

Row 11: Sc in hdc, [ch 4, sc in next ch-4 sp] twice, *ch 3, shell in next shell, ch 2, shell in next shell, ch 3, sk next ch-3 sp **, [sc in next ch-4 sp, ch 4] 4 times, sc in next ch-4 sp, rep from * across, ending last rep at **, [sc in next ch-4 sp, ch 4] twice, sc in 2nd ch of turning ch-4, turn.

Row 12: Ch 6, sc in first ch-4 sp, ch 4, *sc in next ch-4 sp, [ch 3, shell in next shell] twice, ch 3, sk next ch-3 sp **, [sc in next ch-4 sp, ch 4] 3 times, rep from * across, ending last rep at **, sc in next ch-4 sp, ch 4, sc in next ch-4 sp, ch 2, tr in last sc, ch 1, turn.

Row 13: Sc in tr, ch 4, *sc in next ch-4 sp, ch 3, shell in next shell, ch 2, 3 dc in next ch-3 sp, ch 2, shell in next shell, ch 3, sk next ch-3 sp **, [sc in next ch-4 sp, ch 4] twice, rep from * across, ending last rep at **, sc in next ch-4 sp, ch 4, sc in 4th ch of turning ch-6, turn.

Rep Rows 2–13 for patt.

Body Pattern (multiple of 6 sts +2)

Row 1 (RS): Ch 3 (counts as first dc throughout), sk next st, V-st in next st, [sk 2 sts, 3 dc in next st, sk 2 sts, V-st in next st] rep across to last 5 sts, sk 2 sts, 3 dc in next st, sk 1 st, dc in last st, turn.

Row 2 (WS): Ch 3, [3 dc in center dc of next 3-dc group, V-st in ch-1 sp of next V-st (V-st in V-st made)], rep across, ending with dc in 3rd ch of turning ch-3, turn.

Row 3: Ch 3, [V-st in next V-st, 3 dc in center dc of next 3-dc group] rep across, ending with dc in 3rd ch of turning ch-3, turn.

Rep Rows 2 and 3 for patt.

Note: *To dec at beg or end of row in Body Patt, work 1 less st in rem sts of first or last 3-dc group or V-st than was worked on previous row.*

---•---

B A C K

Ch 146, work in Pineapple Patt for 25 rows, ch 1, turn at end of last row.

Edging

Row 1: Sc in each ch, sc and dc across, ch 1, turn.

Row 2: Sc in first sc, [ch 3, sk next sc, sc in next sc] rep across, fasten off.

F R O N T S

Make 2

Ch 74, work Pineapple Patt for 25 rows, ch 1, turn at end of last row.

Edging

Rows 1 & 2: Rep Rows 1 and 2 of edging for back.

JOINING

With WS facing, attach yarn in rem lp of first st of foundation ch of either front, ch 1, working in rem lps of foundation chs of first front, back and 2nd front, sc across, sk 25(19)(13) chs evenly sp across, turn. (266, 272, 278 sc)

Work Row 1 of Body Patt. (266, 272, 278 sts, counting beg ch-3 and ch-1 sps as sts throughout)

Continue working in Body Patt on all sts until 21(21½)(22)" from bottom of pineapple border, ending with a WS row.

Divide for armholes

Work 60(62)(64) sts in Body Patt across, ending with: 2 dc in center dc of 3-dc group for size small, dc in ch-1 sp of V-st for size medium, and V-st in V-st for size large; turn, leaving rem sts unworked.

RIGHT FRONT YOKE

[Dec 1 st at armhole edge every row] 6(8)(10) times, *at same time*, when 22(23)(24)" from beg, [dec at neck edge 1 st every row] 20(18)(16) times, continue on 34(36)(38) sts until 29(30)(31)" from beg, ending with a WS row, fasten off.

BACK YOKE

Sk next 2(1)(2) unworked V-sts and first 2(3)(1) dc of next 3-dc group, attach yarn with a sl st in next dc(V-st sp)(dc), ch 3, 0(1)(2) dc in same st, continue across in Body Patt until a total of 122(124)(126) sts has been worked, ending with dc in ch-1 sp of V-st(2 dc in center dc of 3-dc group)(V-st in V-st), turn.

[Dec 1 st at each edge of every row] 6(7)(8) times, continue in Body Patt on 110 sts until back meas same length as right front yoke, fasten off.

LEFT FRONT YOKE

Sk next 1(2)(2) unworked V-sts and first 3(2)(1) dc of next 3-dc group, attach yarn with a sl st in ch-1 sp of next V-st for size small, and in next dc for sizes medium and large, ch 3, 1(0)(2) dc in same st, continue across to end of row in Body Patt, turn. (60, 62, 64 sts)

Complete as for right front yoke.

Sew shoulder seams.

FINISHING

Edgings

With RS facing, attach yarn with a sl st at lower right front corner, ch 1, sc in same st, *ch 4, sk ½", sc in next sp, rep from * to bottom of left front, fasten off.

Rep around armholes.

Buttons

Sew buttons to left front, placing first button ½" below first neck dec and rem buttons 2½" apart.

Button through corresponding ch-4 sps on right front.

Weave in loose ends. Block as necessary according to yarn label instructions.

—Designed by Maureen Egan Emlet

Tapestry Scarf & Hat

EXPERIENCE LEVEL

Beginner

SIZE

Scarf: 6" x 46" excluding fringe

Hat: Adult

MATERIALS

- Bernat® Berella "4"® worsted weight yarn (3½ oz per skein): 1 skein dark antique rose #8817
- Bernat® Caress® variegated mohair-look yarn (2½ oz per skein): 2 skeins tapestry #6202
- Size G/6 crochet hook or size needed to obtain gauge
- 4" piece of cardboard

GAUGE

Scarf: Rows 1–3 = 1"; [{sc, ch 5} twice, sc] = 3"

Hat: 4 sc and Rnds 1–4 = 1⅛"

To save time, take time to check gauge.

PATTERN NOTES

Leave 9" length of yarn when beg each row and when fastening off, to be worked into fringe.

Join rnds with a sl st unless otherwise stated.

Scarf

Row 1 (RS): With tapestry, ch 206, sc in 2nd ch from hook, *ch 5, sk 5 chs, sc in next ch, rep from * across, fasten off, do not turn. (34 ch-5 sps)

Row 2: Attach dark antique rose with a sl st in first sc, ch 1, sc in same sc, [ch 5, sc in next sc] rep across, fasten off, do not turn.

Row 3: Attach tapestry with a sl st in first sc, ch 1, sc in same sc, [ch 2, sc over ch-5 sps of 2 rows directly below, ch 2, sc in next sc] rep across, ch 1, turn.

Row 4: Sc in first sc, [ch 5, sk {ch-2 sp, sc and ch-2 sp}, sc in next sc] rep across, fasten off, turn.

Rows 5–10: Rep Rows 2–4 twice.

Rows 11 & 12: Rep Rows 2 and 3, at end of Row 12, do not ch 1; fasten off.

Row 13: Working in rem lps on opposite side of foundation ch, with RS facing, attach dark antique rose in end ch, ch 1, sc in same ch, [ch 5, sk 5 chs, sc in next ch] rep across, fasten off, do not turn.

Row 14: Rep Row 3.

Rows 15–23: Rep Rows 4–12.

FRINGE

Cut 18" lengths of yarn to match colors at ends of rows, cutting 2 strands for each row where there is no beg or ending length, and 1 strand for each row where there is beg or ending length.

Fold strands for each st in half. Pull lp end through end st from front to back. Pull loose ends through lp; pull to tighten. Rep in each end st across both ends of scarf.

Hat

Rnd 1: With tapestry, ch 84, join to form a ring, ch 1, beg in same st as joining, sc in each ch around, join in beg sc. (84 sc)

Rnd 2: Ch 1, sc in first sc, [ch 1, sk 1 st, sc in next st] rep around, ending with ch 1, sk last st, join in beg sc.

Rnd 3: Ch 1, sc in each sc and ch-1 sp around, join in beg sc.

Rnd 4: Ch 1, beg in same st as joining, sc in each sc around, working sc dec after every 12 sc, join in beg sc. (78 sts)

Rnd 5: Rep Rnd 2.

Rnds 6–8: Rep Rnds 3–5, working sc dec after every 11 sc on Rnd 7. (72 sc at end of Rnd 7)

Rnds 9–11: Rep Rnds 3–5, working sc dec after every 10 sc on Rnd 10. (66 sc at end of Rnd 10)

Rnds 12–14: Rep Rnds 3–5, working sc dec after every 9 sc on Rnd 13. (60 sc at end of Rnd 13)

Rnds 15–17: Rep Rnds 3–5, working sc dec after every 4 sc on Rnd 16. (50 sc at end of Rnd 16)

Rnds 18–20: Rep Rnds 3–5, working sc dec after every 3 sc on Rnd 19. (40 sc at end of Rnd 19)

Rnds 21–23: Rep Rnds 3–5, working sc dec after every 2 sc on Rnd 22. (30 sc at end of Rnd 22)

Rnds 24–26: Rep Rnds 3–5, working sc dec every other st on Rnd 25. (20 sc at end of Rnd 25)

Rnd 27: Ch 1, sc in each sc around, join in beg sc, fasten off, leaving 12" end. (10 sc)

Weave 12" end through front lps of sc in Rnd 27; pull to tighten, closing center opening.

BOTTOM BAND

Rnd 1: With RS facing, attach dark antique rose with a sl st in any ch of foundation ch, ch 1, sc in same ch, [ch 1, sk 1 ch, sc in next ch] rep around, ending with ch 1, sk last ch, join in beg sc, fasten off. (42 ch-1 sps)

Turn hat inside out; work rem rnds with WS facing.

Rnd 2: Attach tapestry with a sl st in any sc, ch 1, sc in same sc, [ch 5, sk next {ch-1 sp, sc, ch-1 sp}, sc in next sc] rep around, join in beg sc, fasten off. (21 ch-5 sps)

Rnd 3: Attach dark antique rose with a sl st in beg sc, ch 1, sc in same sc, [ch 5, sc in next sc] rep around, join in beg sc, fasten off.

Rnd 4: Attach tapestry with a sl st in beg sc, ch 1, sc in same sc, [ch 2, sc over ch-5 sps of 2 rnds directly below, ch 2, sc in next sc] rep around, join in beg sc.

Rnd 5: Ch 1, sc in same sc, [ch 5, sk next {ch-2 sp, sc, ch-2 sp}, sc in next sc] rep around, join in beg sc, fasten off.

Rnds 6 & 7: Rep Rnds 3 and 4, fasten off at end of Rnd 7.

Weave in loose ends. Turn hat RS out; turn up band to form a cuff.

Edging

Rnd 1: With RS facing, attach tapestry with a sl st in any unworked sc of Rnd 1 of bottom band, [ch 4, sl st in next unworked sc] rep around, join in beg sl st, fasten off.

Weave in loose ends.

POMPON

Wrap tapestry over cardboard 150 times. Slip off cardboard; tie double strand of same color in tight knot through 1 lp end. Cut opposite ends; trim evenly.

Tie pompon onto top of hat with double strand. Trim ends of strand to same length as pompon strands.

—*Designed by Katherine Eng*

Peachy Keen Top

EXPERIENCE LEVEL
Intermediate

SIZE
Women's 12(14)(16) Instructions are given for smallest size, with larger sizes in parentheses. When only 1 number is given, it applies to all sizes.

FINISHED MEASUREMENTS
Chest: 36(41)(45)"

MATERIALS
- 3-ply cotton yarn: 14 oz
- Size G/6 crochet hook or size needed to obtain gauge
- 3 (⅜") matching buttons

GAUGE
[{Dc, jt dc} 6 times, dc] = 4"; 8 rows = 4"

To save time, take time to check gauge.

PATTERN STITCHES

Joint dc (jt dc): Holding back on hook last lp of each st, dc in same st as last dc made, sk next st, dc in next st, yo, draw through all 3 lps on hook.

Beg joint dc (beg jt dc): Ch 2, sk next jt dc, dc in next dc.

Hdc dec: [Yo, insert hook in next st, yo, draw up a lp] twice, yo, draw through all 5 lps on hook.

FRONT RIBBING

Row 1: Ch 11, sc in 2nd ch from hook and in each rem ch across, ch 1, turn. (10 sc)

Row 2: Working in back lps only, sc in each sc across, ch 1, turn.

Rep Row 2 until 13½(15½)(17½)" from beg, do not fasten off, ch 1, do not turn.

Body Front

Row 1 (RS): Working over row ends, work 59(67)(73) sc evenly sp across, turn.

Row 2: Ch 3 (counts as first dc throughout), beg in first st of row, [jt dc, dc in same st as 2nd leg of last jt dc] rep across, turn. (59, 67, 73 sts)

Rep Row 2 for patt until 13(14)(14)" including ribbing, ending with a WS row, turn.

Armhole shaping

Row 1: Sl st in first 5 sts, work in patt across to last 4 sts, turn. (51, 59, 65 sts)

Row 2: Beg jt dc, dc in same st as last dc, continue in patt across, do not work final dc after last jt dc, turn. (49, 57, 63 sts)

Row 3: Ch 3, beg in next dc, work jt dc, continue in patt across, working final dc after last jt dc in top of beg jt dc, turn. (47, 55, 61 sts)

[Rep Rows 2 and 3] 0(1)(1) times. (47, 51, 57 sts)

Row 4(6)(6): Work in patt across, turn. (47, 51, 57 sts)

Yoke

Rows 1–8: Ch 2 (counts as first hdc throughout), hdc in each rem st across, turn. (47, 51, 57 hdc)

Shape neckline (first side)

Row 1: Ch 2, hdc in each of next 16(17)(19) sts, hdc dec over next 2 sts, turn. (18, 19, 21 sts)

Row 2: Ch 2, hdc dec, hdc in each rem st across, turn. (17, 18, 20 sts)

Row 3: Ch 2, hdc in each rem st across to last 2 sts, hdc dec, turn. (16, 17, 19 sts)

Row 4: Rep Row 2. (15, 16, 18 sts)

Row 5: Ch 2, hdc in each rem st across, turn. (15, 16, 18 sts)

Rep Row 5 until 7½(8½)(9)" from beg of armhole shaping, ending at armhole edge, turn.

First shoulder shaping

Row 1: Sl st in first 3(4)(4) sts, ch 2, hdc dec, hdc in each rem st across, turn. (12, 12, 14 sts)

Row 2: Ch 2, hdc in each of next 4 sts, hdc dec, leaving rem sts unworked, fasten off. (6 sts)

Shape neckline (second side)

Row 1: Sk next 9(11)(13) sts on Row 8 of yoke, attach yarn in next st with a sl st, ch 2, hdc dec, hdc in each rem st across, turn. (18, 19, 21 sts)

Rows 2–5: Rep Rows 2–5 of first side, reversing shaping.

Rep Row 5 until 7½(8½)(9)" from beg of armhole shaping, ending at neck edge, turn.

Second shoulder shaping

Row 1: Ch 2, hdc in each rem st across to last 4(5)(5) sts, hdc dec, turn. (12, 12, 14 sts)

Row 2: Sl st in first 6(6)(8) sts, ch 2, hdc dec, hdc in each of next 4 sts, fasten off. (6 sts)

Work as for front ribbing.

Body Back

Work as for body front through Row 4(6)(6) of armhole shaping.

Right back yoke

Row 1: Ch 2, hdc in each of next 22(24)(27) sts, turn. (23, 25, 28 sts)

Row 2: Ch 2, hdc in each rem hdc across, turn.

Rep Row 2 until 7½(8½)(9)" from beg of armhole shaping, ending at armhole edge, turn.

First shoulder shaping

Row 1: Sl st in each of first 3(4)(4) sts, ch 2, hdc dec, hdc in each of next 9(9)(11) sts, hdc dec, leaving rem sts unworked, turn. (12, 12, 14 sts)

Row 2: Ch 2, hdc in each of next 4 sts, hdc dec, fasten off. (6 sts)

Left back yoke

Row 1: Sk next st on last row of armhole shaping, attach yarn to next st, ch 2, hdc in each rem st across, turn. (23, 25, 28 sts)

Row 2: Ch 2, hdc in each rem hdc across, turn.

Rep Row 2 until 7½(8½)(9)" from beg of armhole shaping, ending at neck edge, turn.

Second shoulder shaping

Row 1: Sl st in each of first 8(9)(10) sts, ch 2, hdc dec, hdc in each of next 9(9)(11) sts, hdc dec, leaving rem sts unworked, turn. (12, 12, 14 sts)

Row 2: Sl st in each of first 6(6)(8) sts, ch 2, hdc dec, hdc in each of next 4 sts, fasten off. (6 sts)

SLEEVE

Make 2

Ribbing

Row 1: Ch 8, sc in 2nd ch from hook and in each rem ch across, ch 1, turn. (7 sc)

Row 2: Working in back lps only, sc in each sc across, ch 1, turn.

Rep Row 2 until ribbing meas 10(10¾)(11½)", at end of last row, ch 1, do not turn.

Sleeve body

Row 1 (RS): Working over row ends, work 43(47)(49) sc evenly sp across, turn.

Row 2: Rep Row 2 of body front until sleeve, including ribbing, meas 4", ending with WS row, turn. (43, 47, 49 sts)

Sleeve cap shaping

Rows 1–3: Rep Rows 1–3 of body front armhole shaping. (31, 35, 37 sts at end of Row 3)

Rep Rows 2 and 3 until 21(21)(23) sts rem, do not fasten off at end of last row, turn.

Next Row: Ch 2, [hdc dec, hdc in each of next 2 sts] rep across, ending with hdc dec over last 2 sts for size large only, fasten off. (16, 16, 17 sts)

COLLAR
Make 2

Work as for front ribbing until collar meas 8½(9)(10)", fasten off.

NECKLINE ROSE

Ch 42, sc in 2nd ch from hook, *sk 1 ch, 5 dc in next ch, sk 1 ch, sc in next ch, rep from * across, fasten off. (10 petals)

Roll into rose shape; sew tog on back.

FINISHING

Sew shoulder seams; sew side and sleeve seams. Sew in sleeves.

With RS facing, attach yarn at neckline at back opening, sc evenly sp around neckline and back opening, join with a sl st in beg sc, fasten off.

Sew collars to neckline so they meet at center front.

Sew buttons evenly sp on right back opening; use sps between sts on left back opening for buttonholes.

Attach neckline rose with safety pin to center front between collars. Remove for laundering.

—Designed by Loa Ann Thaxton

Classic Shells Pullover

EXPERIENCE LEVEL
Intermediate

SIZE
Women's small(medium)(large)(extra-large) Instructions are given for small size, with larger sizes in parentheses. When only 1 number is given, it applies to all sizes.

FINISHED MEASUREMENTS
Chest: 36(40)(45)(50)"

MATERIALS
- J. & P. Coats Luster Sheen® sport weight cable twist yarn (50 grams/150 yds per ball): 7(8)(9)(10) balls fuchsia
- Size C/2(E/4)(C/2)(E/4) crochet hook or size needed to obtain gauge

GAUGE
4 shells = 3⅝"; 9 rnds = 4" with size C hook

4 shells and 8 rnds = 4" with size E hook

To save time, take time to check gauge.

PATTERN NOTE
Join rnds with a sl st unless otherwise stated.

PATTERN STITCHES
Beg shell: [Ch 3, 2 dc, ch 3, 3 dc] in indicated sp.

Shell: [3 dc, ch 3, 3 dc] in indicated st or sp.

BOTTOM BORDER

Row 1: Ch 24, [2 dc, ch 3, 3 dc] in 4th ch from hook, [ch 5, sk next 9 chs, shell in next ch] twice, ch 4, turn. (3 shells)

Row 2: Shell in shell sp (shell in shell made), [ch 3, sc over ch-5 sp into 5th ch of ch-9 sp of foundation ch, ch 3, shell in next shell] twice, ch 4, turn.

Row 3: Shell in shell, [ch 7, shell in next shell] twice, ch 2, dc in turning ch-4 sp, ch 3, turn.

Row 4: 3 dc in first ch-2 sp, ch 2, [shell in next shell, ch 5] twice, shell in last shell, ch 4, turn.

Row 5: Shell in shell, [ch 3, sc over ch-5 sp into 4th ch of ch-7 sp in 2nd row below, ch 3, shell in next shell] twice, ch 2, [3 dc, ch 2, dc] in next ch-2 sp, ch 3, turn.

Row 6: 3 dc in first ch-2 sp, ch 2, 3 dc in next ch-2 sp, ch 2, [shell in next shell, ch 7] twice, shell in last shell, ch 4, turn.

Row 7: Shell in shell, [ch 5, shell in next shell] twice, ch 2, [dc in next ch-2 sp, ch 4] twice, [dc, ch 3, dc] in turning ch-3 sp, ch 4, dc over end dc of next row, ch 4, sk next row, dc over end dc of next row, ch 4, [dc, ch 4, dc] over end st of next row *, ch 3, turn.

Row 8: Shell in first ch-4 sp, [ch 3, sk next sp, shell in next sp] 3 times, ch 3, [shell in next shell, ch 3, sc over ch-5 sp into 4th ch of ch-7 sp in 2nd row below, ch 3] twice, shell in last shell, ch 4, turn.

Row 9: Shell in shell, [ch 7, shell in next shell] twice, [ch 4, shell in next shell] 3 times, ch 3, dc in last shell sp, ch 3, turn.

Row 10: Dc in shell sp, [[ch 3, dc] in same sp] 5 times, *ch 3, dc in next shell sp, [ch 3, dc in same sp] 5 times, rep from * once, ch 4, [shell in next shell, ch 5] twice, shell in last shell, ch 4, turn.

Row 11: Shell in first shell, [ch 3, sc over ch-5 sp into 4th ch of ch-7 sp in 2nd row below, ch 3, shell in next shell] twice, ch 4, turn.

Row 12: Shell in shell, [ch 7, shell in next shell] twice, ch 4, turn.

Row 13: Shell in shell, [ch 5, shell in next shell] twice, ch 2, dc in turning ch-4 sp, ch 3, turn.

Row 14: 3 dc in first ch-2 sp, ch 2, [shell in next shell, ch 3, sc over ch-5 sp into 4th ch of ch-7 sp in 2nd row below, ch 3] twice, shell in last shell, ch 4, turn.

Row 15: Shell in shell, [ch 7, shell in next shell] twice, ch 2, [3 dc, ch 2, dc] in next ch-2 sp, ch 3, turn.

Row 16: [3 dc in next ch-2 sp, ch 2] twice, [shell in next shell, ch 5] twice, shell in last shell, ch 4, turn.

Row 17: Shell in shell, [ch 3, sc over ch-5 sp into 4th ch of ch-7 sp in 2nd row below, ch 3, shell in next shell] twice, ch 2, [dc in next ch-2 sp, ch 4] twice, [dc, ch 3, dc] in turning ch, [ch 4, dc over end dc of next row, ch 4, sk next row, dc over end dc of next row, ch 4, [dc, ch 4, dc] over end st of next row, dc in top of last dc of next shell on row below, ch 3, turn.

Row 18: Shell in first ch-4 sp, [ch 3, sk next sp, shell in next sp] 3 times, ch 3, [shell in next shell, ch 7] twice, shell in last shell, ch 4, turn.

Row 19: Shell in shell, [ch 5, shell in next shell] twice, [ch 4, shell in next shell] 3 times, ch 3, dc in last shell sp, ch 3, turn.

Row 20: Dc in shell sp, [[ch 3, dc] in same shell sp] 5 times, *ch 3, dc in next shell sp, [ch 3, dc in same sp] 5 times, rep from * once, ch 4, [shell in next shell, ch 3, sc over ch-5 sp into 4th ch of ch-7 sp in 2nd row below, ch 3] twice, shell in last shell, ch 4, turn.

Row 21: Shell in first shell, [ch 7, shell in next shell] twice, ch 4, turn.

Row 22: Shell in shell, [ch 5, shell in next shell] twice, ch 4, turn.

Row 23: Shell in shell, [ch 3, sc over ch-5 sp into 4th ch of ch-7 sp in 2nd row below, ch 3, shell in next shell] twice, ch 2, dc in turning ch-4 sp, ch 3, turn.

Row 24: 3 dc in first ch-2 sp, ch 2, [shell in next shell, ch 7] twice, shell in last shell, ch 4, turn.

Row 25: Shell in shell, [ch 5, shell in next shell] twice, ch 2, [3 dc, ch 2, dc] in next ch-2 sp, ch 3, turn.

Row 26: [3 dc in next ch-2 sp, ch 2] twice, [shell in next shell, ch 3, sc over ch-5 sp into 4th ch of ch-7 sp in 2nd row below, ch 3] twice, shell in last shell, ch 4, turn.

Row 27: Shell in shell, [ch 7, shell in next shell] twice, ch 2, [dc in next ch-2 sp, ch 4] twice, [dc, ch 3, dc] in turning ch, ch 4, dc over end dc of next row, ch 4, sk next row, dc over end dc of next row, ch 4, [dc, ch 4, dc] over end st of next row, dc in top of last dc of next shell on row below, ch 3, turn.

Row 28: Shell in first ch-4 sp, [ch 3, sk next sp, shell in next sp] 3 times, ch 3, [shell in next shell, ch 5] twice, shell in last shell, ch 4, turn.

Row 29: Shell in shell, [ch 3, sc over ch-5 sp into 4th ch of ch-7 sp in 2nd row below, ch 3, shell in next shell] twice, [ch 4, shell in next shell] 3 times, ch 3, dc in last shell sp, ch 3, turn.

Row 30: Dc in shell sp, [[ch 3, dc] in same sp] 5 times, *ch 3, dc in next shell sp, [ch 3, dc in same sp] 5 times, rep from * once, ch 4, [shell in next shell, ch 7] twice, shell in last shell, ch 4, turn.

Row 31: Shell in shell, [ch 5, shell in next shell] twice, ch 4, turn.

Row 32: Shell in shell, [ch 3, sc over ch-5 sp into 4th ch of ch-7 sp in 2nd row below, ch 3, shell in next shell] twice, ch 4, turn.

Rows 33–36: Rep Rows 3–6.

Row 37: Rep Row 7 across to *, dc in top of last dc of next shell on row below, ch 3, turn.

Rows 38–62: Rep Rows 8–32.

Sizes small & medium only

Rows 63–79: Rep Rows 33–49. (8 scallops)

Row 80 (Joining): Dc in shell sp, [ch 3, dc in same sp] 5 times, *ch 3, dc in next shell sp, [ch 3, dc in same sp] 5 times, rep from * once, ch 3, dc in last sp at end of Row 7, [3 dc in next shell sp, ch 1, sl st in base of next shell on Row 1, ch 1, 3 dc in same sp as last 3 dc, ch 3, sc over ch-5 sp into 4th ch of ch-7 sp in 2nd row below, ch 3] twice, 3 dc in last shell sp, ch 1, sl st in base of last shell on Row 1, ch 1, 3 dc in same sp as last 3 dc, ch 4, turn, join in 4th ch of turning ch-4 on Row 1, do not fasten off, turn.

Sizes large & extra-large only

Rows 63–92: Rep Rows 33–62.

Rows 93–99: Rep Rows 33–39. (10 scallops)

Row 100 (Joining): Dc in shell sp, [ch 3, dc in same sp] 5 times, *ch 3, dc in next shell sp, [ch 3, dc in same sp] 5 times, rep from * once, ch 3, dc in last sp at end of Row 7, [3 dc in next shell sp, ch 1, sl st in base of next shell on Row 1, ch 1, 3 dc in same sp as last 3 dc, ch 3, sc in 4th ch of ch-7 sp in 2nd row below, ch 3] twice, 3 dc in last shell sp, ch 1, sl st in base of last shell on Row 1, ch 1, 3 dc in same sp as last 3 dc, ch 4, turn, join in 4th ch of turning ch-4 on Row 1, do not fasten off, turn.

BODY

All sizes

Rnd 1: Beg shell in ch-4 sp just made, shell in each ch-4 sp around, join in 3rd ch of beg ch-3, turn. (40, 40, 50, 50 shells)

Rnds 2–17(17)(20)(20): Sl st in next 3 dc and shell sp, beg shell in same sp, shell in each shell around, join in 3rd ch of beg ch-3, turn. (body measures 7½", 8½", 9", 10" above border)

BACK

Sizes small & medium only

Row 18: Sl st in next 3 dc, sc in shell sp, ch 2, shell in each of next 17 shells, dc in next shell sp, turn.

Row 19: Sl st in next 3 dc, sc in shell sp, ch 3, shell in each of next 15 shells, tr in next shell sp, ch 3, turn.

Rows 20–28: Shell in each shell across, dc in last dc of end shell, ch 3, turn. (15 shells)

First shoulder

Row 29: Shell in next 3 shells, tr in next shell sp, ch 3, turn.

Rows 30–37: Rep Row 20, at end of Row 37 fasten off. (3 shells)

Second shoulder

Row 29: Sk next 7 shells on Row 28 after last tr of Row 29 of first shoulder, attach yarn with a sl st in next shell sp, ch 4, shell in each of last 3 shells, dc in last dc of end shell, ch 3, turn.

Rows 30–37: Rep Rows 30–37 of first shoulder. (3 shells)

Sizes large & extra-large only

Row 21: Sl st in next 3 dc, sc in shell sp, ch 2, shell in each of next 23 shells, dc in next shell sp, turn.

Row 22: Sl st in next 3 dc, sc in shell sp, ch 2, shell in each of next 21 shells, dc in next shell sp, turn.

Row 23: Sl st in next 3 dc, sc in shell sp, ch 2, shell in each of next 19 shells, dc in next shell sp, ch 3, turn.

Rows 24–31: Shell in each shell across, dc in last dc of end shell, ch 3, turn. (19 shells)

First shoulder

Row 32: Shell in each of first 4 shells, tr in next shell sp, ch 3, turn.

Rows 33–41: Rep Row 24, at end of Row 41 fasten off. (4 shells)

Second shoulder

Row 32: Sk next 9 shells on Row 31 after last tr of Row 32 of first shoulder, attach yarn with a sl st in next shell sp, ch 4, shell in each of last 4 shells, dc in last dc of end shell, ch 3, turn.

Rows 33–41: Rep Rows 33–41 of first shoulder. (4 shells)

FRONT

Sizes small & medium only

Row 18: Sk next shell on Row 17 at underarm, attach yarn with a sl st in next shell, ch 3, shell in each of next 17 shells, dc in next shell sp, ch 3, turn.

Rows 19–28: Rep Rows 19–28 of back. (15 shells)

First shoulder

Rows 29–36: Rep Rows 29–36 of first shoulder of back.

Row 37: Dc in end dc on back shoulder, [3 dc in next shell sp on front, ch 1, sl st in corresponding shell sp on back, ch 1, 3 dc in same sp on front] 3 times, dc in end dc on back shoulder, dc in last dc of end shell on front, fasten off.

Second shoulder

Rows 29–36: Rep Rows 29–36 of 2nd shoulder of back.

Row 37: Rep Row 37 of first shoulder of front.

Sizes large & extra-large only

Row 21: Attach yarn with a sl st in next shell on Rnd 20, ch 3, shell in each of next 23 shells, dc in next shell sp, turn.

Rows 22–31: Rep Rows 22–31 of back.

First shoulder

Rows 32–40: Rep Rows 32–40 of first shoulder of back.

Row 41: Dc in end dc on back shoulder, [3 dc in next shell sp on front, ch 1, sl st in corresponding shell sp on back, ch 1, 3 dc in same sp on front] 4 times, dc in end dc on back shoulder, dc in last dc of end shell on front, fasten off.

Second shoulder

Rows 32–40: Rep Rows 32–40 of 2nd shoulder of back.

Row 41: Rep Row 41 of first shoulder of front.

NECK EDGING

All sizes

With RS facing, attach yarn in shell sp at bottom right corner of neck, ch 6 (counts as first dc, ch 3), [[dc, ch 3] in same sp] 4 times, dc in same sp, *ch 1, sc in next shell sp, ch 1, dc in next shell sp, [[ch 3, dc] in same sp] 5 times, rep from * 3(3)(4)(4) times, ch 1, sc in end dc of shell in next row, sk next sp, **dc in next sp, [[ch 3, dc] in same sp] 5

times, ch 1, sk next sp, sc in end dc in next row, ch 1, sk next sp, rep from ** to shoulder joining, continue around to correspond, join in 3rd ch of beg ch-6, fasten off.

ARMHOLE EDGING

All sizes

With RS facing attach yarn in shell sp at bottom of armhole, work as for neck edging.

—Designed by Marion L. Kelly

Raspberry Winter Ensemble

EXPERIENCE LEVEL
Intermediate

SIZE
Hooded Scarf: 10" wide x 39" long excluding fringe

Mittens: Ladies' size 6–7

MATERIALS
- Caron® Wintuk® 4 worsted weight yarn (3.5 oz per skein): 5 skeins strawberry #26
- Size I/9 crochet hook or size needed to obtain gauge
- 6¼" piece cardboard

GAUGE
Hooded Scarf: 8 dc = 2"; 4 dc rows = 3"

Mittens: 4 sc and 4 sc rows = 1"

To save time, take time to check gauge.

PATTERN NOTES
Join rnds with a sl st unless otherwise stated.

Always work beg sc in same st as joining.

PATTERN STITCHES
Beg shell: [Ch 3, 2 dc, ch 2, 3 dc] in indicated st or sp.

Shell: [3 dc, ch 2, 3 dc] in indicated st or sp.

Beg V-st: [Ch 5, dc] in indicated st or sp.

V-st: [Dc, ch 2, dc] in indicated st or sp.

Hooded Scarf

HOOD

First side

Row 1 (WS): Beg at top of hood, ch 47, dc in 4th ch from hook and in next ch, *sk 3 chs, shell in next ch, [sk 3 chs, V-st in next ch, sk 3 chs, shell in next ch] rep across to last 6 chs, sk 3 chs, dc in each of last 3 chs, turn.

Row 2: Ch 3 (counts as first dc throughout), dc in each of next 2 dc, ch 2, [V-st in next shell sp, shell in next V-st sp] rep across, ending with V-st in last shell sp, ch 2, dc in each of last 3 sts, turn.

Row 3: Ch 3, dc in each of next 2 dc, sk first ch-2 sp, [shell in next V-st sp, V-st in next shell sp] rep across, ending with shell in last V-st sp, dc in each of last 3 sts, turn.

Rows 4–19: Rep Rows 2 and 3 alternately, fasten off at end of Row 19.

Second side

Row 1: With RS facing, attach yarn with a sl st in first ch on opposite side of foundation ch, ch 3, dc in each of next 2 chs, rep Row 1 of first side from * across, turn.

Rows 2–19: Rep Rows 2 and 3 alternately, fasten off at end of Row 19, leaving length for sewing seam.

Fold hood WS out, with foundation ch at center top, st back seam over last 19 rows, matching row ends.

SCARF

With RS facing and back seam of hood at left side, fold front opening edge of hood to RS after first shell of Row 19, attach yarn with a sl st through shell sp of same first shell and V-st sp directly behind it.

First side

Row 1: Ch 3, 2 dc in same sp, ch 2, V-st in end st of Row 19 and in next shell sp directly behind it at the same time, [shell in next V-st sp, V-st in next shell sp] 3 times, ch 2, dc in each of last 3 sts, turn.

Row 2: Rep Row 3 of hood.

Rows 3–42: Rep Rows 2 and 3 of scarf alternately, fasten off at end of Row 42.

Second side

Row 1: With RS facing, beg at center back seam of hood, attach yarn with a sl st in first dc of last 3-dc group of Row 19 of hood, ch 3, dc in each of next 2 dc, ch 2, [V-st in next shell sp, shell in next V-st sp] 3 times, fold front edge of hood to RS after first shell of Row 19, V-st in end st of Row 19 and in next shell sp directly behind it at the same time, ch 2, 3 dc in next shell sp and in V-st directly behind it at the same time, turn.

Rows 2–42: Rep Rows 2–42 of first side.

FRINGE

Make 9 for each side

Wrap yarn around cardboard 19 times. Remove from cardboard; cut 1 end. Inserting hook from WS to RS, pull looped end through end st at corner of scarf. Pull loose ends through lp; pull to tighten. Rep in each ch-2 sp across scarf, ending in end st. Rep for 2nd side.

Mittens

Rnd 1: Ch 2, 7 sc in 2nd ch from hook, join in beg sc.

Rnd 2: Ch 1, 2 sc in each sc around, join in beg sc. (14 sc)

Rnd 3: Ch 1, sc in first sc, [2 sc in next sc, sc in next sc] rep around, ending with 2 sc in last sc, join in beg sc. (21 sc)

Rnd 4: Ch 1, sc in each of first 6 sc, [2 sc in next sc, sc in each of next 6 sc] twice, 2 sc in next sc, join in beg sc. (24 sc)

Rnd 5: Ch 1, sc in each sc around, join in beg sc.

Rnd 6: Ch 1, sc in each of first 7 sc, [2 sc in next sc, sc in each of next 7 sc] twice, 2 sc in next sc, join in beg sc. (27 sc)

Rnd 7: Ch 1, sc in each sc around, join in beg sc.

Rnd 8: Ch 1, sc in each of first 8 sc, [2 sc in next sc, sc in each of next 8 sc] twice, 2 sc in next sc, join in beg sc. (30 sc)

Rnds 9–20: Ch 1, sc in each sc around, join in beg sc.

Rnd 21: Ch 1, sc in first sc, ch 10 (thumb opening), sc in each sc around, join in beg sc.

Rnd 22: Ch 1, sc in first sc, sc in each of next 10 chs, sc in each rem sc around, join in beg sc. (40 sc)

Rnd 23: Ch 1, sc in each of first 5 sc, sc dec over next 2 sc, sc in each of next 6 sc, sc dec over next 2 sc, sc in each of next 21 sc, sc dec over next 2 sc, sc in each of next 2 sc, join in beg sc. (37 sts)

Rnd 24: Ch 1, sc in each of first 16 sts, sc dec over next 2 sts, sc in each rem st around, join in beg sc. (36 sc)

Rnd 25: Ch 1, sc in each of first 10 sts, [sc dec over next 2 sts, sc in each of next 10 sts] twice, sc dec over last 2 sts, join in beg sc. (33 sts)

Rnd 26: Ch 1, sc in each st around, join in beg sc. (33 sc)

Rnd 27: Ch 1, sc in each of first 25 sts, sc dec over next 2 sts, sc in each rem st around, join in beg sc. (32 sts)

Rnd 28: Ch 1, sc in each st around, join in beg sc.

Rnd 29: Ch 1, sc in each of first 14 sts, sc dec over next 2 sts, sc in each of next 14 sts, sc dec over last 2 sts, join in beg sc. (30 sts)

Rnd 30: Ch 1, sc in each of first 8 sts, [sc dec over next 2 sts, sc in each of next 8 sts] twice, sc dec over last 2 sts, join in beg sc. (27 sts)

Rnd 31: Ch 1, sc in each of first 6 sts, [sc dec over next 2 sts, sc in each of next 6 sts] twice, sc dec over next 2 sts, sc in each rem sc around, join in beg sc. (24 sts)

CUFF EDGING

Rnd 32: Beg shell in same st as joining, [sk next st, V-st in next st, sk next st, shell in next st] 5 times, sk next st, V-st in next st, sk last st, join in 3rd ch of beg ch-3.

Rnd 33: Sl st in each of next 2 dc and in ch-2 sp, beg V-st in same sp, [shell in next V-st sp, V-st in next shell sp] rep around, ending with shell in last V-st sp, join in 3rd ch of beg ch-5.

Rnd 34: Sl st in ch-2 sp, beg shell in same sp, [V-st in next shell sp, shell in next V-st sp] rep around, ending with V-st in last shell sp, join in 3rd ch of beg ch-3, fasten off.

THUMB

Rnd 1: Holding mitten with thumb opening to the left, attach yarn with a sl st in rem lp of first ch of ch-10, ch 1, beg in same st as joining, work 13 sc evenly sp around thumb opening, join in beg sc. (13 sc)

Rnds 2–7: Ch 1, sc in each sc around, join in beg sc, do not fasten off.

FINISHING

Note: *Do not join rnds.*

Ch 1, [sc dec over next 2 sts] rep around until opening is closed, fasten off.

Weave yarn end inside thumb.

—Designed by Lucille LaFlamme

Toddler's Hooded Scarf

EXPERIENCE LEVEL

Intermediate

SIZE

Toddler 2–4

MATERIALS

- Baby fingering yarn (1¾ oz per skein): 2 skeins variegated pink, white, blue and lavender
- Size 0 steel crochet hook or size needed to obtain gauge

GAUGE

12 sts = 2"; 8 rows = 1½" in patt

To save time, take time to check gauge.

PATTERN NOTE

Join rnds with a sl st unless otherwise stated.

PATTERN STITCH

Shell: 5 dc in indicated st.

HOOD

Row 1: Ch 41, sc in 2nd ch from hook, [dc in next ch, sc in next ch] rep across, ending with dc in last ch, ch 1, turn. (40 sts)

Row 2: Sc in first dc, [dc in next sc, sc in next dc] rep across, ending with dc in last sc, ch 1, turn.

Rows 3–78: Rep Row 2, do not fasten off at end of last row.

Fold in half so top of last row and foundation ch meet; working through both thicknesses over row ends, sl st 1 edge tog for center back seam, fasten off (WS). Turn RS out.

SCARF

Right side

Row 1: Ch 33, sc in 2nd ch from hook, [dc in next ch, sc in next ch] rep across, ending with dc in last ch, ch 1, turn. (32 sts)

Rows 2–26: Rep Row 2 of hood, at end of Row 26, do not ch 1; turn.

Row 27: Ch 2, sk first 2 sts, [sc in next dc, dc in next sc] rep across to last 2 sts, sk next dc, hdc in last sc, turn. (28 patt sts, not counting beg ch-2 or last hdc as sts)

Rows 28–31: Rep Row 27, at end of Row 31, ch 1, turn. (12 patt sts at end of Row 31)

Right neck band

Rep Row 2 of hood on rem 12 sts until neck band meas 3", do not ch 1 or turn at end of last row, do not fasten off.

Joining to hood

Row 1: With WS of hood facing, sl st in first st at bottom right front corner of hood, ch 1, turn so RS is facing, work in patt across 12 sts of neck band, ch 1, turn.

Row 2: Work in patt across 12 neck band sts, sk next 2 sts at bottom of hood, sl st in next st, ch 1, turn.

Row 3: Work in patt across 12 neck band sts, ch 1, turn.

Rep last 2 rows across bottom of hood until last st at bottom left front corner is joined, do not fasten off; ch 1, turn.

Left neck band

Work in est patt across 12 sts until piece meas 3", to correspond with right side, ending with a RS row, do not fasten off; ch 1, turn.

Left side

Rows 1–5: [Sc, dc, sc] in first dc, dc in next sc, work in est patt across to last st, [dc, sc, dc] in last sc, ch 1, turn. (32 sts at end of Row 5)

Rows 6–31: Continuing in est patt, work even on 32 sts, do not fasten off at end of last row; ch 1, turn.

SCARF EDGING

Row 1: Sc in first st, [sk next st, shell in next st, sk next st, sc in next st] 7 times, sk next st, shell in next st, sc in next st, fasten off.

With RS facing, attach yarn with a sl st in rem lp of first ch of foundation ch of opposite scarf end, ch 1, beg in same st, rep Row 1 of scarf edging, fasten off.

HOOD EDGING

Attach yarn with a sl st at lower right corner of hood where neck band joins hood bottom, ch 1, sc in same st, working shells and sc alternately over row ends, work 28 shells evenly sp across hood front, ending with sc over last row end, fasten off.

—Designed by Margaret Dick

Striped Slippers

EXPERIENCE LEVEL

Advanced beginner

SIZE

Men's small(medium)(large) Instructions are given for smallest size, with larger sizes in parentheses. When only 1 number is given, it applies to all sizes.

FINISHED MEASUREMENTS

9"–9½"(10"–10¼")(11"–11½")

MATERIALS

- Worsted weight yarn: 3(4)(5) oz maroon and 1(1¼)(1½) oz off-white
- Size G/6 crochet hook or size needed to obtain gauge
- Tapestry needle

GAUGE

4 sts and 4 rows/rnds = 1"

To save time, take time to check gauge.

PATTERN NOTES

Join rnds with a sl st unless otherwise stated.

To change color at end of rnd, drop working color to WS after last st is completed, join in beg sc with next color.

Do not fasten off color not in use unless otherwise stated; drop to WS of work and pick up again when needed, drawing up not too tightly to top of next row to be worked in that color.

———— • ————

SLIPPER

Make 2

Toe

Row 1 (RS): With maroon, ch 13(15)(17), sc in 2nd ch from hook and in each rem ch across, ch 1, turn. (12, 14, 16 sc)

Rows 2–26: Working in back lps only, sc in each sc across, ch 1, turn, at end of Row 26, do not ch 1, fasten off, leaving length for sewing seam.

With tapestry needle and maroon, RS tog, sew Row 1 and Row 26 tog, do not fasten off.

Weave rem length through ends of rows; pull up tightly and secure. Turn RS out.

Instep

Rnd 1: Working in ends of rows on opposite side of toe, attach maroon with a sl st at seam, ch 1, 34 sc evenly sp around, join in beg sc with off-white.

Rnd 2: Ch 1, beg in same st as joining, ch 1, sc in each sc around, join in beg sc with maroon.

Rnd 3: Ch 1, beg in same st as joining, sc in each sc around, join in beg sc with off-white.

Rnd 4: Ch 1, beg in same st as joining, sc in each sc around, join in beg sc.

Rnd 5: Rep Rnd 4, joining with maroon.

Rnd 6: Rep Rnd 3.

Rnds 7–9: Rep Rnd 4, joining with maroon at end of Rnd 9.

Rnd 10: Rep Rnd 3, fasten off maroon.

Rnds 11 & 12: Rep Rnd 4.

Rnds 13 & 14: Ch 1, 2 sc in same st as joining (inc made), sc in each rem sc around, join in beg sc, fasten off at end of Rnd 14. (36 sc at end of Rnd 14)

Heel

Row 1: With RS facing, attach maroon with a sl st in 12th st to right of joining st, ch 1, beg in same st, sc in each of next 24 sc, leaving rem 12 sts unworked for instep, ch 1, turn. (24 sc)

Rows 2–15(17)(19): Sc in each sc across, ch 1, turn, at end of Row 15(17)(19) do not ch 1, fasten off, leaving length for sewing seam.

Fold heel in half with RS tog; with tapestry needle and maroon, sew center back seam, matching sts.

Trim

Rnd 1: With RS facing, attach maroon with a sl st at center back seam of heel, ch 1, beg in same st, sc in each row end across to instep, sk 1 st on instep, sc in each of next 10 sts of instep, sk 1 st, sc in each row end of heel across, join in beg sc, fasten off.

Rnd 2: With RS facing, attach off-white with a sl st at center back, ch 1, sc in each sc around, join in beg sc.

Rnd 3: Ch 1, sc in each sc around, join in beg sc, fasten off.

Rnd 4: With WS facing, attach maroon with a sl st at center back, sl st in each sc around, join in beg sl st, fasten off.

—Designed by Ruth G. Shepherd

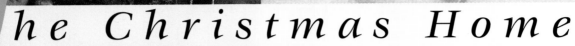

The Christmas Home

Gifts for Making Christmas Memories to Treasure

Making special memories is a gift every crocheter holds in her or his hands. By stitching holiday decorations and accents for the family to enjoy year after year, you create family traditions that will be cherished for years to come.

Victorian Treasures

Three enchanting patterns, including a cozy throw, our holly Christmas bear and a balsam-and-lace stocking, make up this collectible Victorian Treasures Christmas set (left). Crochet the complete set for yourself or as a very special gift for someone you love. Instructions begin on page 142.

Country Christmas Stockings

Delight all those country folks at heart in your family by making special Country Christmas Stockings (right) just for them! Bright stars, cheery stripes and fun hearts, all worked in cotton yarn, will add a touch of charm to your holiday home. Instructions begin on page 145.

Holly Place Mat

Add a delicate touch of crochet to your Christmas dinner by stitching a set of these festive Holly Place Mats (below). They are sure to become an anticipated tradition as you use them year after year. Instructions begin on page 147.

Holiday Shawl

Look your festive best with this elegant Holiday Shawl (right)! Perfect for a fancy Christmas party or special holiday concert, this shawl is crocheted with a specialty gold-and-white yarn. Instructions begin on page 149.

Festive Snowballs Set

Give your holiday decor a coordinated look by crocheting a vibrant Festive Snowballs Set (below), including a tree skirt with matching stockings, for the family! Christmas red and green accented with white embroidery and edging make this set a feast for the eyes! Instructions begin on page 150.

Christmas Table Topper

Cover a small round table with this festive Christmas Table Topper (above) for a holiday party or just as a cheerful accent throughout the Christmas season. Instructions begin on page 154.

Starry Night

If you like Scandinavian-style decor, then you'll enjoy crocheting this eye-catching Starry Night tree skirt and stocking set (left). A black background accented with white, red, green and yellow cross-stitching makes for a striking combination. Instructions begin on page 152.

Victorian Treasures

EXPERIENCE LEVEL
Bear & Throw: Beginner
Balsom & Lace Stocking: Intermediate

SIZE
Victorian Throw: Approximately 49" x 36" including border

Balsam & Lace Stocking: 16" long

Holly Christmas Bear: Approximately 11" tall standing

MATERIALS
- Caron® Victorian Christmas Gold worsted weight yarn (1¾ oz per skein): 9 skeins lace #1902 and 8 skeins each cranberry #1900 and balsam #1901
- Worsted weight yarn: small amount black
- Size F/5 crochet hook or size needed to obtain gauge
- Size G/6 crochet hook or size needed to obtain gauge
- Tapestry needle
- Polyester fiberfill
- 1 yd ¼"-wide white satin ribbon
- 4 (⅝"-diameter) gold jingle bells

GAUGE
Victorian Throw: 18 dc = 5"; 4 dc rows = 2¼" with larger hook

Holly Christmas Bear: 4 sc and 4 sc rnds = 1" with smaller hook

Balsam & Lace Stocking: 3 sc and 4 sc rows = 1" with larger hook

To save time, take time to check gauge.

PATTERN NOTES
To change color in dc, work last dc in working color until 2 lps rem on hook, drop working color to WS, yo with next color and complete dc.

Join rnds with a sl st unless otherwise stated.

Do not join rnds for Holly Christmas Bear; mark last st of each rnd with CC.

PATTERN STITCH
Cable twist: Sk 2 sts, fpdc over each of next 2 sts, fpdc over first sk st, fpdc over 2nd sk st.

Victorian Throw

MOTIF

Make 35

Row 1: With larger hook and cranberry, ch 27, dc in 4th ch from hook and in each rem ch across, turn. (25 dc, counting last 3 chs of beg ch as first dc)

Rows 2–4: Ch 3 (counts as first dc throughout), dc in each rem dc across, turn, at end of Row 4, change to lace in last st, fasten off cranberry, turn. (25 dc)

Rows 5–8: Ch 3, dc in each dc across, turn, at end of Row 8, change to balsam in last st, fasten off lace, turn.

Rows 9–12: Ch 3, dc in each dc across, turn, at end of Row 12, fasten off.

JOINING
With tapestry needle and matching yarn, sew motifs tog in 5 rows of 7 motifs each, following Fig. 1.

FIG. 1

EDGING

Rnd 1: With larger hook, attach lace with a sl st in any st on outer edge of throw, ch 1, beg in same st, sc evenly sp around, working 3 sc in each corner, join in beg sc.

Rnd 2: Ch 1, sc in same st as joining, [ch 4, sk 2 sts, sc in next sc] rep around, adjusting number of sts sk at end of rnd, if necessary, join in beg sc.

Rnd 3: Sl st in each of first 2 chs, ch 1, sc in same sp, [ch 5, sc in next ch-4 sp] rep around, join in beg sc.

Rnd 4: Ch 1, sc in same st as joining, [5 hdc in next ch-5 sp, sc in next sc] rep around, join in beg sc, fasten off.

Holly Christmas Bear

HEAD

Rnd 1: With smaller hook and cranberry, ch 2, 6 sc in 2nd ch from hook. (6 sc)

Rnd 2: 2 sc in each sc around. (12 sc)

Rnds 3 & 4: Sc in each sc around.

Rnd 5: [Sc in next sc, 2 sc in next sc] rep around. (18 sc)

Rnd 6: Sc in each of next 3 sc, 2 sc in each of next 12 sc, sc in each of last 3 sc. (30 sc)

Rnds 7–12: Sc in each sc around.

Rnd 13: [Sc in each of next 3 sc, sc dec over next 2 sc] rep around. (24 sc)

Rnd 14: [Sc in each of next 2 sts, sc dec over next 2 sts] rep around. (18 sc)

Stuff head with polyester fiberfill.

Rnd 15: [Sc in next sc, sc dec over next 2 sc] rep around. (12 sc)

Rnd 16: [Sc dec over next 2 sc] rep around, fasten off, leaving end.

Thread end onto tapestry needle; weave through Rnd 16 sts and pull to close, adding more stuffing as necessary.

EAR

Make 2

Rnds 1–4: Rep Rnds 1–4 of head. (12 sc)

Rnd 5: Sc in each sc around, fasten off, leaving end for sewing.

Thread end onto tapestry needle; holding ear flat, sew across bottom opening, gathering slightly.

BODY

Rnd 1: Beg at bottom with smaller hook and cranberry, ch 2, 6 sc in 2nd ch from hook. (6 sc)

Rnd 2: 2 sc in each sc around. (12 sc)

Rnd 3: [Sc in next sc, 2 sc in next sc] rep around. (18 sc)

Rnd 4: [Sc in each of next 2 sc, 2 sc in next sc] rep around. (24 sc)

Rnd 5: [Sc in each of next 3 sc, 2 sc in next sc] rep around. (30 sc)

Rnds 6–18: Sc in each sc around.

Rnd 19: [Sc in each of next 3 sc, sc dec over next 2 sc] rep around. (24 sc)

Rnd 20: Sc in each sc around.

Rnd 21: [Sc in each of next 2 sc, sc dec over next 2 sc] rep around. (18 sc)

Stuff body with polyester fiberfill.

Rnd 22: [Sc in next sc, sc dec over next 2 sc] rep around, fasten off, leaving length for sewing. (12 sc)

LEG

Make 2

Rnd 1: Beg at heel with smaller hook and cranberry, ch 5, sc in 2nd ch from hook, sc in each of next 2 chs, 3 sc in last ch, working on opposite side of foundation ch, sc in each of next 3 chs. (9 sc)

Rnd 2: 2 sc in next sc, sc in each of next 2 sc, 2 sc in each of next 3 sc, sc in each of next 2 sc, 2 sc in next sc. (14 sc)

Rnd 3: Sc in each of next 5 sc, 2 sc in each of next 4 sc, sc in each of next 5 sc. (18 sc)

Rnd 4: [Sc in each of next 2 sc, 2 sc in next sc] rep around. (24 sc)

Rnds 5–7: Sc in each sc around.

Rnd 8: Sc in each of next 6 sc, [sc dec over next 2 sc] 6 times, sc in each of next 6 sc. (18 sc)

Rnd 9: Sc in each of next 3 sc, [sc dec over next 2 sc] 6 times, sc in each of next 3 sc. (12 sc)

Rnds 10–20: Sc in each sc around, fasten off at end of Rnd 20, leaving end for sewing.

Stuff leg. Thread end into tapestry needle and weave through sts of Rnd 20; pull to close, adding more stuffing as necessary. Knot to secure.

ARM

Make 2

Rnd 1: With smaller hook and cranberry, ch 2, 5 sc in 2nd ch from hook. (5 sc)

Rnd 2: 2 sc in each sc around. (10 sc)

Rnds 3–15: Sc in each sc around, fasten off, leaving end.

Stuff arm. Thread end onto tapestry needle and weave through sts of Rnd 15; pull to close, adding more stuffing as necessary. Knot to secure.

COLLAR

Row 1: With smaller hook and lace, ch 26, sc in 2nd ch from hook, [ch 1, sk 1 ch, sc in next ch] rep across, ch 1, turn. (12 ch-1 sps)

Row 2: 2 sc in first sc, [sc in next ch-1 sp, 2 sc in next sc] rep across, ch 1, turn. (38 sc)

Row 3: Sc in first sc, ch 4, sk 1 sc, sc in next sc, [ch 4, sk 2 sc, sc in next sc] rep across to last 2 sc, ch 4, sk 1 sc, sc in last sc, ch 1, turn. (13 ch-4 sps)

Row 4: Sc in first sc, ch 5, sc in first ch-4 sp, [ch 5, sc in next ch-4 sp] rep across, ending with ch 5, sc in last sc, ch 1, turn. (14 ch-5 sps)

Row 5: Sc in first sc, [5 hdc in next ch-5 sp, sc in next sc] rep across, fasten off.

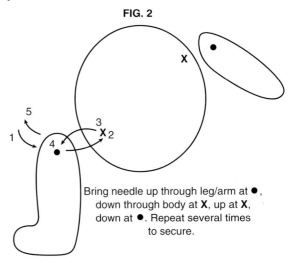

FIG. 2

Bring needle up through leg/arm at ●, down through body at **X**, up at **X**, down at ●. Repeat several times to secure.

With tapestry needle and cranberry, using photo as a guide, sew ears to head. Sew head to body.

With black and tapestry needle embroider eyes and nose with satin st; embroider mouth with straight st.

With tapestry needle and cranberry, sew arms and legs to body as shown in Fig. 2 so limbs are movable.

Weave ribbon through Rnd 1 of collar; place collar around bear's neck, tying bow in front.

Balsam & Lace Stocking

CUFF

Rnd 1: With larger hook and lace, ch 40, join to form a ring, ch 1, beg in same st as joining, sc in each ch around, join in beg ch. (40 sc)

Rnds 2 & 3: Ch 1, beg in same st, sc in each sc around, join in beg sc.

Rnd 4: Ch 1, sc in same st as joining, ch 1, [sk 1 sc, sc in next sc, ch 1] rep around, join in beg sc. (20 ch-1 sps)

Rnd 5: Ch 1, beg in same st, sc in each sc and ch-1 sp around, do not join, mark first st of each rnd with CC or small safety pin. (40 sc)

Rnds 6–11: Sc in each sc around, do not join, at end of Rnd 11, join in beg sc, fasten off.

Edging

Rnd 1 (RS): With larger hook, working on opposite side of foundation ch, attach lace with a sl st in any st, ch 1, sc in same st, [ch 3, sk 1 st, sc in next st] rep around, join in beg sc. (20 ch-3 sps)

Rnd 2: Sl st in first ch-3 sp, ch 3 (counts as first dc), 4 dc in same sp, [sc in next sp, 5 dc in next sp] rep around, ending with sc in last sp, join in 3rd ch of beg ch-3, fasten off.

UPPER STOCKING

Note: Upper stocking is worked inside out, so WS rows of upper stocking are worked with RS of cuff facing, and vice versa.

Rnd 1 (WS): With larger hook, RS of cuff facing, working in back lps only of Rnd 11 of cuff, attach balsam with a sl st in any st, ch 2 (counts as first hdc throughout), hdc in each rem sc around, join in 2nd ch of beg ch-2, turn. (40 hdc)

Rnd 2: Ch 2, hdc in each rem hdc around, join in 2nd ch of beg ch-2, turn. (40 hdc)

Rnd 3: Ch 2, [bpdc over each of next 4 hdc, hdc in each of next 4 hdc] rep around, ending with hdc in each of last 3 hdc, join in 2nd ch of beg ch-2, turn.

Rnd 4 (RS): Ch 2, hdc in each of next 3 hdc, [cable twist over next 4 bpdc, hdc in each of next 4 hdc] rep around, ending with cable twist over each of last 4 bpdc, join in 2nd ch of beg ch-2, turn.

Rnd 5: Ch 2, [bpdc over each of next 4 fpdc of cable twist, hdc in each of next 4 hdc] rep around, ending hdc in each of last 3 hdc, join in 2nd ch of beg ch-2, turn.

Rnd 6: Ch 2, hdc in each of next 3 hdc, [fpdc over each of next 4 bpdc, hdc in each of next 4 hdc] rep around, ending with fpdc over each of last 4 bpdc, join in 2nd ch of beg ch-2, turn.

Rnd 7: Ch 2, [bpdc around each of next 4 fpdc, hdc in each of next 4 hdc] rep around, ending with hdc in each of last 3 hdc, join in 2nd ch of beg ch-2, turn.

Rnds 8–23: Rep Rnds 4–7 alternately, fasten off at end of Rnd 23, turn.

HEEL SHAPING

Row 1: With RS of upper stocking facing, attach lace with a sl st in same st as joining, ch 1, sc in same st, sc in each of next 3 hdc, [sc in each of next 4 post sts, sc in each of next 4 hdc] twice, ch 1, turn. (20 sc)

Rows 2–9: Sk first sc, sc in each sc across to last 2 sc, sk next sc, sc in last sc, ch 1, turn. (4 sc at end of Row 9)

Row 10: [Sc dec over next 2 sc] twice, ch 1, turn. (2 sts)

Row 11: Sc in each st across, ch 1, turn. (2 sc)

Rows 12–20: 2 sc in first sc, sc in each sc across to last sc, 2 sc in last sc, ch 1, turn. (20 sc at end of Row 20)

Row 21: Sc in each sc across, fasten off.

FOOT

Rnd 1: With larger hook, RS of upper stocking facing, attach balsam with a sl st in first sc to right on Row 21 of heel, ch 2, hdc in each of next 19 sc, [cable twist over next 4 bpdc, hdc in each of next 4 hdc] rep across 20 sts of upper stocking, ending with cable twist over last 4 bpdc, join in 2nd ch of beg ch-2, turn.

Rnd 2: Ch 2, [bpdc over each of next 4 fpdc of cable twist, hdc in each of next 4 hdc] twice, bpdc over each of next 4 fpdc, [hdc in each of next 4 hdc, bpdc over each of next 4 hdc] twice, hdc in each of next 3 hdc, join in 2nd ch of beg ch-2, turn.

Rnds 3–12: Beg with Rnd 6, rep Rnds 4–7 of upper stocking alternately, fasten off at end of Rnd 12.

TOE SHAPING

Note: Do not join rnds unless otherwise stated; mark last st of each rnd with CC.

Rnd 1: With RS of upper stocking facing and larger hook, attach lace with a sl st in same st as joining, ch 1, beg in same st, sc in each sc around. (40 sc)

Rnd 2: [Sc in each of next 6 sc, sc dec over next 2 sc] 5 times. (35 sts)

Rnd 3: [Sc in each of next 5 sc, sc dec over next 2 sc] 5 times. (30 sts)

Rnd 4: [Sc in each of next 4 sc, sc dec over next 2 sc] 5 times. (25 sts)

Rnd 5: [Sc in each of next 3 sc, sc dec over next 2 sc] 5 times. (20 sts)

Rnd 6: [Sc in each of next 2 sc, sc dec over next 2 sc] 5 times. (15 sts)

Rnd 7: [Sc in next sc, sc dec over next 2 sc] 5 times, join in beg sc, fasten off, leaving end for sewing.

FINISHING

Assembly

Turn stocking inside out; turn cuff down. Thread end at toe into tapestry needle; weave through sts of Rnd 7 of toe and pull tightly to gather. Take a few small sts to secure.

Sew heel seam, matching sts.

Top edging

With larger hook and RS facing, attach lace in rem lp of any st on Rnd 11 at top of cuff, sl st in each st around, join in beg sl st, fasten off.

Hanger

With larger hook, attach lace with a sl st at center back of cuff at top edge, ch 16, sl st in beg sl st, fasten off.

Tie (make 2)

With larger hook and balsam, leaving 4" end, ch 60, fasten off, leaving 4" end.

Beg in middle of cuff front, weave 1 tie through Rnd 4 of cuff to middle of cuff back. Weave 2nd tie through Rnd 4 on rem of cuff. Tie jingle bell to each end of both ties. Tie ends in bows at front and back.

—Victorian Throw and Holly Christmas Bear designed by Michele Wilcox
Balsam & Lace Stocking designed by Colleen Sullivan

Country Christmas Stockings

EXPERIENCE LEVEL
Intermediate

SIZE
22" long

MATERIALS

- Bernat® Handicrafter® Cotton worsted weight yarn (1¾ oz/50 grams per skein): 6 skeins off-white #02 (MC), 2 skeins red #16, and 1 skein each emerald #17, lemon #05 and French blue #10
- Size F/5 crochet hook or size needed to obtain gauge
- Yarn needle
- 1 package 5mm silver star sequins
- 1 package glass transparent seed beads
- Sewing needle
- Nylon thread

GAUGE
14 sc and 15 sc rows = 4"
To save time, take time to check gauge.

PATTERN NOTE
Join rnds with a sl st unless otherwise stated.

PATTERN STITCH
2-sc dec: Draw up a lp in each of next 3 indicated sts, yo, draw through all 4 lps on hook.

Heart Stocking

UPPER STOCKING

Row 1: Beg at top with MC, ch 44, sc in 2nd ch from hook and in each rem ch across, ch 1, turn. (43 sc)

Row 2: Sc in each sc across, ch 1, turn.

Rows 3–47: Rep Row 2, fasten off at end of Row 47.

Embroidery

With tapestry needle, using a single strand of yarn, work cross sts as shown on Chart A (see page 146).

HEEL

Row 1: With RS facing, sk first 33 sts, attach emerald with a sl st in next st, ch 1, sc in same st as joining and in each of next 9 sts, bring beg of Row 47 around as if to join, sc across first 10 sk sts, ch 1, turn. (20 sc)

Row 2: Sc in each of next 13 sts, ch 1, turn. (13 sc)

Row 3: Sc in each of next 6 sts, ch 1, turn. (6 sc)

Row 4: Sc in each sc across last row, sc in next unworked sc on Row 1, ch 1, turn. (7 sc)

Row 5: Sc in each sc across last row, sc in next unworked sc on Row 2, ch 1, turn. (8 sc)

Rows 6–17: Rep Rows 4 and 5 alternately, fasten off at end of Row 17. (20 sc at end of Row 17)

FOOT

Rnd 1: With RS facing, attach MC with a sl st in 11th sc of Row 17 of heel, ch 1, sc in same st and in each of next 9 sc, sk next 2 sc of upper stocking, sc in each of next 19 sc, sk 2 sc, sc in each of last 10 sc on heel, join in beg sc, ch 1, turn. (39 sc)

Rnds 2–14: Beg in same st as joining, sc in each sc around, join in beg sc, ch 1, turn, fasten off at end of Rnd 14.

Embroidery

With tapestry needle and 1 strand of emerald, cross-st 4 additional rows on foot in patt est on upper stocking.

TOE

Note: *Do not join rnds or turn unless otherwise stated; mark first st of each rnd with a small safety pin or piece of CC.*

Rnd 1: With RS facing, attach emerald with a sl st in same st as joining on Rnd 14 of foot, ch 1, sc in same st and in each of next 38 sc. (39 sts)

Rnd 2: [Sc dec over next 2 sc, sc in each of next 2 sc, sc dec over next 2 sc, sc in each of next 7 sc] 3 times. (33 sts)

Rnds 3, 5, 7, 9 & 11: Sc in each st around, at end of Rnd 11, fasten off, leaving 10" length.

Rnd 4: [Sc dec over next 2 sc, sc in each of next 2 sc, sc dec over next 2 sc, sc in each of next 5 sc] 3 times. (27 sts)

CHART A

Row 1

Row 47

COLOR KEY
∴ Red
⊠ Emerald
☐ Off-white

Rnd 6: [Sc dec over next 2 sc, sc in each of next 2 sc, sc dec over next 2 sc, sc in each of next 3 sc] 3 times. (21 sts)

Rnd 8: [Sc dec over next 2 sc, sc in each of next 2 sc, sc dec over next 2 sc, sc in next sc] 3 times. (15 sts)

Rnd 10: [Sc dec over next 2 sc, sc in each of next 2 sc] 3 times, sc dec over next 2 sc, sc in next sc. (11 sts)

Thread 10" length onto tapestry needle; weave through sts of Rnd 11 and pull to close opening. Secure in place on WS of stocking.

Join back seam and close openings at heel.

HEART

Make 2

Row 1: Beg at bottom with red, ch 2, sc in 2nd ch from hook, ch 1, turn.

Row 2: 2 sc in sc, ch 1, turn.

Row 3: 2 sc in first sc, sc in next sc, ch 1, turn. (3 sc)

Row 4: 2 sc in first sc, sc in next sc, 2 sc in last sc, ch 1, turn. (5 sc)

Row 5: 2 sc in first sc, sc in each of next 3 sc, 2 sc in last sc, ch 1, turn. (7 sc)

Top
First side

Row 6: Sc in each of first 3 sc, ch 1, turn.

Row 7: Sk 1 sc, sc in each of last 2 sc, fasten off.

Second side

Rows 6 & 7: Attach red with a sl st in sc at opposite edge, ch 1, beg in same st, rep Rows 6 and 7 of first side.

Holding hearts tog, working through both thicknesses, attach red with a sl st at indention of top, sl st evenly sp around, join in beg sl st, ch 5, sl st at indention, fasten off.

CUFF

Rnd 1: With RS facing, attach MC with a sl st at top of seam, working in rem lps on opposite side of foundation ch, ch 3 (counts as first dc), dc in each of next 42 chs, join in 3rd ch of beg ch-3.

Rnd 2: Sl st in each dc around, join in beg sl st, [ch 15, sl st in joining] twice, ch 10, remove hook, draw ch through ch-5 sp of heart, ch 10, sl st in joining, [ch 15, sl st in joining] 5 times, fasten off.

Star Stocking

UPPER STOCKING

Row 1 (RS): With MC, ch 44, sc in 2nd ch from hook and in each rem ch across, fasten off. (43 sts)

Row 2: With RS facing, attach red with a sl st in first sc, ch 1, sc in same st and in each rem sc across, fasten off.

Row 3: With RS facing, attach MC with a sl st in first sc, ch 1, sc in same st and in each sc across, ch 1, turn.

Rows 4–8: Sc in each sc across, ch 1, turn, do not ch 1 at end of Row 8; fasten off.

Rows 9–43: Rep Rows 2–8 alternately.

Rows 44–47: Rep Rows 2–5, fasten off at end of Row 47.

HEEL

Rows 1–17: Rep Rows 1–17 of heel for Heart Stocking using French blue.

FOOT

Row 1: With RS facing, attach MC with a sl st in 11th sc of Row 17 of heel, ch 1, sc in same st and in each of next 9 sc, sk next 2 sc of upper stocking, sc in each of next 19 sc, sk 2 sc, sc in each of last 10 sc on heel, ch 1, turn. (39 sc)

Rows 2 & 3: Sc in each sc across, ch 1, turn, fasten off at end of Row 3.

Rows 4–10: Rep Rows 2–8 of upper stocking.

Rows 11–14: Rep Rows 2–5 of upper stocking, fasten off at end of Row 14.

Join back and foot seams; close heel openings.

TOE

Rnds 1–11: With RS facing, attach French blue with a sl st at seam, rep Rnds 1–11 of toe for Heart Stocking.

LARGE STAR

Rnd 1: With lemon, ch 4, 14 dc in 4th ch from hook, join in 4th ch of beg ch-4. (15 dc, counting last 3 chs of beg ch as first dc)

Rnd 2: [Ch 7, sc in 2nd ch from hook, hdc in next ch, dc in each of next 2 chs, tr in each of next 2 chs, sk next 2 sts on Rnd 1, sl st in next st] 5 times.

Rnd 3: Ch 1, working in rem lps of next ch-7, sc in first rem lp, *sc in each of next 5 rem lps, 3 sc in rem lp at tip, sc in each of next 5 sts **, 2-sc dec over next tr, next sl st and rem lp of next ch, rep from * around, ending last rep at **, sc dec over last tr and next sl st, join in beg sc.

Rnd 4: Sl st in each st around, join in beg sc, fasten off.

SMALL STAR

Make 2

Rnd 1: With lemon, ch 3, 9 hdc in 3rd ch from hook, join in 3rd ch of beg ch-3. (10 hdc, counting last 2 chs of beg ch as first hdc)

Rnd 2: [Ch 4, sc in 2nd ch from hook, hdc in next ch, dc in next ch, sk next st on Rnd 1, sl st in next st] 5 times, fasten off.

Holding both stars tog, working through both thicknesses, attach lemon with a sl st at tip of any point, ch 5, sl st in same st, sl st in each st around, join in beg sl st, fasten off.

CUFF

Rnds 1 & 2: Rep Rnds 1 and 2 of cuff for Heart Stocking, drawing ch-10 lp through ch-5 sp of small star.

FINISHING

Large star

With sewing needle and nylon thread, sew seed beads over star sequins, having 5 in each line from center of star to end of each point.

With tapestry needle and lemon, sew large star to front of upper stocking as shown in photo.

Heel & toe

With sewing needle and nylon thread, randomly sew star sequins with seed beads over toe and heel.

With tapestry needle and lemon, randomly embroider 3 (5-point) line stars on heel and 6 on toe.

—Designed by Ann E. Smith

Holly Place Mat

EXPERIENCE LEVEL
Advanced

SIZE
Approximately 13" x 18"

MATERIALS
- DMC® Cebelia® crochet cotton size 10 (50 grams per ball): 1 ball each cream #712 (MC), very dark Christmas red #816 (A) and Christmas green #699 (B)
- Size 7 steel crochet hook or size needed to obtain gauge
- 8 bobbins

GAUGE
15 sps and 16 rows = 4"

To save time, take time to check gauge.

PATTERN NOTES
Wind 6 bobbins of B and 2 bobbins of A.

Read all odd-numbered (RS) rows of chart from right to left; read all even-numbered (WS) rows from left to right.

To change colors in dc, work dc with working color until 2 lps rem on hook, drop working color to WS of work, yo with next color and complete dc.

To carry color not in use across sp to its next working area, wrap color not in use around working color while working ch sts of sp.

CHART A

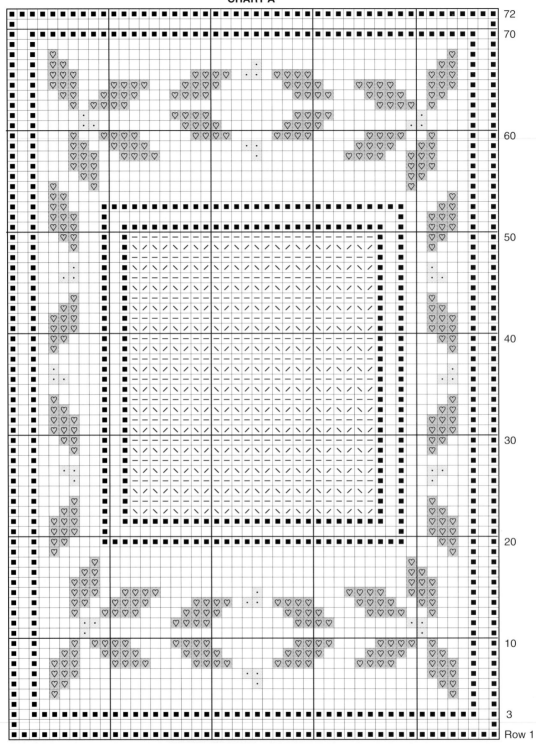

COLOR AND STITCH KEY
- ♡ Christmas green bl
- ■ Cream bl
- · Very dark Christmas red pc
- ⊠ Cream lacet
- − Cream bar
- ☐ Cream sp

Do not carry CCs across more than 1 sp; attach new bobbin. Carry MC at wrong side of work when not in use, working over it with CC in use.

PATTERN STITCHES

Block (bl): Dc in each of next 3 sts.

Beg bl: Ch 3, dc in each of next 3 sts.

Sp: Ch 2, sk next 2 dc or next ch-2 sp, dc in next indicated st.

Popcorn (pc): 5 dc in designated st or sp, remove hook from lp, insert hook from RS to WS in top of first of 5 dc just made, pull lp through dc to form pc, ch 1 to close.

Bar: Ch 5, dc in next indicated dc.

Lacet: Ch 3, sk 2 sts, sc in next st, ch 3, sk 2 sts, dc in next dc.

Pc bl: Pc in indicated st or sp, dc in next dc.

Bar over a lacet: Ch 5, sk [ch-3, sc, ch-3], dc in next dc.

Bl over a bl: Dc in each of next 3 dc.

Bl over sp: Dc in each of next 2 chs, dc in next dc.

2 bls over a bar: Dc in each of next 5 chs, dc in next dc.

Sp over a bl: Ch 2, sk 2 dc, dc in next dc.

Sp over a sp: Ch 2, dc in next dc.

Sp over a pc bl: Ch 2, sk pc, dc in next dc.

Pc bl over a sp: Pc in ch-2 sp, dc in next dc.

Pc bl over a pc bl: Pc in top of pc, dc in next dc.

PLACE MAT

Row 1 (RS): With MC, ch 147, dc in 4th ch from hook and in each rem ch across, turn. (48 bls; 145 dc, counting last 3 chs of foundation ch as first dc)

Row 2: Beg bl over a bl, 46 sps over 46 bls, bl over a bl.

Rows 3–72: Follow Chart A, fasten off at end of Row 72. Block to size.

—Designed by Nancy Hearne

Holiday Shawl

EXPERIENCE LEVEL
Intermediate

SIZE
Approximately 60" wide across top x 36" long including fringe

MATERIALS
- Muench® Valentina® 95 percent viscose/5 percent polyester yarn (50 grams/140 yds per skein): 7 skeins white with gold #2900
- Size H/8 crochet hook or size needed to obtain gauge
- 6" piece cardboard
- Seam sealant

GAUGE
First 5 rows = 3¾" wide x 2⅝" long

To save time, take time to check gauge.

PATTERN NOTE
Shawl is worked in 1 piece from bottom point to upper edge.

PATTERN STITCHES

Front post tr (fptr): Yo hook twice, insert hook from front to back and to front again around vertical post (upright part) of indicated st, yo and draw yarn through, yo and complete tr.

2-dc cl: Holding back on hook last lp of each st, work 2 dc in indicated st, yo, draw through all 3 lps on hook.

Shell: [2-dc cl, {ch 1, 2-dc cl} twice] in indicated st.

Beg inc: Ch 5 (counts as first tr, ch-1), tr in first tr.

End inc: [Tr, ch 1, tr] in 4th ch of turning ch-5.

SHAWL

Row 1: Ch 3, dc in 3rd ch from hook, [ch 1, 2-dc cl] twice in same ch as last dc (beg shell made), turn.

Row 2: Ch 5 (counts as first tr, ch-1 throughout), tr in first 2-dc cl of shell, ch 1, tr in next 2-dc cl, ch 1, [tr, ch 1, tr] in next dc, turn. (4 ch-1 sps)

Row 3: Beg inc, ch 1, [fptr, ch 1] over each tr across, end inc, turn. (6 ch-1 sps)

Row 4: Beg inc, ch 1, [fptr, ch 1] over each tr and fptr across, end inc, turn.

Row 5: Beg inc, ch 1, fptr over next tr, ch 1, fptr over next fptr, ch 1, sk next fptr, shell in top of next fptr, ch 1, sk next fptr, fptr over next fptr, ch 1, fptr over next tr, ch 1, end inc, turn.

Row 6: Beg inc, ch 1, fptr over next tr, *[ch 1, fptr over next fptr] twice *, [ch 1, tr in next 2-dc cl] 3 times, rep from * to *, ch 1, fptr over next tr, ch 1, end inc, turn. (12 ch-1 sps)

Rows 7 & 8: Rep Row 4. (16 ch-1 sps at end of Row 8)

Row 9: Beg inc, ch 1, fptr over next tr, *[ch 1, fptr over next fptr] twice, ch 1, sk next fptr, shell in top of next fptr, ch 1, sk next fptr, fptr over next fptr *, rep from * to *, ch 1, fptr over next fptr, ch 1, fptr over next tr, ch 1, end inc, turn.

Row 10: Beg inc, ch 1, fptr over next tr, [ch 1, fptr over next fptr] 3 times, {ch 1, tr in top of next 2-dc cl} 3 times] twice, [ch 1, fptr over next fptr] 3 times, ch 1, fptr over next tr, ch 1, end inc, turn.

Rows 11 & 12: Rep Row 4.

Row 13: Beg inc, ch 1, fptr over next tr, ch 1, [[fptr over next fptr, ch 1} 3 times, sk next fptr, shell in top of next fptr, ch 1, sk next fptr] 3 times, [fptr, ch 1] over each rem fptr and tr, end inc, turn.

Row 14: Beg inc, ch 1, fptr over next tr, ch 1, [fptr over next fptr, ch 1] 4 times, [[tr in top of next 2-dc cl, ch 1} 3 times, {fptr over next fptr, ch 1} 3 times] 3 times, [fptr, ch 1] over each rem fptr and tr, end inc, turn. (28 ch-1 sps)

Rows 15 & 16: Rep Row 4. (32 ch-1 sps at end of Row 16)

Rows 17–65: Continue in est patt, working incs at beg and end of every row and positioning each shell on every 4th row midway between 2 shells of last shell row, with 3 fptr between shells, ending with shell row, fasten off.

FRINGE

Wrap yarn several times around cardboard; cut 1 end and remove cardboard. Fold 1 strand in half, insert hook in side edge of shawl, draw folded lp of strand through st, pull cut ends through folded lp, pull to tighten. Rep evenly sp closely tog across 2 sides of shawl.

Following Fig. 1, tie overhand knots in strands; apply a drop of seam sealant to each knot.

FIG. 1

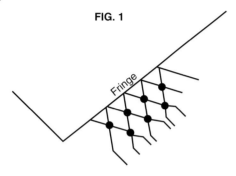

Fringe

FINISHING

Weave in loose ends; secure with a few sts of white sewing thread.

Spray shawl with water; pin to size. Spray a 2nd time; allow to dry thoroughly.

—Designed by Maureen Egan Emlet

Festive Snowballs Set

EXPERIENCE LEVEL
Intermediate

SIZE
Tree Skirt: 35" in diameter including edging

Stocking: Approximately 18" long

MATERIALS
• Red Heart® Super Saver® worsted weight yarn (8 oz/225 grams per skein): 2 skeins each cherry red #319 and paddy green #368, and 1 skein white #311
• Size H/8 crochet hook or size needed to obtain gauge
• Tapestry needle

GAUGE
13 sc and 14 rows = 4"

To save time, take time to check gauge.

PATTERN NOTE
Join rnds with a sl st unless otherwise stated.

PATTERN STITCH
Popcorn (pc): 5 dc in indicated st, remove hook from lp, insert hook in top of first dc of 5-dc group, pick up dropped lp, draw lp through dc.

Tree Skirt

PANEL

Make 4 cherry red & 4 paddy green

Row 1: Ch 45, sc in 2nd ch from hook and in each rem ch across, ch 1, turn. (44 sc)

Row 2: Sc in each st across, ch 1, turn.

Row 3: Sc dec over first 2 sc, sc in each rem sc across to last 2 sc, sc dec over last 2 sc, ch 1, turn.

Rep Rows 2 and 3 until 6 sts rem, fasten off, leaving end for sewing.

With tapestry needle, sew panels tog, alternating red and green.

EMBROIDERY

With white and tapestry needle, work embroidery along each seam as shown in Fig. 1.

FIG. 1 EMBROIDERY CHART

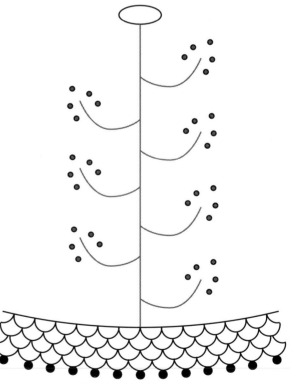

Rep along each seam line

STITCH KEY
↜ Outline st
● French knot (wrap 4 times around needle)

TOP EDGING

Rnd 1: With RS facing, attach white with a sl st at top edge of skirt, ch 1, beg in same st, sc in each sc around, join in beg sc. (48 sc)

Rnd 2: Ch 1, sc in same st as joining, ch 3, [sk 1 sc, sc in next sc, ch 3] rep around, join in beg sc, fasten off.

BOTTOM EDGING

Rnd 1: Attach white with a sl st in any rem lp of foundation ch on bottom edge, ch 1, beg in same st, sc in each rem ch lp around, join in beg sc. (44 sc per panel; 352 sc total)

Rnd 2: Ch 1, sc in same st as joining, [ch 5, sk next 3 sc, sc in next sc] rep around, ending with ch 2, dc in beg sc to form last ch-5 sp.

Rnd 3: Ch 1, sc in sp just formed, [ch 6, sc in next ch-5 sp] rep around, ending with ch 3, dc in beg sc to form last ch-6 sp.

Rnd 4: Ch 1, sc in sp just formed, [ch 7, sc in next ch-6 sp] rep around, ending with ch 3, tr in beg sc to form last ch-7 sp.

Rnd 5: Ch 1, sc in same sp, [ch 6, pc in 3rd ch from hook, ch 3, sc in next ch-7 sp] rep around, join in beg sc, fasten off. Weave in loose ends.

Stocking

HEEL

Rnd 1: With white, ch 2, 6 sc in 2nd ch from hook, do not join.

Rnd 2: 2 sc in each sc around, do not join. (12 sc)

Rnd 3: [3 sc in next sc, sc in each of next 5 sc] twice, join in beg sc. (16 sc)

Rnd 4: Ch 1, 3 sc in same st as joining, sc in each of next 7 sc, 3 sc in next sc, sc in each of last 7 sc, join in beg sc. (20 sc)

Rnd 5: Ch 1, 3 sc in same st as joining, sc in each of next 9 sc, 3 sc in next sc, sc in each of last 9 sc, join in beg sc. (24 sc)

Rnd 6: Ch 1, 3 sc in same st as joining, sc in each of next 11 sc, 3 sc in next sc, sc in each of last 11 sc, join in beg sc. (28 sc)

Rnd 7: Ch 1, 3 sc in same st as joining, sc in each of next 13 sc, 3 sc in next st, place piece of CC yarn or other small marker in next-to-last sc just made, sc in each of last 13 sc, fasten off, set aside. (32 sc)

TOE

Note: *Do not join rnds unless otherwise stated; mark last st of each rnd with CC or other small marker.*

Rnd 1: With white, ch 4, join to form a ring, 8 sc in ring.

Rnd 2: 2 sc in each sc around. (16 sc)

Rnd 3: [Sc in each of next 3 sc, 2 sc in next sc] 4 times. (20 sc)

Rnd 4: [Sc in each of next 4 sc, 2 sc in next sc] 4 times. (24 sc)

Rnd 5: Sc in each sc around.

Rnd 6: [Sc in each of next 5 sc, 2 sc in next st] 4 times. (28 sc)

Rnds 7–9: Rep Rnd 5, at end of Rnd 9, join in beg sc, fasten off.

Rnd 10: Attach cherry red with a sl st in next sc, ch 1, beg in same st, sc in each sc around. (28 sc)

Rnd 11: 2 sc in first sc, sc in each rem sc around. (29 sc)

Rnd 12: Sc in each sc around.

Rnds 13–15: Rep Rnds 11 and 12 alternately, ending with Rnd 11, fasten off at end of Rnd 15. (31 sc at end of Rnd 15)

Rnds 16 & 17: Attach paddy green with a sl st in next sc, ch 1, beg in same st, rep Rnd 12 and Rnd 11. (32 sc at end of Rnd 17)

Rnd 18: Sl st in each of next 3 sc, sc in each of next 29 sc.

Rnd 19: Sc in each st around. (32 sc)

Rnd 20: Rep Rnd 18.

Rnd 21: Rep Rnd 19, fasten off.

BODY

Rnd 22: Attach cherry red with a sl st in next sc, ch 1, sc in same st and in each of next 9 sc, sc in marked st on heel, sc in each of next 15 heel sts, sk next 16 sc on toe, sc in each of next 6 sc. ***Note:*** *Half of sts on foot and heel will be left unworked and sewn tog later. (32 sc)*

Rnd 23: Sc in next sc, sl st in next 3 sc, sc in each of next 5 sc, hdc in each of next 3 sc, sc in each of next 6 sc, 2 sc in next sc (center back of stocking), sc in each of next 6 sc, hdc in each of next 3 sc, sc in each of next 4 sc. (33 sts)

Rnd 24: Sc in each of next 9 sts, hdc in each of next 3 sts, sc in each of next 14 sts, hdc in each of next 3 sts, sc in each of next 4 sts. (33 sts)

Rnd 25: Sc in next st, sl st in next 3 sts, sc in each of next 5 sts, hdc in each of next 3 sts, sc in each of next 7 sts, 2 sc in next sc, sc in each of next 7 sts, hdc in each of next 3 sts, sc in each of next 3 sts. (34 sts)

Rnd 26: Sc in each st around.

Rnd 27: Sc in each sc around, working 2 sc in sc at center back of stocking, fasten off. (35 sc)

Rnds 28–33: Attach paddy green with a sl st in next sc, ch 1, beg in same st as joining, rep Rnds 26 and 27 alternately, fasten off paddy green at end of Rnd 33. (38 sc at end of Rnd 33)

Rnds 34–39: Attach cherry red with a sl st in next sc, ch 1, beg in same st as joining, rep Rnds 26 and 27 alternately, fasten off at end of Rnd 39. (41 sc at end of Rnd 39)

Rnds 40–57: Rep Rnd 26, alternately working 6 rnds each paddy green and cherry red, join in beg sc at end of Rnd 57, fasten off.

CUFF

Rnd 1: Attach white with a sl st in back lp only of center back st, ch 1, working in back lps only this rnd and beg in same st, sc in each sc around. (41 sc)

Rnds 2–12: Sc in each sc around, at end of Rnd 12, join in beg sc, do not fasten off.

Hanging loop

Ch 16, sc in same st as joining, fasten off.

EDGING

Rnd 1: With top of stocking pointing up, attach white with a sl st at center back in rem lp of Rnd 57, ch 1, beg in same st, sc in each rem lp around, join in beg sc. (41 sc)

Rnd 2: Sk first sc, [sc in next sc, pc in next sc] rep around, join in beg sc, fasten off.

With tapestry needle and white, sew rem heel flap to stocking with blind sts.

Weave in loose ends.

—Designed by Maureen Egan Emlet

Starry Night

·

EXPERIENCE LEVEL
Advanced beginner

SIZE
Tree Skirt: Approximately 48" in diameter

Stocking: Approximately 6" wide at top x 16½" long

MATERIALS
- Red Heart® Super Saver® worsted weight yarn (8 oz per skein): 5 skeins black #12 (MC), 3 skeins white #311 (CC), and 2 skeins each paddy green #368 (A), hot red #390 (B)
- Red Heart® Sport™ sport weight yarn (2½ oz per skein): 3 skeins yellow #230
- Size H/8 crochet hook
- Size I/9 crochet hook or size needed to obtain gauge
- Large-eyed, blunt-tipped tapestry needle
- Cardboard: 1", 2" and 2½" pieces
- 4 snaps

GAUGE
7 sc = 2"; 4 sc rows = 1" with larger hook

To save time, take time to check gauge.

PATTERN NOTE
Join rnds with a sl st unless otherwise stated.

·

Tree Skirt

SKIRT SECTION

Make 8

Row 1 (RS): With larger hook and MC, beg at inside edge, ch 16, dc in 4th ch from hook and in each rem ch across, ch 1, turn. (14 dc, counting last 3 chs of beg ch as first dc)

Row 2 (WS): 2 sc in first dc, sc in each dc across to last dc, 2 sc in last dc, turn. (16 sc)

Row 3: Ch 3 (counts as first dc throughout), dc in each rem sc across, ch 1, turn. (16 dc)

Rows 4–47: Rep Rows 2 and 3 alternately, fasten off at end of Row 47. (60 sts in Rows 46 and 47)

Row 48: With RS facing, using larger hook, attach A with a sl st at right edge of skirt section, ch 1, 2 sc in first st, sc in each st across to last st, 2 sc in last st, ch 1, turn. (62 sc)

Row 49: Sc in each sc across, fasten off A, attach B with a sl st in last st, ch 1, turn.

Rows 50 & 51: Sc in each sc across, ch 1, turn, at end of Row 51, fasten off B, attach MC with a sl st in last st, ch 1, turn.

Row 52: 2 sc in first sc, sc in each rem sc across to last sc, 2 sc in last sc, ch 1, turn. (64 sc)

Rows 53–55: Sc in each sc across, ch 1, turn.

Rows 56–63: Rep Rows 52–55 twice, fasten off MC at end of Row 63. (68 sc in Rows 60–63)

Rows 64 & 65: With B, rep Rows 48 and 49, fasten off B at end of Row 65, attach A with a sl st in last st, ch 1, turn.

Rows 66 & 67: Rep Rows 50 and 51, fasten off.

Top edging

Row 1: With larger hook, RS facing, attach B with a sl st at right edge, ch 1, sc in each rem lp of beg ch across, ch 1, turn. (14 sc)

Row 2: Sc in each sc across, fasten off B, attach A with a sl st in last sc, ch 1, turn.

Rows 3 & 4: Sc in each sc across, ch 1, turn, at end of Row 4, fasten off.

Side edging

Row 1: With smaller hook, RS facing, attach MC with a sl st at end of 1 side of skirt section, working over row ends, work 90 sc evenly sp across side, fasten off.

Rep on opposite side of same section.

Rep for rem 7 sections.

FINISHING

Border (4 panels only)

Row 1: With smaller hook, RS facing, attach B in first MC sc of Row 1 of side edging, sc in each sc across, ch 1, turn.

Row 2: Sc in each sc across, fasten off B, attach A with a sl st in last sc, ch 1, turn.

Rows 3 & 4: Sc in each sc across, ch 1, turn, fasten off at end of Row 4.

Rep on opposite side of same section.

Embroidery

With tapestry needle, follow Chart A (see page 157) to embroider Back stitching on borders, top edging, and Rows 48–51 and 64–67 of each skirt section.

Follow Chart B to embroider cross-sts over Rows 2–46 of each skirt section.

Follow Chart C to embroider snowflakes over Rows 54–62 of each skirt section.

Joining

With tapestry needle and black, sew panels tog, alternating

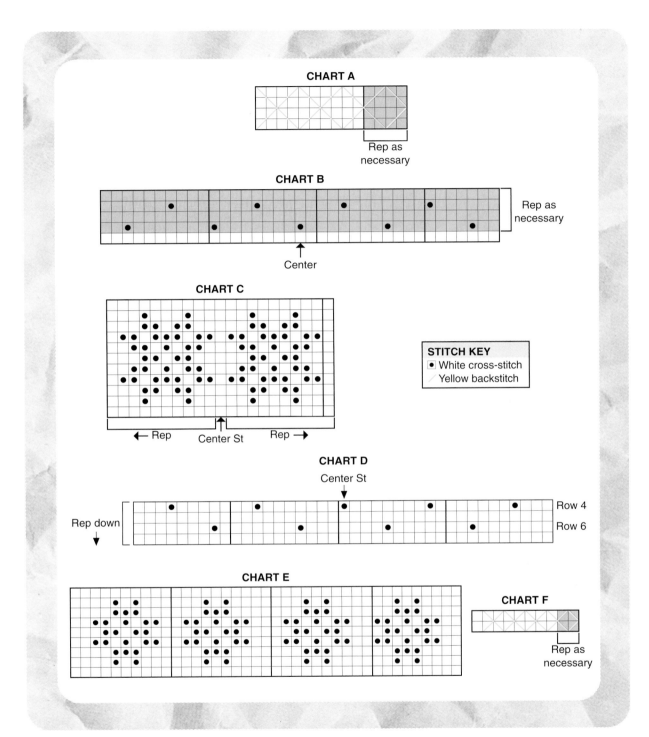

CHART A

Rep as necessary

CHART B

Rep as necessary

Center

CHART C

← Rep   Center St   Rep →

STITCH KEY
• White cross-stitch
╱ Yellow backstitch

CHART D

Center St

Rep down
↓

Row 4
Row 6

CHART E

CHART F

Rep as necessary

bordered panels with unbordered panels and leaving a back opening.

Sew 4 snaps evenly sp along back opening edges.

Drawstring

With smaller hook and 1 strand each MC and CC, ch 48, fasten off.

Weave through Row 1 of skirt panels, beg and ending at back opening.

Tassel (make 2)

Wrap MC around 2½" piece cardboard 20 times. Slip off cardboard; tie through lp at top. Tie again 1" down from top. Cut bottom lps.

Tie 1 tassel to each end of drawstring.

Fringe

Wrap MC several times around 2" piece of cardboard; cut bottom lps. Rep with CC. Fold 1 strand MC in half. Pull lp end through first st on bottom edge of skirt; draw cut ends through lp and pull to tighten.

Rep in next st with CC strand.

Continue in each st across outer edge of skirt, alternating MC and CC strands.

Stocking

UPPER STOCKING

Row 1: Beg at top with larger hook and MC, ch 41, sc in 2nd ch from hook and in each rem ch across, turn. (40 sc)

Row 2: Ch 3 (counts as first dc), dc in each rem sc across, ch 1, turn. (40 dc)

Row 3: Sc in each dc across, turn.

Rep Rows 2 and 3 alternately until upper stocking meas approximately 9", ending with Row 2, fasten off.

HEEL

Row 1: Sk first 30 sts of last row of upper stocking, with larger hook, attach MC with a sl st in next st, ch 1, sc in same st and in each of rem 9 sts, bring end of last row of upper stocking around as if to join, sc in each of next 11 sk sc of last row, ch 1, turn. (21 sc)

Row 2: Sc in each of next 14 sc, ch 1, turn.

Row 3: Sc in each of next 7 sc, ch 1, turn.

Row 4: Sc in each sc across last row, sc in next unworked sc of Row 1, ch 1, turn. (8 sc)

Row 5: Sc in each sc across last row, sc in next unworked sc of Row 2, ch 1, turn. (9 sc)

Rows 6–17: Rep Rows 4 and 5 alternately, fasten off at end of Row 17. (21 sc at end of Row 17)

FOOT

Row 1: Sk first 10 sc of Row 17 of heel, attach MC with a sl st in next st, ch 1, sc in same st and in each of rem 10 sc across, sk next 2 sts of last row of upper stocking, sc in each of next 15 sts of upper stocking, sk last 2 sts, sc in each of rem 10 sc of Row 17 of heel, turn. (36 sc)

Rep Rows 2 and 3 of upper stocking until foot meas 4½" from Row 17 of heel, ending with Row 2.

TOE

First half

Row 1: Sc in each of first 18 sc, ch 1, turn.

Rows 2–8: Sc dec, sc in each rem sc across to last 2 sc, sc dec, ch 1, turn, fasten off at end of Row 8. (4 sc at end of Row 8)

Second half

Row 1: With larger hook, attach MC with a sl st in next unworked st in last row of foot, ch 1, sc in same st and in each of next 17 sc, ch 1, turn.

Rows 2–8: Rep Rows 2–8 of first half of toe.

STOCKING EMBROIDERY

With tapestry needle, beg at Row 4 of upper stocking, fol-low Chart B (see page 153) to embroider cross-sts over upper stocking, stopping embroidery sts at heel and contin-uing in est patt over foot of stocking, ending at toe.

CUFF

Row 1: With larger hook and MC, ch 41, sc in 2nd ch from hook and in each rem ch across, ch 1, turn. (40 sts)

Rows 2–8: Sc in each sc across, ch 1, turn, at end of Row 8, fasten off.

Having Row 1 of cuff even with Row 1 of upper stocking, both RS facing, working through both thicknesses, attach MC with a sl st at right edge, ch 1, sc in same st and in each st across, fasten off. (40 sc)

TOP CUFF EDGING

Row 1: With RS facing, using larger hook, attach B at right edge of cuff, ch 1, sc in same st and in each sc across, fas-ten off, attach A with a sl st in last st, ch 1, turn.

Row 2: Sc in each sc across, fasten off.

BOTTOM CUFF EDGING

Rows 1 & 2: Rep Rows 1 and 2 of top cuff edging, working in rem lps of foundation ch of cuff.

CUFF EMBROIDERY

Follow Chart D to embroider snowflakes on cuff.

Follow Chart E to embroider cross-sts over top and bottom cuff edgings.

Sew foot, back and cuff seams.

FRINGE

Wrap MC several times around 1" piece of cardboard; cut bottom lps. Rep with CC. Apply fringe in same manner as for Tree Skirt, working in sts of Row 2 of bottom cuff edging.

—Designed by Michele Maks Thompson
for Monsanto's Designs for America Program

Christmas Table Topper

EXPERIENCE LEVEL
Advanced beginner

SIZE
Approximately 32½" square

MATERIALS
- South Maid® Super Saver crochet cotton size 10 (600 yds per ball): 2 balls white #1
- South Maid® crochet cotton size 10 (350 yds per ball): 1 ball each victory red #494 and myrtle #484
- Size 6 steel crochet hook or size needed to obtain gauge
- Spray starch

GAUGE
Motif Rnds 1–3 = 2¼"

To save time, take time to check gauge.

PATTERN NOTE

Join rnds with a sl st unless otherwise stated.

PATTERN STITCHES

Beg 3-tr cl: Ch 4 (counts as first tr), holding back on hook last lp of each tr, 2 tr in indicated sp, yo, draw through 3 lps on hook.

3-tr cl: Holding back on hook last lp of each tr, 3 tr in indicated sp, yo, draw through 4 lps on hook.

Trtr: Yo 4 times, insert hook in indicated st, yo, draw up a lp, [yo, draw through 2 lps on hook] 5 times.

Quadtr: Yo 5 times, insert hook in indicated st, yo, draw up a lp, [yo, draw through 2 lps on hook] 6 times.

Beg shell: [Ch 3, dc, ch 3, 2 dc] in indicated st.

Shell: [2 dc, ch 3, 2 dc] in indicated st.

Beg 3-dc cl: Ch 3 (counts as first dc), holding back on hook last lp of each st, 2 dc in indicated sp, yo, draw through 3 lps on hook.

3-dc cl: Holding back on hook last lp of each st, 3 dc in indicated sp, yo, draw through 4 lps on hook.

———•———

FIRST MOTIF

Rnd 1: With victory red, ch 8, join to form a ring, beg 3-tr cl in ring, ch 5, [3-tr cl in ring, ch 5] 7 times, join in top of beg 3-tr cl, fasten off. (8 3-tr cls)

Rnd 2: Attach myrtle in any ch-5 sp, ch 1, beg in same sp, [4 sc, ch 3, 4 sc] in each ch-5 sp around, join in beg sc, fasten off.

Rnd 3: Attach white in any ch-3 sp, ch 1, sc in same sp, [ch 9, sc in next ch-3 sp] rep around, ending with ch 3, trtr in beg sc to form last ch-9 sp. (8 ch-9 sps)

Rnd 4: Ch 1, [sc, ch 3, sc] in sp just formed, [ch 9, {sc, ch 3, sc} in next ch-9 sp] rep around, ending with ch 3, trtr in beg sc to form last ch-9 sp.

Rnd 5: Ch 1, [sc, ch 3, sc] in sp just formed, [ch 11, {sc, ch 3, sc} in next ch-9 sp] rep around, ending with ch 4, quadtr in beg sc to form last ch-11 sp.

Rnd 6: Ch 1, [sc, ch 3, sc] in sp just formed, [ch 13, {sc, ch 3, sc} in next ch-11 sp] rep around, ending with ch 6, quadtr in beg sc to form last ch-13 sp.

Rnd 7: Beg shell in top of quadtr, [ch 7, sc in next ch-3 sp, ch 7, shell in 7th ch of next ch-13 sp] rep around, ending with ch 7, sc in last ch-3 sp, ch 7, join in 3rd ch of beg ch-3, fasten off.

SECOND & SUBSEQUENT MOTIFS

Rnds 1–6: Rep Rnds 1–6 of first motif.

Joining

Rnd 7: Ch 3, dc in top of quadtr, ch 1, sc in any shell sp on previous motif, *ch 1, 2 dc in same st as last dc on working motif, ch 3, sc in next ch-7 sp on previous motif, ch 3, sc in next ch-3 sp on working motif, ch 3, sc in next ch-7 sp on

previous motif, ch 3, [2 dc, ch 1] in 7th ch of next ch-13 sp on working motif, sc in next shell sp on previous motif, ch 1, 2 dc in same ch as last 2 dc on working motif * (1 side joined), complete as for Rnd 7 of first motif.

Make and join a total of 49 motifs in 7 rows of 7 motifs each. When subsequent motifs require joining on 2 sides, work joining Rnd 7 until first side has been joined, ch 7, sc in next ch-3 sp on working motif, ch 7, [2 dc, ch 1] in 7th ch of next ch-13 on working motif, sc in corresponding shell on next motif to be joined, rep from * to * of joining rnd, complete as for first motif.

FILLER MOTIF

Note: Make 36, joining each on Rnd 2 to the 8 unworked Rnd 7 ch-7 sps where 4 motifs meet.

Rnd 1: With white, ch 8, join to form a ring, beg 3-tr cl in ring, [ch 5, 3-tr cl in ring] 7 times, ch 2, dc in top of beg 3-tr cl.

Rnd 2: Ch 1, sc in sp just formed, ch 4, sc in any unworked Rnd 7 ch-7 sp to be joined, ch 4, sc in next ch-5 sp on filler motif, [ch 4, sc in next unworked Rnd 7 ch-7 sp to be joined, ch 4, sc in next ch-5 sp on filler motif] rep around, join in beg sc, fasten off.

EDGING

Rnd 1: Attach white in first unworked shell sp to the right on any corner motif, ch 1, sc in same sp, [{ch 7, sc in next ch-7 sp} twice, ch 7, sc in next shell sp] 3 times, *[ch 7, sc in next ch-7 sp] twice, ch 7, sc in sp between joined shells, **[{ch 7, sc in next ch-7 sp} twice, ch 7, sc in next shell sp] twice **, rep from * to corner, rep from ** to **, rep from * around, ending with [ch 7, sc in next ch-7 sp] twice, ch 7, join in beg sc, fasten off.

Rnd 2: Attach victory red in any ch-7 sp, beg shell in same sp, ch 3, [shell in next sp, ch 3] rep around, join in 3rd ch of beg ch-3, fasten off.

Rnd 3: Attach myrtle in any shell sp, beg 3-dc cl in same sp, [ch 3, sc in next sp, ch 3, 3-dc cl in next shell sp], rep around, ending with ch 3, join in top of beg 3-dc cl, fasten off.

Starch lightly; press on WS.

—Designed by Emma Willey

General Instructions

Please review the following information before working the projects in this book. Important details about the abbreviations and symbols used and finishing instructions are included.

Hooks

Crochet hooks are sized for different weights of yarn and thread. For thread crochet, you will usually use a steel crochet hook. Steel crochet hook sizes range from size 00 to 14. The higher the number of hook, the smaller your stitches will be. For example, a size 1 steel crochet hook will give you much larger stitches than a size 9 steel crochet hook. Keep in mind that the sizes given with the pattern instructions were obtained by working with the size thread or yarn and hook given in the materials list. If you work with a smaller hook, depending on your gauge, your project size will be smaller; if you work with a larger hook, your finished project's size will be larger.

Gauge

Gauge is determined by the tightness or looseness of your stitches, and affects the finished size of your project. If you are concerned about the finished size of the project matching the size given, take time to crochet a small section of the pattern and then check your gauge. For example, if the gauge called for is 10 dc = 1 inch, and your gauge is 12 dc to the inch, you should switch to a larger hook. On the other hand, if your gauge is only 8 dc to the inch, you should switch to a smaller hook.

If the gauge given in the pattern is for an entire motif, work one motif and then check your gauge.

Understanding Symbols

As you work through a pattern, you'll quickly notice several symbols in the instructions. These symbols are used to clarify the pattern for you: Brackets [], curlicue brackets {}, asterisks *.

Brackets [] are used to set off a group of instructions worked a number of times. For example, "[ch 3, sc in ch-3 sp] 7 times" means to work the instructions inside the [] seven times. Brackets [] also set off a group of stitches to be worked in one stitch, space or loop. For example, the brackets [] in this set of instructions, "Sk 3 sc, [3 dc, ch 1, 3 dc] in next st" indicate that after skipping 3 sc, you will work 3 dc, ch 1 and 3 more dc all in the next stitch.

Occasionally, a set of instructions inside a set of brackets needs to be repeated too. In this case, the text within the brackets to be repeated will be set off with curlicue brackets {}. For example, "[Ch 9, yo twice, insert hook in 7th ch from hook and pull up a loop, sk next dc, yo, insert hook in next dc and pull up a loop, {yo and draw through 2 lps on hook} 5 times, ch 3] 8 times." In this case, in each of the eight times you work the instructions included in brackets, you will work the section included in curlicue brackets five times.

Asterisks * are also used when a group of instructions is repeated. They may either be used alone or with brackets. For example, "*Sc in each of the next 5 sc, 2 sc in next sc, rep from * around, join with a sl st in beg sc" simply means you will work the instructions from the first * around the entire round.

"*Sk 3 sc, [3 dc, ch 1, 3 dc] in next st, rep from * around" is an example of asterisks working with brackets. In this set of instructions, you will repeat the instructions from the asterisk around, working the instructions inside the brackets together.

Stitch Abbreviations

beg ....begin(ning)	p ....picot
bl(s) ....block(s)	rem ....remain(ing)
bpdc ....back post dc	rep ....repeat
ch(s) ....chain(s)	rnd(s) ....round(s)
cl(s) ....cluster(s)	RS ....right side facing you
CC ....contrasting color	sc ....single crochet
dc ....double crochet	sk ....skip
dec ....decrease	sl st..slip stitch
dtr ....double treble crochet	sp(s) ....space(s)
fpdc ....front post dc	st(s) ....stitch(es)
hdc ....half-double crochet	tog ....together
inc ....increase	tr ....treble crochet
lp(s) ....loop(s)	trtr ....triple treble crochet
MC ....main color	WS ....wrong side facing you
meas ....measures(s)	yo ....yarn over

Basic Stitches

Front Loop (a)   Back Loop (b)

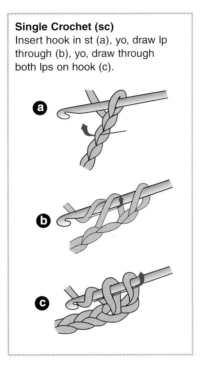

Chain (ch)
Yo, draw lp through hook.

Slip Stitch
Insert hook in beg ch, yo, draw lp through.

Single Crochet (sc)
Insert hook in st (a), yo, draw lp through (b), yo, draw through both lps on hook (c).

Half-Double Crochet (hdc)
Yo, insert hook in st (a), draw lp through (b), yo, draw through all 3 lps on hook (c).

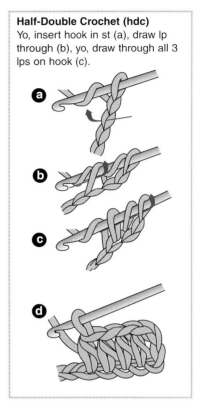

Double Crochet (dc)
Yo, insert hook in st (a), yo, draw through 1 lp (b), [yo, draw through 2 lps] twice (c, d).

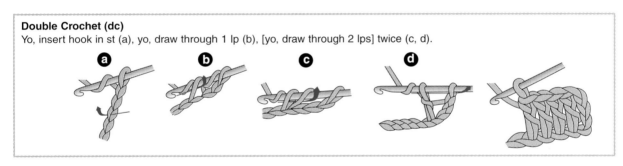

Treble Crochet (tr)
Yo hook twice, insert hook in st (a), yo, draw lp through (b), [yo, draw through 2 lps on hook] 3 times (c, d, e).

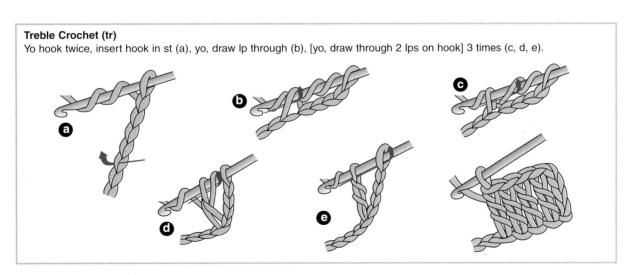

Decreasing

Single Crochet Decrease

Dec 1 sc over next 2 sc as follows: Draw up a lp in each of next 2 sts, yo, draw through all 3 lps on hook.

Half-Double Crochet Decrease

Dec 1 hdc over next 2 hdc as follows: [Yo, insert hook in next st, yo, draw lp through] twice, yo, draw through all 5 lps on hook.

Double Treble Crochet (dtr)

Yo hook 3 times, insert hook in st (a), yo, draw lp through (b), [yo, draw through 2 lps on hook] 4 times (c, d, e, f).

Double Crochet Decrease

Double Crochet next 2 stitches together: Decreasing 1 dc over next 2 dc

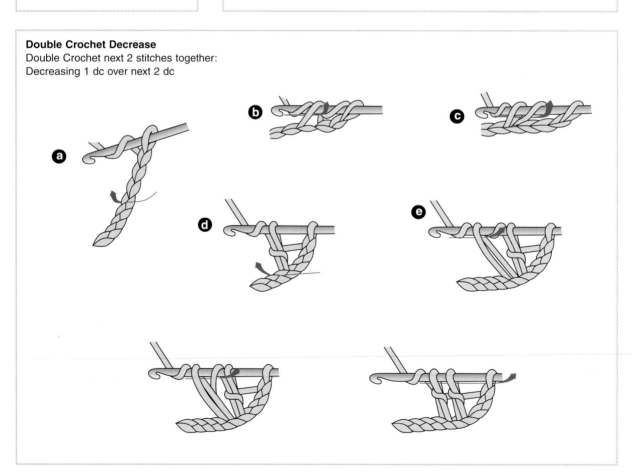

Special Stitches

Shell (sh)
[2 dc, ch 2, 2 dc] in next st or ch sp.

Reverse Single Crochet (reverse sc)
Working from left to right, insert hook in next st to the right (a), yo, draw through st, complete as for sc (b).

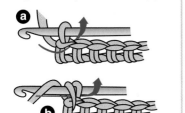

Picot (p)
Ch 3, sl st in 3rd ch from hook.

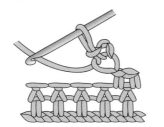

Front Post (a)/Back Post (b)

Chain color change (ch color change)
Yo with new color, draw through last lp on hook.

Double Crochet color change (dc color change)
Drop first color, yo with new color, draw through last 2 lps of st.

Yarn Conversion

Ounces to Grams		Grams to Ounces	
1	28.4	25	⅞
2	56.7	40	1⅔
3	85.0	50	1¾
4	113.4	100	3½

Hairpin Lace Stitch

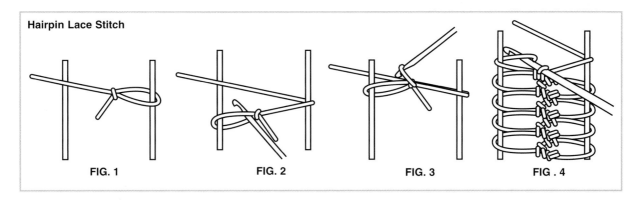

FIG. 1   FIG. 2   FIG. 3   FIG . 4

Cross-Stitch Diagram

FIG. 1   FIG. 2   FIG. 3   FIG. 4

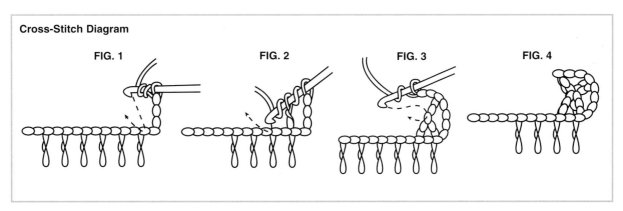

~ Index ~

Monsanto's Designs for America Program

Double Border Granny, Easy Clusters Pillow, Geometric Stripes, Girl's Button Vest, Pine Tree Jacket, Rainbow of Hearts, Starry Night Set, White-on-White, Winter Pineapple